Day Trading

FOR

DUMMIES®

Day Trading

FOR

DUMMIES®

by Ann C. Logue

Wiley Publishing, Inc.

Day Trading For Dummies®

Published by
Wiley Publishing, Inc.
111 River St.
Hoboken, NJ 07030-5774
www.wiley.com

About the Author

Ann C. Logue is the author of *Hedge Funds for Dummies* (Wiley, 2006). She has written for *Barron's*, *The New York Times*, *Newsweek Japan*, *Wealth Manager*, and the International Monetary Fund. She is a lecturer at the Liautaud Graduate School of Business at the University of Illinois at Chicago. Her current career follows 12 years of experience as an investment analyst. She has a B.A. from Northwestern University and an M.B.A. from the University of Chicago, and she holds the Chartered Financial Analyst (CFA) designation.

Dedication

Once again, to Rik and Andrew, for their love and support.

Author's Acknowledgments

So many wonderful people helped me with this book! I talked to many day traders, brokers, and others in the investment business, including Jack Alogna and Beth Cotner, Michael Browne of DTN Inc., Nihar Dalil, Greg Gocek and Robert Cohen of the CFA Society of Chicago, Mary Haffenberg and Curt Zuckert at the Chicago Mercantile Exchange, Anil Joshi of NuFact, Karen H. at Gamblers Anonymous, James Kupfer of Waterston Financial, James Lee of TradersLaboratory.com, Wayne Lee of NASDAQ, Khurram Naik and James Cagnina at Infinity Brokerage Services, Don Padou, Chris Tabaka, Elizabeth Tabaka, and Allen Ward. I also talked to several other traders who asked to remain anonymous; they know who they are, and I hope they also know how much I appreciate their help.

As for the mechanics of putting together the book, Corbin Collins and Stacy Kennedy of Wiley were great to work with through this tough schedule. (Dummies authors do not get to take time off!) Finally, my agent, Marilyn Allen, made it all happen.

Thanks, everyone!

Publisher's Acknowledgments

We're proud of this book; please send us your comments through our Dummies online registration form located at www.dummies.com/register/.

Some of the people who helped bring this book to market include the following:

Acquisitions, Editorial, and Media Development

Project Editor: Corbin Collins

Acquisitions Editor: Stacy Kennedy

Copy Editor: Corbin Collins

Technical Editor: Robert L. Cohen, FSA, CFA

Media Project Supervisor: Laura Moss-Hollister

Media Development Specialist: Kit Malone

Editorial Manager: Michelle Hacker

Editorial Supervisor and Reprint Editor:
Carmen Krikorian

Editorial Assistants: Erin Calligan Mooney,
Joe Niesen, David Lutton, Leeann Harney

Cartoons: Rich Tennant
(www.the5thwave.com)

Composition Services

Project Coordinator: Kristie Rees

Layout and Graphics: Stacie Brooks,
Carl Byers, Stephanie D. Jumper,
Laura Pence, Christine Williams

Proofreaders: John Greenough, Linda Seifert

Indexer: Potomac Indexing LLC

Publishing and Editorial for Consumer Dummies

Diane Graves Steele, Vice President and Publisher, Consumer Dummies

Joyce Pepple, Acquisitions Director, Consumer Dummies

Kristin A. Cocks, Product Development Director, Consumer Dummies

Michael Spring, Vice President and Publisher, Travel

Kelly Regan, Editorial Director, Travel

Publishing for Technology Dummies

Andy Cummings, Vice President and Publisher, Dummies Technology/General User

Composition Services

Gerry Fahey, Vice President of Production Services

Debbie Stailey, Director of Composition Services

Contents at a Glance

Table of Contents

Part III: Day Trading Strategies 193

Introduction

So you want to make money from home, eh?

If you love the thrill of the markets and have the patience to sit and stare at a screen for hours waiting for the right moment to get in and get out of securities, then day trading might be a great career option. But it has risks, too. It requires the right psychological makeup. Good day traders are patient and decisive, confident but not arrogant. They most certainly are not gamblers, although day trading attracts gamblers who discover it's a great way to *lose* money from home. Any day can be your best day, but it can also put you out of business forever.

Day Trading For Dummies is for people who are looking for a career change or who simply want to supplement investment return with new techniques. I give you what you need to know, from determining whether you are cut out for it, to laying out your home office, to researching and planning trades.

Maybe you'll decide day trading is not for you — if so, you'll be glad that you spent only the price of this book and not thousands on research and training. A lot of people make a lot of money selling services to neophyte day traders, claiming to be the best thing going. And maybe so — for some people. I give a wider perspective. If you decide to day trade, this book shouldn't be your only guide. Find a trading system that works for you.

About This Book

First, let me tell you what this book is not: It's not a textbook, and it's not a guide for professional investors. Several of those are on the market already, and they are fabulous — but often dry and assume underlying knowledge.

This book assumes you don't know much about day trading, but that you are a smart person who is thinking about doing it. It contains straightforward explanations of how day trading works, how to get started, what the pitfalls are, and what some of the alternatives are for your portfolio and for your career. If you really want to read some textbooks, I list a few in the Appendix.

Conventions Used in This Book

I'll start with the basics: I put important words that I define in *italics*. I often **bold** the key words of lists to bring the important ideas to your attention. And I place all Web addresses in `monofont` to set them apart.

I cover investment research in this book, and I make an effort to introduce you to some technical terms that will come up in the investment world. You don't need to know everything in this book to day trade; most successful day traders pick one system that works for them and stick to it. I think it's helpful to show the array of possibilities to help you make decisions about what might suit *you*. Sometimes I throw in references to deeper, academic investment theories. To alert you to these topics, I flag them with Technical Stuff icons (see the section "Icons Used in This Book").

During printing of this book, some of the Web addresses may have broken across two lines of text. If you come across such an address, rest assured that I haven't put in any extra characters (such as hyphens) to indicate the break. When using a broken Web address, type in exactly what you see on the page, pretending that the line break doesn't exist.

I include sidebars in the book that you don't really need to read in order to follow the chapter text. With that stated, though, I do encourage you to go back and read through this extra material when you have the time. Many of the sidebars contain practice examples that help you get an even better idea of how some of the investment concepts work.

Foolish Assumptions

The format of this book requires me to make some assumptions about you, the reader. I assume that you're someone who needs to know a lot about day trading in a short period of time. You may be considering a career change or looking for a productive hobby in retirement, and you want to know how to decide whether day trading is right for you. And if you determine that day trading *is* right for you, you want to know how to get started, right down to the setup for your computer monitors.

I assume that you're someone who has extra money to trade (whether it's yours or not) and who wants to try day trading techniques to goose up your portfolio returns.

I also assume that you have some understanding of the basics of investing — that you know what mutual funds and brokerage accounts are, for example. If you don't feel comfortable with that much, you may want to read *Investing For Dummies* or *Mutual Funds For Dummies* and then come back here.

No matter your situation or motives, my goal is to give you enough information so that you can ask smart questions, do careful research, and handle your money so that you can meet *your* goals. And if you don't have enough money right now to make a living from day trading, I want you to discover plenty of information from this book so that you will have it at the ready someday. Some research and trading techniques used by day traders can help you make better buy and sell decisions for the securities that you hold now. You can find more strategies than you may expect.

How This Book Is Organized

Day Trading For Dummies is sorted into four parts so that you can find what you need to know quickly.

Part I: Day Trading Fundamentals

The first part describes what day trading is, how it works, and what basic asset classes are used by day traders. It distinguishes between investing, trading, and gambling; knowing which is which can help you avoid costly mistakes. And it covers regulatory issues that will affect you as a day trader.

Part II: Day Trading Tools

Here, you'll find a guide to the practicalities: how to set up your office to improve your response times; choose the support services you need to research trades; get through the treacherous days with your sanity intact and your positions under control; pay taxes on your gains; and figure out how well you performed. This is the nitty-gritty, day-in-the-life stuff that separates day trading from video games. (Because, yes, in some ways, they're similar.)

Part III: Day Trading Strategies

This part is all about the different strategies and research techniques that day traders use to determine where and when to buy and sell their positions. This includes selling short to profit from securities that are declining in price and using leverage to make bigger trades in hopes of bigger returns.

The information here can help you make better portfolio decisions, even if you decide not to become a day trader. And it's just a start. The markets teach traders new things every day, and the smart ones pay attention.

Part IV: The Part of Tens

In this . . . *For Dummies*-only part, you get to enjoy some top-ten lists. I present ten reasons to day trade, ten reasons to avoid day trading, ten common mistakes that day traders make, and ten alternative careers for people who love the excitement of trading but who don't want to work for themselves as day traders.

I also include an Appendix full of references so that you can get more information if you desire.

Icons Used in This Book

You'll see four icons scattered around the margins of the text. Each icon points out a certain type of information, most of which you should know or may find interesting about day trading. They go as follows:

This icon notes something you should keep in mind about day trading. It may refer to something I covered earlier in the book, or it may highlight something you need to remember for future investing decisions.

Tip information tells you how to invest a little better, a little smarter, a little more efficiently. The information can help you make better day trades or ask better questions of people who want to supply you with research, training, and trading systems.

I've included nothing in this book that can cause death or bodily harm, as far as I can figure out, but plenty of things in the world of day trading can cause you to lose big money or, worse, your sanity. These points help you avoid big problems.

I put the boring (but sometimes helpful) academic stuff here. I even throw in a few equations here and there. By reading this material, you get the detailed information behind the investment theories or, sometimes, some interesting trivia or background information.

Where to Go from Here

Well, open up the book and get going! Allow me to give you some ideas. You may want to start with Chapter 1 if you know nothing about day trading so you can get a good sense of what I'm talking about. If you need to get set up to start trading, look at Chapters 6 and 7. If you want to know about some of the potential problems in day trading, turn to Chapters 5, 8, 10, and 19.

If you are thinking about day trading as a career, Chapter 2 describes what day traders do all day, and Chapter 20 can give you some good alternatives. For ideas about developing strategies, whether you're going to hold for a few minutes or several years, go to Part III. If you have a particular area of interest, use the index and table of contents to go to the topic you want. If you're not sure, you may as well turn the page and start at the beginning.

Part I
Day Trading Fundamentals

The 5th Wave   By Rich Tennant

"She had a great first week day trading. We're hoping for another so she can buy the matching desk."

In this part . . .

Day trading seems like an exciting way to make money, but is it right for you? And how is it different from investing — or gambling? Well, you've come to the right place. This part describes what day trading is, how it works, and what basic asset classes are used by day traders. It also covers some of the basic regulatory issues that will affect you as a day trader.

Chapter 1

Wake Up to Day Trading

*M*ake money from the comfort of your home! Be your own boss! Beat the market with your own smarts! Build real wealth! Tempting, isn't it? Day trading can be a great way to make money all on your own. It's also a great way to lose a ton of money, all on your own. Are you cut out to take the risk?

Day trading is a crazy business. Traders work in front of their computer screens, reacting to blips, each of which represents real dollars. They make quick decisions, because their ability to make money depends on successfully executing a large number of trades that generate small profits. Because they close out their positions in the stocks, options, and futures contracts they own at the end of the day, some of the risks are limited. Each day is a new day, and nothing can happen overnight to disturb an existing profit position.

But those limits on risk can limit profits. After all, a lot can happen in a year, increasing the likelihood that your trade idea will work out. But in a day? You have to be patient and work fast. Some days there is nothing good to buy. Other days it seems like every trade loses money. Do you have the fortitude to face the market every morning?

In this chapter, I give you an overview of day trading. I cover what exactly day traders do all day, go through the advantages and disadvantages of day trading, cover some of the personality traits of successful day traders, and give you some information on your likelihood of success.

You may find that day trading is a great career option that takes advantage of your street smarts and clear thinking — or that the risk outweighs the potential benefits. That's okay: The more you know before you make the decision to trade, the greater the chance of being successful. If it turns out that day trading isn't right for you, you can apply strategies and techniques that day traders use to improve the performance of your investment portfolio.

It's All in a Day's Work

The definition of day trading is that day traders hold their securities for only one day. They close out their positions at the end of every day and then start all over again the next day. By contrast, *swing traders* hold securities for days and sometimes even months, whereas *investors* sometimes hold for years.

The short-term nature of day trading reduces some risks, because there's no chance of something happening overnight to cause big losses. Meanwhile, many investors have gone to bed, thinking their position is in great shape, then woke up to find that the company has announced terrible earnings or that its CEO is being indicted on fraud charges.

But there's a flip side (there's always a flip side, isn't there?): The day trader's choice of securities and positions has to work out in a day, or it's gone. There's no tomorrow for any specific position. Meanwhile, the swing trader or the investor has the luxury of time, as it sometimes takes a while for a position to work out the way your research shows it should. In the long run, markets are efficient, and prices reflect all information about a security. Unfortunately, it can take a few days of short runs for this efficiency to kick in.

Day traders are speculators working in zero-sum markets one day at a time. That makes the dynamics different from other types of financial activities you may have been involved in.

When you take up day trading, the rules that may have helped you pick good stocks or find great mutual funds over the years will no longer apply. This is a different game with different rules.

Speculating, not hedging

Professional traders fall into two categories: speculators and hedgers. Speculators look to make a profit from price changes. Hedgers are looking to protect against a price change. They're making their buy and sell choices as insurance, not as a way to make a profit, so they choose positions that offset their exposure in another market. For example, a food-processing company might look to hedge against the risks of the prices of key ingredients — like corn, cooking oil, or meat — going up by buying futures contracts on those ingredients. That way, if prices do go up, the company's profits on the contracts help fund the higher prices that it has to pay to make its products. If the prices stay the same or go down, it loses only the price of the contract, which may be a fair tradeoff to the company.

The farmer raising corn, soybeans, or cattle, on the other hand, would benefit if prices went up and would suffer if they went down. To protect against a price decline, the farmer would sell futures on those commodities. Then, his futures position would make money if the price went down, offsetting the decline on his products. And if the prices went up, he'd lose money on the contracts, but that would be offset by his gain on his harvest.

The commodity markets were intended to help agricultural producers manage risk and find buyers for their products. The stock and bond markets were intended to create an incentive for investors to finance companies. Speculation emerged in all of these markets almost immediately, but it was not their primary purpose.

Markets have both hedgers and speculators in them. Day traders are all speculators. They look to make money from the market as they see it now. They manage their risks by carefully allocating their money, using stop and limit orders (which close out positions as soon as predetermined price levels are reached) and closing out at the end of the night. Day traders don't manage risk with offsetting positions the way a hedger does. They use other techniques to limit losses, like careful money management and stop and limit orders (all of which you can learn about in Chapter 2).

Knowing that different participants have different profit and loss expectations can help a day trader navigate the turmoil of each day's trading. And that's important, because to make money in a zero-sum market, you only make money if someone else loses.

Understanding zero-sum markets

In a zero-sum game, there are exactly as many winners as losers. There's no net gain, which makes it really hard to eke out a profit. And here's the thing: Options and futures markets, which are popular with day traders, are zero-sum markets. If the person who holds an option makes a profit, then the person who *wrote* (which is option-speak for *sold*) that option loses the same amount. There's no net gain or net loss in the market as a whole.

Now, some of those buying and selling in zero-sum markets are hedgers who are content to take small losses in order to prevent big ones. Speculators may have the profit advantage in certain market conditions. But they can't count on having that advantage all the time.

So who wins and loses in a zero-sum market? Some days, it all depends on luck, but over the long run, the winners are the people who are the most disciplined. They have a trading plan, set limits and stick to them, and can trade based on the data on the screen — not based on emotions like hope, fear, and greed.

Unlike the options and futures markets, the stock market is not a zero-sum game. As long as the economy grows, company profits will grow, and that will lead to growing stock prices. There really are more winners than losers over the long run. That doesn't mean there will be more winners than losers today, however. In the short run, the stock market should be treated like a zero-sum market.

If you understand how profits are divided in the markets that you choose to trade, you'll have a better understanding of the risks that you face as well as the risks that are being taken by the other participants. People do make money in zero-sum markets, but you don't want those winners to be making a profit off of you.

Some traders make money — lots of money — doing what they like. Trading is all about risk and reward. Those traders who are rewarded risked the 80 percent washout rate. Knowing that, do you want to take the plunge? If so, read on. And if not, read on anyway, as you might get some ideas that can help you manage your other investments.

Keeping the discipline: closing out each night

Day traders start each day fresh and finish each day with a clean slate. That reduces some of the risk, and it forces discipline. You can't keep your losers longer than a day, and you have to take your profits at the end of the day before those winning positions turn into losers.

And that discipline is important. When you are day trading, you face a market that does not know and does not care who you are, what you are doing, or what your personal or financial goals are. There's no kindly boss who might cut you a little slack today, no friendly coworker to help through a jam, no great client dropping you a little hint about her spending plans for the next fiscal year. Unless you have rules in place to guide your trading decisions, you will fall prey to hope, fear, doubt, and greed — the Four Horsemen of trading ruin.

So how do you start? First, you develop a business plan and a trading plan that reflect your goals and your personality. Then, you set your working days and hours and you accept that you will close out every night. Both of these steps are covered in Chapter 2. As you think about the securities that you will trade (Chapter 3) and how you might trade them (Chapters 12 and 13), you'll also want to test your trading system (Chapter 11) to see how it might work in actual trading.

In other words, you do some preparation and have a plan. That's a basic strategy for any endeavor, whether it's running a marathon, building a new garage, or taking up day trading.

Committing to Trading as a Business

For many people, the attraction of day trading is that traders can very much control their own hours. Many markets, like foreign exchange, trade around the clock. And with easy Internet access, day trading seems like a way to make money while the baby is napping, on your lunch hour, or working just a few mornings a week in between golf games and woodworking.

That myth of day trading as an easy activity that can be done on the side makes a lot of traders very rich, because they make money when traders who are not fully committed lose their money.

Day trading is a business, and the best traders approach it as such. They have business plans for what they will trade, how they will in invest in their business, and how they will protect their trading profits. So, much of this book is about this business of trading: how to do a business plan (Chapter 2), how to set up your office (Chapter 6), tax considerations (Chapter 10), and performance evaluation (Chapter 11). If you catch a late-night infomercial about trading, the story will be about the ease and the excitement. But if you want that excitement to last, you have to make the commitment to doing trading as a business to which you dedicate your time and your energy.

Trading part-time: an okay idea if done right

Can you make money trading part-time? You can, and some people do. To do this, they approach trading as a part-time job, not as a little game to play when they have nothing else to going on. A part-time trader may commit to trading three days a week, or to closing out at noon instead of at the close of the market. A successful part-time trader still has a business plan, still sets limits, and still acts like any professional trader would, just for a smaller part of the day.

Part-time trading works best when the trader can set and maintain fixed business hours. Your brain knows when it needs to go to work and concentrate on the market, because the habit is ingrained.

The successful part-timer operates as a professional with fixed hours. Think of it this way: My son is a patient in a group pediatric practice that has some part-time doctors. They keep set hours and behave like any other doctors in the practice; it's just that they do it for fewer hours each week. They commit their attention to medicine when they are on the job, and patients only know about their part-time hours when it comes time to make an appointment. These doctors don't pop into the office and start giving shots during their lunch break from their "real" job, sneaking around so that their "real" boss doesn't find out. And what patient would want to be seen by a doctor who won't dedicate themselves to providing health care, even if it's just for a few hours a day?

If you want to be a part-time day trader, approach it the same way that a part-time doctor, part-time lawyer, or part-time accountant would approach work. Find hours that fit your schedule and commit to trading during them. Have a dedicated office space with high-speed Internet access and a computer that you use just for trading. If you have children at home, you may need to have child care during your trading hours. And if you have another job, set your trading hours away from your work time. Trading via cell phone during your morning commute is a really good way to lose a lot of money (not to mention your life if you try it while driving).

Trading as a hobby: a bad idea

Because of the excitement of day trading and the supposed ease of doing it, you may be thinking that it would make a great hobby. If it's a boring Saturday afternoon, you could just spend a few hours day trading in the forex market (foreign exchange), and that way you'd make more money than if you spent those few hours playing video games! Right?

Uh, no.

Trading without a plan and without committing the time and energy to do it right is a route to losses. Professional traders are betting that there will be plenty of suckers out there, because that creates the losers that allow them to take profits in a zero-sum market.

The biggest mistake an amateur trader can make is to make a lot of money the first time trading. That first success was almost definitely due to luck, and that luck can turn against a trader on a dime. If you make money your first time out, take a step back and see if you can figure out why. Then test your strategy, using Chapter 11 as a guide, to see if it's a good one that you can use often.

Yes, I have two warnings in this section, and for good reason: Successful day traders commit to their business. Even then, most day traders fail in their first year. Brokerage firms, training services, and other traders have a vested interest in making trading seem like an easy activity that you can work into your life. But it's a job — a job that some people love, but a job nonetheless.

If you really love the excitement of the markets, there are ways to invest on a hobbyist's schedule. First, you can spend your time doing fundamental research to find long-term investments, which is described a little bit in Chapter 12. You can look into alternative investments to help diversify your portfolio; Chapter 3 can get you started on that. You can also trade with play money, either in demo accounts or in trading contests, to try out trading without committing real money. Chapter 20 has some ideas on that.

Working with a Small Number of Assets

Most day traders pick one or two markets and concentrate on those to the exclusion of all others. That way, they can learn how the markets trade, how news affects prices, and how the other participants react to new information. Also, concentrating on just one or two markets helps a trader maintain focus.

And what do day traders trade? Chapter 3 has information on all of the different markets and how they work, but here's a quick summary of the most popular assets with day traders right now:

- **Financial futures:** Futures contracts allow traders to profit from price changes in such market indexes as the S&P 500 or the Dow Jones Industrial Average. They give traders exposure to the prices at a much lower cost than buying all of the stocks in the index individually. Of course, they tend to be more volatile than the indexes they track, because they are based on expectations.

- **Forex:** *Forex*, short for *foreign exchange*, involves trading in currencies all over the world to profit from changes in exchange rates. Forex is the largest and most liquid market there is, and it's open for trading all day, every day except Sunday. Traders like the huge number of opportunities. Because most price changes are small, they have to use *leverage* (borrowed money) to make a profit. The borrowings have to be repaid no matter what happens to the trade, which adds to the risk of forex.

✔ **Common stock:** The entire business of day trading began in the stock market, and the stock market continues to be popular with day traders. They look for news on company performance and investor perception that affect stock prices, and they look to make money from those price changes. Day traders are a big factor in some industries, such as technology. The big drawback? Stock traders can get killed at tax time if they are not careful. (See Chapter 10 for more information.)

Managing your positions

A key to successful trading is knowing how much you are going to trade and when you are going to get out of your position. Sure, day traders are always going to close out at the end of the day — or they wouldn't be day traders — but they also need to cut their losses and take their profits as they occur during the day.

Traders rarely place all their money on one trade. That's a good way to lose it! Instead, they trade just some of it, keeping the rest to make other trades as new opportunities in the market present themselves. If any one trade fails, the trader still has money to place new trades. Some traders divide their money into fixed proportions, and others determine how much money to trade based on the expected risk and expected return of the security that they are trading. Careful money management helps a trader stay in the game longer, and the longer a trader stays in, the better the chance of making good money. Chapter 2 has more information on this.

To protect their funds, traders use *stop and limit orders*. These are placed with the brokerage firm and kick in whenever the security reaches a predetermined price level. If the security starts to fall in price more than the trader would like, *bam*! It's sold, and no more losses will occur on that trade. The trader doesn't agonize over the decision or second-guess herself. Instead, she just moves on to the next trade, putting her money to work on a trade that's likely to be better.

Day traders make a lot of trades, and a lot of those trades are going to be losers. The key is to have more winners than losers. By limiting the amount of losses, the trader makes it easier for the gains to be big enough to generate more than enough money to make up for them.

Focusing your attention

Day traders are often undone by stress and emotion. It's hard, looking at screens all day, working alone, to keep a steady eye on what's happening in the market. But traders have to do that. They have to concentrate on the market and stick to their trading system, staying as calm and rational as possible.

Those who do well have support systems in place. They are able to close their positions and spend the rest of the day on other activities. They do something to get rid of their excess energy and clear their minds, such as running or yoga or meditation. They understand that their ability to maintain a clear mind when the market is open is crucial.

Traders sometimes think of the market itself, or everyone else who is trading, as the enemy. The real enemies are emotions: doubt, fear, greed, and hope. Those four feelings keep traders from concentrating on the market and sticking to their systems.

One of the frustrations of trading is that some days, there will be more opportunities to trade than you have time or money to trade. Good trades are getting away from you. You simply don't have the resources to take advantage of every opportunity you see. That's why it's important to have a plan and to concentrate on what works for you.

Personality Traits of Successful Day Traders

Traders are a special breed. They can be blunt and crude, because they act fast against a market that has absolutely no consideration for them. For all their rough exterior, they maintain strict discipline about how they approach their trading day and what they do during market hours.

The discipline begins with a plan for how to start the day, including reviews of news events and trading patterns. It includes keeping track of trades made during the day, to help the trader figure out what works and why. And it depends on cutting losses as they occur, reaping all profits that appear, and refining a set of trading rules so that tomorrow will be even better. No, it's not as much fun as just jumping in and placing orders, but it's more likely to lead to success.

Not everyone can be a day trader, nor should everyone try it. In this section I cover some of the traits that make up the best of them.

Independence

For the most part, day traders work by themselves. Although some cities have offices for traders, known as *trading arcades*, the number of these places has been declining over the years because the cost of setting up at home has gone down dramatically. Computers and monitors are relatively inexpensive, high-speed Internet connectivity is easier to get, and many brokerage firms cater to the needs of traders who are working by themselves.

So that leaves the day trader at home, alone, stuck in a room with nothing but the computer screen for company. It can be boring, and it can make it hard to concentrate. Some people can't handle it.

But other traders thrive on being alone all day, because it brings out their best qualities. They know that their trading depends on them alone, not on anyone else. The trader has sole responsibility when something goes wrong, but he also gets to keep all the spoils. He can make his own decisions about what works and what doesn't, with no pesky boss or annoying corporate drone telling him what he needs to do today.

If the idea of being in charge of your own business and your own trading account is exciting, then day trading might be a good career option for you.

And what if you want to trade but don't want to be working by yourself? Consider going to work for a brokerage firm, a hedge fund, a mutual fund, or a commodities company. These businesses need traders to manage their own money, and they usually have large numbers of people working together on their trading desks to share ideas, cheer each other on, and give each other support when things go wrong.

No matter how independent you are, your trading will benefit if you have friends and family to offer you support and encouragement. That network will help you better manage the emotional aspects of trading. Besides, it's more fun to celebrate your success with someone else!

Quick-wittedness

Day trading is a game of minutes. An hour may as well be a decade when the markets are moving fast. And that means a day trader can't be deliberative or panicky. When it's time to buy or sell, it's time to buy or sell, and that's all there is to it.

Many investors prefer to spend hours doing a careful study of a security and markets before committing money. Some of these people are enormously successful. Warren Buffett, the CEO of Berkshire Hathaway, amassed $37 billion from his careful investing style, money that he is giving to charity. But Buffett and people like him are not traders.

Traders have to have enough trust in their system and enough experience in the markets that they can act quickly when they see a buy or sell opportunity.

Many brokerage firms offer their clients demonstration accounts or backtesting services that allow traders to work with their system before committing actual dollars, helping them learn to recognize market patterns that signal potential profits.

A trader with a great system who isn't quick on the mouse button has another option: automating trades. Many brokerage firms offer software that will execute trades automatically whenever certain market conditions occur. For many traders, it's a perfect way to take the emotion out of a trading strategy. Others dislike automatic trading, because it takes some of the fun out of it. And let's face it, successful traders find the whole process to be a good time.

Decisiveness

Day traders have to move quickly, so they also have to be able to make decisions quickly. There's no waiting until tomorrow to see how the charts play out before committing capital. If the trader sees an opportunity, she has to go with it. Now.

But what if it's a bad decision? Well, of course some decisions are going to be bad. That's the risk of making any kind of an investment, and without risk, there is no return. Anyone playing around in the markets has to accept that.

But two good day trading practices help limit the effects of making a bad decision. The first is the use of stop and limit orders, which automatically close out losing positions. The second is closing out all positions at the end of every day, which lets traders start fresh the next day.

If you have some downside protection in place, then it's psychologically easier to go ahead and make the decisions you need to make in order to make a profit. And if you are one of those people who has a hard time making a decision, day trading probably isn't right for you.

What Day Trading Is Not

There is much mythology about day trading: Day traders lose money. Day traders make money. Day traders are insane. Day traders are cold and rational. Day trading is easy. Day trading is a direct path to alcoholism and ruin.

I'm going to bust a few day trading myths. Someone has to do it, right? There's both good news and bad news in this section, so read it through to get some perspective on what, exactly, the day trader can expect from this new endeavor.

It's not investing . . .

Day traders never hold a position for more than a day. Swing traders hold positions for a few days, maybe even a few weeks, but rarely longer than that. Investors hold their stakes for the long term, with some looking to hang onto their securities for decades and maybe even hand them down to their children.

Day trading is most definitely not investing. It's an important function to the capital markets because it forces the price changes that bring the supply and demand of the market into balance, but it doesn't create new sources of funding for companies and governments. It doesn't generate long-term growth.

Many day traders withdraw their trading capital on a regular basis to put into investments, helping them build a long-term portfolio for their retirement or for other ventures they might want to take on. There's a good chance the trader will have someone else manage this money, because investing and trading have different mindsets.

But it's not gambling . . .

One of the biggest knocks on day trading is that it's just another form of gambling. And as everyone knows, or should know: In gambling, the odds always favor the house.

In day trading, the odds are even in many markets. The options and futures markets, for example, are zero-sum markets with as many winners as losers, but those markets also include people looking to hedge risk and who thus have lower profit expectations than do day traders.

The stock market has the potential for more winning trades than losing trades, especially over the long run, so it's not a zero-sum market. The odds are ever-so-slightly in the trader's favor.

And in all markets, the prepared and disciplined trader can do better than the frantic, naïve trader. That's not the case when gambling, because no matter how prepared the gambler is, the casino has the upper hand.

 People with gambling problems sometimes turn to day trading as a socially acceptable way to feed their addiction. If you know you have a gambling problem or suspect you are at risk, it's probably not a good idea to take up day trading. Day traders who are closet gamblers tend to make bad trades and have trouble setting limits and closing out at the end of the day. They turn the odds against them. Chapter 4 has some information on the line between day trading and gambling.

It's hardly guaranteed . . .

Given the participation of day traders in securities markets, researchers are always trying to figure out whether they make money. And the answers aren't good. Here I review some of the literature to show you the current state of day trading success rates. Note that they are low. Few people who take this up succeed, in part because few people who take this up are prepared. And even many of the prepared traders fail.

Much of the research covers performance in the late 1990s, when day trading became wildly popular. It grew along with the commercial Internet, and it fell out of favor when the Internet bubble burst.

Day trading is difficult, but it is not impossible. You can improve your chances of success by taking the time to prepare and by having enough money to fund your initial trading account. During the first year, you'll want to handle trading losses and still be able to pay your rent and buy your groceries. Knowing that the basics of your life are taken care of will give you more confidence, and that will help your performance.

"Do Day Traders Make Money? Evidence from Taiwan"

This paper, written in 2004 by Brad Barber, Yi-Tsung Lee, Yu-Jane Liu, and Terrance Odean (and available at http://faculty.haas.berkeley.edu/odean/papers/Day%20Traders/Day%20Trade%20040330.pdf) found that only 20 percent of day traders in Taiwan tracked between 1995 and 1999 made money in any six-month period, after considering transaction costs. Median profits, net of costs, were U.S. $4,200 for any six-month period, although the best traders showed semi-annual profits of $33,000. The study also found that those who placed the most trades made the most money, possibly because they are the most experienced traders in the group.

"Report of the Day Trading Project Group"

In 1999, the North American Securities Administrators Association, which represents state and provincial securities regulators in the United States, Canada, and Mexico, researched day trading so that its members could provide appropriate oversight. The report, which you can see at www.nasaa.org/content/Files/NASAA_Day_Trading_Report.pdf, did not include performance data. However, it cited several cases where brokerage firms were sanctioned by regulators for misrepresenting their clients' performance numbers, including one firm that had no clients with profits.

"Trading Profits of SOES Bandits"

Paul Schultz and Jeffrey Harris looked into the profits made by the so-called SOES bandits, day traders who took advantage of loopholes that existed in NASDAQ's Small Order Entry System in the 1990s. These people were the first day traders. Did they make money? The authors looked at a few weeks of trade data from two different firms. What they found was that about a third of all round-trip trades (buying and then later selling the same security) lost money before commissions. Only a quarter of the round-trip trades had a profit of $250 or more before commissions. The 69 traders in the study made anywhere from one to 312 round-trip trades per week. They had an average weekly profit after commission of $1,690; however, almost half of the traders, 34 of them, lost money in an average week.

You can see the abstract at `http://papers.ssrn.com/sol3/papers.cfm?abstract_id=137949`. The full article is available through many libraries.

But it's not exactly dangerous . . .

Yes, a lot of day traders lose money, and some lose everything that they start out with. Many others don't lose all of their trading capital; they just decide that there are better uses of their time and better ways to make money.

A responsible trader works with _risk capital_, which is money that she can afford to lose. She uses stop and limit orders to minimize her losses, and she always closes out at the end of the day. She understands the risks and rewards of trading, and that keeps her sane.

Many day trading strategies rely on _leverage_, which is the use of borrowed money to increase potential returns. That carries the risk of the trader losing more money than is in his account. However, the brokerage firm doesn't want that to happen, so it will probably close a leveraged account that's in danger of going under. That's good, because it limits your potential loss.

It's not easy . . .

Along with the relatively low rate of success, day trading is really stressful. It takes a lot of energy to concentrate on the markets, knowing that real money is at stake. The profit amounts on any one trade are likely to be small, which means the trader has to be persistent and keep placing trades until the end of the day.

Some traders can't handle the stress. Some get bored. Some get frustrated. And some can't believe that they can make a living doing something that they love.

But then, neither are a lot of other worthwhile activities

Day trading is tough, but many day traders can't imagine doing anything else. The simple fact is that a lot of occupations are difficult ways to make a living, and yet they are right for some people. Every career has its advantages and disadvantages, and day trading is no different.

When you finish this book, you should have a good sense of whether or not day trading is right for you. If you realize that it's the career you have been searching for, I hope it leaves you with good ideas for how to get set up and learn more so that you are successful.

And if you find that maybe day trading isn't right for you, I hope you get some ideas that can help you manage your long-term investments better. After all, the attention to price movements, timing, and risk that is critical to a day trader's success can help any investor improve their returns. What's not to like about that?

Putting day trading success rates in perspective

When I was doing research for this book, I talked to one very successful trader who told me two things. First, he was suspicious of all the books and training programs on day trading, because he didn't think that they really helped people learn to trade. Despite that, he liked that they existed, because trading had proven to be a great way for him to make a good living and support his family, and he thought it would be great if those people who are cut out for trading discovered the business.

Yes, most day traders fail — about 80 percent in the first year, as I noted earlier. But so do a large percentage of people who start new businesses or enter other occupations. That's why I've combed through several different reports and databases to show how well people do in other fields. (My sources are *Realty Times*; Barber, Lee, Liu, and Odean; American College of Sports

Medicine; ACT; Ohio State University; and the National Center for Education Statistics.)

Field	First Year Failure Rate (%)
Real estate sales	86
Day trading	80
Training for a marathon	70
College	33
Restaurants	26
Teaching	13

If you understand the risks and keep them in perspective, you'll be better able to handle the slings and arrows of misfortune on the way to your goal.

Chapter 2

Making a Day Trade of It

Day trading is sometimes presented as a profitable hobby. Anyone who buys a day trading DVD course via infomercial can make money easily in just a few hours a week, right? Well, no. Day trading is a job. It can be a full-time job or a part-time job, but it requires the same commitment to working regular hours and the same dedication to learning a craft and honing skills as any other job.

The best traders have plans for their business and for their trades. They know in advance how they want to trade and what they expect to do when they face the market. They may find themselves deviating from their plans at times, due to luck or circumstance or changing markets, but in those cases at least they understand why they are trying something else.

Failing to plan is planning to fail. And if you can't remember that right now, don't worry. I repeat it several times in this book.

Here's another reason for planning: Trading comes in many flavors, and many of those who call themselves day traders are actually doing other things with their money. If you know in advance what you want to do, you'll be less likely to panic or follow fads. You'll be in a better position to take advantage of opportunities in a way that suits your personality, trading skills, and goals. And that's why this entire chapter is devoted to planning.

Planning Your Trading Business

The day trader is an entrepreneur who has started a small business that trades in securities in hopes of making a return. You'll get your business off to a good start if you have a plan for what you want to do and how you're going to do it. That way, you know what your goals are and what you need to do to achieve them.

You can find a lot of sample business plans in books and on the Internet, but most of them are not appropriate for a trader. A typical business plan is designed to not only guide the business, but also to attract outside financing. Unless you are going to take in partners or borrow money from an outside source, your day trading business plan is for you only. No executive summary and no pages of projections needed.

So what do you need instead? How about a list of your goals and a plan for what you will trade, what your hours will be, what equipment you'll need, and how much to invest in the business?

Setting your goals

The first thing you need in your plan is a list of your goals, both short term and long term. Here is a sample list to get you started:

- ✔ Where do you want to be in the next three months, six months, nine months, a year, three years, five years, and ten years?
- ✔ How many days a year do you want to trade?
- ✔ What do you need to know to trade better?
- ✔ How much do you want to make?
- ✔ What will you do with your profits?
- ✔ How will you reward yourself when you hit your goals?

Be as specific as possible when you think about what you want to do with your trading business and don't worry if your business goals overlap with your personal goals. When you are in business for yourself, the two often mix.

You might be tempted to say, "I want to make as much money as I possibly can," and forget the rest, but that's not a goal that's quantifiable. If you don't know that you've reached your goal, how can you go on to set new ones? And if you don't meet your goal, how will you know how to make changes?

Picking the markets

There are so many different securities and derivatives that you can day trade! Sure, you want to trade anything that makes money for you, but what on earth is that? Each market has its own nuances, so if you flit from futures to forex (foreign exchange), you might be courting disaster. That's another reason why you need a plan. If you know what markets you want to trade, you'll have a better sense of what research services you'll need, what ongoing training you might want to consider, and how to evaluate your performance.

Chapter 3 covers different asset classes and how day traders might use them in great detail. For now, Table 2-1 gives a little cheat sheet that covers those that are most popular with day traders. Think about your chosen markets in the same way: What do you want to trade, where will you trade it, what is the risk and return, and what are some of the characteristics that make this market attractive to you?

And what do zero sum, leverage, and upward bias mean? Well, *zero sum* means that for every winner, there is a loser. There is no net gain in the market. *Leverage* is the use of borrowed money, which increases potential return and also increases risk. *Upward bias* means that in the long run, the market is expected to increase in price, but that doesn't mean it will go up on any given day that you are trading.

Table 2-1	Popular Things for Day Traders to Trade		
Item	*Main Exchange*	*Risk/Reward*	*Characteristics*
Stock index futures	CME	Zero sum/ leverage	Benefits from movements of broad markets
Treasury bond futures	CBT	Zero sum/ leverage	Best way for day traders to play the bond market
Foreign exchange	OTC	Zero sum/ leverage	Markets open all day, every day, except Sunday
Corn	CBT	Zero sum/ leverage	An agricultural market liquid enough for day traders
Large-cap stocks	NYSE, NASDAQ	Upward bias	Good stocks for day trading, large and volatile

Key: CME = Chicago Mercantile Exchange, CBT = Chicago Board of Trade, OTC = Over the counter, NYSE = New York Stock Exchange

The characteristics of the different markets and assets will affect both your business plan and your trading plan. The business plan should include information on what you will trade and why, as well as on what you hope to learn to trade in the future. The trading plan looks at what you want to trade each day and why, so that you can channel your efforts.

Many day traders work in a few different markets, depending on their temperament and trading conditions, but successful traders have narrowed down the few markets where they want to concentrate their efforts. Start slowly, working just one or two different securities, but consider adding new markets as your experience and trading capital grows.

Fixing hours, vacation, and sick leave

The markets are open more or less continuously. Although many exchanges have set trading hours, there are traders working after hours who are willing to sell if you want to buy. Some markets, such as foreign exchange, take only the briefest of breaks over the course of a week. This gives day traders incredible flexibility — no matter what hours and what days are best for you to trade, you can find something that works for you. If you are sharpest in the evenings, you might be better off trading Asian currencies, because those markets are active when you are. Of course, this can be a disadvantage, because no one is setting limits for you. Few markets are great places to trade every hour of every day.

If you want to, you can trade almost all the time. But you probably don't want to. To keep your sanity, maintain your perspective, and have a life outside of your trading, you should set regular hours and stick to them. In your business plan, determine when you are going to trade, how often you are going to take a vacation, how many sick days you'll give yourself, and how you'll know to take a day off. One of the joys of self-employment is that you can take time off when you need to, so give yourself that little perk in your business plan.

Trading is a stressful business. You need to take time off to clear your head, and you'll probably find that working while sick is a sure-fire route to losses. Build in some sick and vacation time — and read Chapter 8 for more information on how to manage the stress of the markets.

Getting yourself set up

Part of your business plan should cover where you work and what equipment you need. (Chapter 6 has some ideas on that subject.) What can you afford now, and what is on your wish list? Do you have enough computing equipment, the right Internet connection, and a working filing system? This is part of your plan for getting your business underway, so put some thought into your infrastructure.

And yes, this is important. You don't want to lose a day of trading because your computer has crashed, nor do you want to be stuck with an open position because your Internet service provider has a temporary outage. And you certainly don't want to lose your concentration because you are trying to work in the family room while other members of your household are playing video games.

Investing in your business

You won't have the time and money to do everything you want to do in your trading business, so part of your business plan should include a list of things that you want to add over time. A key part of that is continuous improvement: No matter how good a trader you are now, you can always be better. Furthermore, the markets are always changing. New products come to market, new trading regulations are passed, and new technologies appear. You will always need to absorb new things, and part of your business plan should consider that. Ask yourself

- ✔ What percentage of your time and trade gains will go into expanding your knowledge of trading?
- ✔ Do you want to do that by taking seminars or by allocating the time to simulation testing?
- ✔ What upgrades will you make to your trading equipment?
- ✔ How are you going to set yourself up to stay in trading for the long haul?

It takes money to make money — another cliché. It doesn't mean that you should spend money willy-nilly on any nifty gadget or fancy video seminar that comes your way. Instead, it means that an ongoing, thoughtful investment in your trading business will pay off in a greater likelihood of long-run success.

Evaluating and revising your plan

One component of your business plan should be a plan for revising it. Things are going to change. You may be more or less successful than you hope, market conditions may change on you, and you may simply find out more about how you trade best. That's why you should set a plan for updating your business plan to reflect where you are and where you want to be as you go along. At least once a year, and more often if you feel the need for a change, go through your business plan and revise it to reflect where you are now. What are your new goals? What are your new investment plans? What are you doing right, and what needs to change?

A sample business plan

Not sure what should be in a business plan? Here's a sample to get you thinking about how to plan your trading business.

Where I Am Now

I am about to start a career as a day trader. I have $50,000 in capital that I can risk without affecting my livelihood. I will rely on my spouse's job to cover our family spending needs and our health insurance. This trading account will be used to meet our long-term goals: paying off the mortgage, sending the children to college, paying for our retirement, and ultimately buying a vacation house in the mountains.

This business plan covers what I need to get started.

My Business Goals

In three months, I will have spent $5,000 of my capital on a functional office and will have a tested trading strategy that works well in simulation.

In six months, I will be trading daily. I will have lost no more than $5,000 of my trading capital.

In nine months, I will be trading daily, and I will have more winning trades than losing trades.

In a year, I will have gained 10 percent on my account. I will withdraw $1,000 to pay toward our mortgage and another $1,000 toward an ergonomic chair and other office equipment upgrades. I will have mastered my first trading system and will be testing a second one in order to expand my trading opportunities.

In three years, my trading account will have $150,000 in it from my trading successes, after making investments in my business and paying an additional $10,000 in principal on the mortgage. I will be trading three different systems with satisfactory success.

In five years, I will have $300,000 in my trading account. I will have made enough money to have paid off our mortgage, after making regular payments on principal and interest every month, paying $10,000 in year three, and paying off the rest with the profits that I expect to earn between years three and five. I will be known as a successful trader.

In ten years, I will have a second house, and I will continue my record of trading success. I will take $100,000 out of my trading account to cover college tuition.

Markets Traded

My primary trading strategy will involve momentum trades on the E-Mini S&P 500, E-Mini NASDAQ, and E-Mini Russell 2000 futures contracts traded on the Chicago Mercantile Exchange. I will put no more than 10 percent of my capital into any one trade and I will close out positions each night.

I am interested in news-driven *swing trading* (holding for short periods of time but longer than a day) in large technology companies, so I will research and test strategies with those. I am also interested in trading Asian currencies, so I will make the time to learn more about those markets and determine if I can trade them effectively during my preferred trading hours.

Trading Hours and Days

Because my primary strategy is equity driven, I will trade only while the equity markets are open, from 9:30 a.m. until 4:00 p.m. Monday through Friday. I will spend an hour before the markets open researching current trends and news events so that I know what people will be looking for that day. I will spend an hour after the market closes doing paperwork and reviewing the day's trades.

I will take off three full weeks for vacation: the week of my children's spring break, a week in August for a family vacation, and the last week of December. I will also take off any day that I am ill so that I can maintain my health and my concentration.

My Business Setup

I work from a home office. I use my startup funds to purchase two monitors working off of one computer, with a second clone computer on hand in case something goes wrong. I have cable Internet access as well as a DSL backup through my phone line. I have a wireless router, so that I can check my email and instant messages through a third computer, a laptop, instead of through my trading computer.

I have an account with a full-service online brokerage firm that can offer me the necessary research services. I also subscribe to *Investor's Business Daily* and *The Wall Street Journal*, which I read each morning to help me gauge sentiment.

I track my trades on a paper form that I collect in ring binders. I collect my other paperwork in ring binders that I keep on the shelf in my office.

Investing in My Business

To stay successful in the long run, I need to keep my skills sharp. To do this, I will read one book on trading psychology or a successful trader's memoir each month. I will also work on simulation trading for swing trading in technology stocks, as I plan to add that to my trading system.

As my trade profits grow, I will invest some of them in trying new trading techniques, knowing that I may have short-term losses until I understand a market better. I will spend one day at the end of each quarter on backtesting and simulation of new strategies.

My wish list includes a more comfortable chair for my office.

Evaluating my Business Plan

Before each vacation, I will read over this business plan. I will use the time away from the markets to think about what changes I need to make in it and will revise the plan upon my return.

Business plans are living documents. Use your plan to run your trading business; as your business runs, use the results to update your plan. You can keep the old ones around to show you how much progress you have made, if you are so inclined.

Planning Your Trades

A good trader has a plan. She knows what she wants to trade and how to trade it. She knows what her limits are before she places the order. She's not afraid to take a loss now in order to prevent a bigger loss in the future, and she's willing to sit out the market if nothing is happening that day. Her plan gives her the discipline to protect her capital so that she has money in her account to profit when the opportunities present themselves.

In this section, I cover the components of trade planning. When you start trading, you'll probably write notes to set up a trading plan for each day that covers what you expect for the day, what trades you hope to make, and what your profit goals and loss limit are. As you develop experience, trade planning may become innate. You develop the discipline to trade according to plan, without needing to write it all down — although you might find it useful to tape a list of the day's expected announcements to your monitor.

Like a business plan, a trading plan is flexible. The markets don't know what you've planned, and you'll probably end up deviating on more than one occasion. The key thing is knowing *why* you deviated: Was it because of the information that you saw when you were looking at your screen, or was it because you became panicky?

What do you want to trade?

The first step in your trading plan should also be addressed in your business plan: What is it that you want to trade? Many traders work in more than one market, and each market is a little different. Some trade different products simultaneously, whereas others choose one for the day and work only on that.

You need to figure out which markets give you the best chance of getting a profit that day. It's going to be different. Some days, no trades will be good for you in one market. If you are too antsy for that, then find another market to keep you busy so that you don't trade just to stay awake. (Of course, many traders report that the big money opportunities are in the slower, less glamorous markets.)

As a day trader, you are self-employed. You don't answer to a boss and don't have to trade today if you don't want to. So if you have a headache, or if no good trades are available to you, or if recent losses have gotten you down, take the day off and do something fun.

How do you want to trade it?

Figuring out how to trade an asset involves a lot of considerations: What is your mood today? What will other traders be reacting to today? How much risk do you want to take? How much money do you want to commit? This is the nitty-gritty stage of trade planning that can help you manage your market day better.

Starting the day with a morning review

Before you start trading, take some time to determine where your head is relative to the market. Is today a day that you can concentrate? Are there things happening in your life that might distract you, are you coming down with the flu, or were you out too late last night? Or are you rearing to go, ready to take on whatever the day brings? Your mindset should influence how aggressively you want to trade and how much risk you want to take. You have to pay attention to do well in the markets, but you also have to know when to hang back during the day's activities. For example, many traders find that their strategies work best at certain times of the day, such as at the open or before major news announcements.

Think about what people will be reacting to. Go through the newspapers and check the online newswires to gather information. Then figure out the answers to these questions:

✔ Are there big news announcements scheduled for today? At what time? Do you want to trade ahead of the news or want to wait and see what the market does?

✔ Did something happen overnight? Will that affect trading on the open, or is it already in the markets? Do you want to trade on the open or wait?

✔ What are the other people who trade the same future, commodity, stock, or currency that you do worried about today? How are they likely to respond? Do you want to go with the market or strike a contrary position?

For a handy list of expected news announcements on any given trading day, check out www.tradethenews.com/weekly-calendar.php.

Drawing up a sample order

Once you have a sense of how you are going to tackle the day, you want to determine how much you are going to trade. The key considerations are the following:

✔ Do you want to be long or short? That is, do you want to bet that the asset you are trading is going up in price or down?

✔ Do you want to borrow money? If so, how much? Borrowing — also known as *margin* or *leverage* — increases your potential return as well as your risk. (Margin, leverage, and short selling are discussed in Chapter 14.)

Some contracts, such as futures, have built-in leverage. As soon as you decide to trade them, you are borrowing money.

✔ How much money do you want to trade — in dollars, and as a percentage of your total account size? (Money management is discussed in detail in Chapter 9.)

Once you have those items detailed, you're in good shape to get started for the day.

Figuring out when to buy and when to sell

Once you get insight into what the day might be like and how much money you want to allocate to the markets, your next step is to figure out when you will buy and when you will sell. Ah, but if that were easy, do you think I'd be writing a book on day trading? No. If knowing when to buy and sell were easy, I would be too busy taking private surfing lessons in front of my beachfront mansion on Maui to be writing a book.

The very best traders aren't selling trading advice, because they are already retired. Everyone else is figuring it out as they go along, with varying degrees of success.

Many traders rely on *technical analysis*, which involves looking at patterns in charts of the price and volume changes. I discuss technical analysis in Chapter 12. Other traders look at news and price information as the market changes, rather than looking at price patterns, and that's discussed in Chapter 13. Still others care only about very short-term price discrepancies, covered in Chapter 14. But the most important thing, no matter what approach you prefer, is that you *backtest* and simulate your trading before you commit real dollars. That way, you have a better sense of how you'll react in real market conditions. That key step is covered in Chapter 11.

Setting profit goals

When you trade, you want to have a realistic idea how much money you can make. What's a fair profit? Do you want to ride a winning position until the end of the day or do you want to get out quickly once you've made enough money to compensate for your risk? There's no one answer to this question, as so much depends on market conditions and your trading style. In this section are some guidelines that can help you determine what's best for you.

But first, I take a detour and define all the different terms for profits that you might come across.

The language of money

Profits are discussed differently in different markets, and you may as well have the right lingo when you write your plan:

- ✔ **Pennies:** Stocks trade in decimal form, so each price movement is worth at least a penny — one cent. It's an obvious way to measure to a profit.

- ✔ **Pips:** A *pip* is the smallest unit of currency that can be traded. In foreign exchange markets (forex), a pip is generally equal to one one-hundredth of a cent. If the value of the euro moves from $1.2934 to $1.2935, it has moved a pip.

Do not confuse a pip in the forex market with an investment scheme known as *PIP*, sometimes called People in Profit or Pure Investor. (The fraud also operates as *HYIP*, for High Yield Investment Program.) PIP has been promoted as a trading system with a guaranteed daily return, but it's really a pyramid scheme that takes money from participants and returns little or nothing. You can get more information from the SEC's Web site, `www.sec.gov/divisions/enforce/primebank.shtml`.

✔ **Points:** A *point* is a single percentage. A penny is a point, as is a 1 percent change in a bond price. A related number, a *basis point*, is a percent of a percent, or .0001.

✔ **Teenies:** Many securities, especially bonds and derivatives on them, trade in increments of ⅛ of a dollar. Half of an eighth is a sixteenth, also known as a *teeny*.

✔ **Ticks:** A *tick* is the smallest trading increment in a futures contract. It varies from product to product. How much it works out to be depends on the contract structure. For the Chicago Mercantile Exchange's E-Mini S&P 500 contract, a tick is equal to $12.50, calculated as a 0.25 change in the underlying S&P 500 index multiplied by $50 multiplier. A tick on a Chicago Board of Trade E-Mini soybean contract is $1.25, calculated as 1/8 cent on a bushel of soybeans in a contract covering 1000 bushels. You can get information on the tick size of contracts that interest you on the Web site of the offering exchange, which are listed in Chapter 3.

No one ever lost money taking a profit, as the cliché goes. (The trading business is rife with clichés, if you haven't noticed.) The newer you are to day trading, the more sense it makes to be conservative. Close your positions and end your day when you reach a target profit — and then make note of what happens afterward. Can you afford to hold on to your positions longer in order to make a greater profit?

Thinking about profits

Your profit goals can be sliced and diced a few different ways. The first is the *gain per trade*, on both a percentage basis and an absolute basis. The second is the *gain per day*, on both a percentage basis and an absolute basis. What do you have to do to reach these goals? How many successful trades will you have to make? Do you have the capital to do that? And what is right for the trade you are making right now, regardless of what your longer-term goals are?

Setting limits on your trades

It's a good idea to set a *loss limit* along with a profit goal.

For example, many futures traders have a rule to risk two ticks in pursuit of three ticks. That means that they will sell a position as soon as it loses two ticks in value, and they will also sell a position as soon as it gains three ticks in value. And for anything in between? Well, they close out their positions at the end of the day, so whatever happens happens.

Even traders who do not have a rule like that often set a limit on how much they will lose per trade. Other traders use computer programs to guide their buys and their sells, so they need to sell their positions automatically. Brokers make this easy by giving customers the choice of a stop order or a limit order to protect their positions.

You want to limit your loss per trade *as well as* your loss per day. If today is not a good one, close up shop, take a break, and come back fresh tomorrow.

Stop orders

A *stop order*, also known as a *stop loss order*, is an order to sell a security at the market price as soon as it hits a predetermined level. If you want to make sure you sell a block of stock when it falls below $30 per share, for example, you could enter a stop order at $30 (telling your broker "Sell Stop 30"). As soon as the stock hits $30, the broker sells it, even if the price goes to $29 or $31 before all the stock is sold.

Limit orders

A *limit order* is an order to buy or sell a security at a specific price or better: lower than the current price for the buy order, higher than the specific price for a sell order. If you want to make sure you sell a block of stock when it falls below $30 per share, for example, you could enter a limit order at $30 (telling your broker "Sell Limit 30"). As soon as the stock hits $30, the broker sells it, as long as the price stays at $30 or higher. If the price goes even a penny below $30, the limit is no longer enforced. After all, no buyers are going to want to pay an above-market price just so you can get your order filled all the way!

Stop limit orders

A *stop limit* order is a combination of a stop order and a limit order. It tells the broker to buy or sell at a specific price or better, but only after the price reaches a given stop price. If you want to make sure you sell a block of stock when it falls below $30 per share, but you do not want to sell it if it starts to go back up, for example, you could enter a stop order at $30 with a limit of $31 (telling your broker "Sell 30 Limit 31"). As soon as the stock hits $30, the broker sells it as long as the price stays under $31. If the price goes above $31, the order is no longer enforced. There's a very small price range where this order will be executed.

Are you confused? Well, the differences may be confusing, but understanding them is important to helping you manage your risks. That's why Table 2-2 is a handy break-out of the different types of orders.

Table 2-2	Different Types of Orders		
Buy Orders			
	Stop Order	**Limit Order**	**Stop Limit Order**
Order instructions	Buy Stop 30	Buy Limit 30	Buy Stop 30 Limit 31
Market Price ($)	Action after the stock hits $30		
28.50	Buy	Buy	Buy
29.00	Buy	Buy	Buy
29.50	Buy	Buy	Buy
30.00	Buy	Buy	Buy
30.50	Buy	Nothing	Buy
31.00	Buy	Nothing	Nothing
31.50	Buy	Nothing	Nothing
Sell Orders			
	Stop Order	**Limit Order**	**Stop Limit Order**
Order Instructions	Sell Stop 30	Sell Limit 30	Sell Stop 30 Limit 29
Market Price ($)	Action after the stock hits $30		
28.50	Sell	Nothing	Nothing
29.00	Sell	Nothing	Sell
29.50	Sell	Nothing	Sell
30.00	Sell	Sell	Sell
30.50	Sell	Sell	Sell
31.00	Sell	Sell	Sell
31.50	Sell	Sell	Sell

What if the trade goes wrong?

No matter how in tune you feel with the market, no matter how good your track record, and no matter how disciplined you are with setting stops, stuff is going to happen. Just as you can make more money than you plan to, you can also *lose* a lot more. If you are going to day trade, you have to accept that there are going to be some really bad days.

A sample trading plan

A trading plan may only be good for a short time, but having an idea of what to expect in the market and how you will react goes a long way toward keeping trading discipline, which improves your likelihood of long-run profits. What does such a plan look like? Well, here's a sample to get you started.

What I'm Trading Today

Today, I'll be trading the E-Mini S&P 500 futures. They closed down yesterday, but I'm expecting an uptick in the market today as companies report good earnings, so I am going to trade on the long side. My plan is to start the day buying two contracts with stop orders to sell if they decline more than three ticks each. These contracts will remain open until the end of the day unless the stop is reached. I will add a third contract if the market shows momentum in the morning and a fourth contract if it shows momentum in the afternoon. These two additional contracts can be long or short, depending on the market direction, although it is unlikely that the purchasing manager or home sales surveys will have a large effect on the market's direction. (Naturally, I will not take out a short contract during the day if my two initial long contracts are still open.) I will close all positions at the end of the day, if not sooner.

Because the margin on each contract is $3,500, my maximum exposure today will be approximately 28 percent of my total account, with no contract accounting for more than 7 percent of my account.

Today's Expected News Announcements

Before the open: earnings announcements from ADM (expect $0.62), PG (expect $0.74)

10:00 a.m. ISM Index — survey of purchasing managers — market expects 51.0

10:00 a.m. Pending Home Sales — market expects up 0.5 percent

After the close: earnings announcements from UA (expect $0.20), MET (expect $1.29)

5:00 p.m. Auto Sales — market expects 5.1m

5:00 p.m. Truck Sales — market expects 7.2m

My Profit and Loss Goals for the Day

My profit goal is five ticks or $62.50 per contract traded, for a target of $250 if I acquire my planned maximum of four contracts, but I plan to ride my profits until the end of the day. If all four contracts decline in value, I will close when they fall three ticks apiece, for a maximum loss of $37.50 per contract or $150 for the day.

So what do you do? You suck it up, take the loss, and get on with your life.

Yes, the market may have blown past your stops. That happens sometimes, and it's hard to watch real dollars disappear into someone else's account, someone you will never know. Still, close your position and just remember that tomorrow is another day with another chance to do better.

Don't hold in hopes of making up a loss. The market does not know what you own and will not reward your loyalty and best hopes.

After you take the loss and clear your head, see if there is something you can learn for next time. Sometimes a loss can teach you valuable lessons that make you a smarter, more disciplined trader in the long run.

Closing Out Your Position

By definition, day traders only hold their investment positions for a single day. This is important for a few reasons:

- ✔ Closing out daily reduces your risk of something happening overnight.

- ✔ Margin rates — the interest rates paid on money borrowed for trading — are low and in some cases zero for day traders, but the rates go up on overnight balances.

- ✔ It's good trade discipline that can keep you from making expensive mistakes.

But like all rules, the single day rule can be broken and probably should be broken sometimes. In this section, I cover a few longer-term trading strategies that you may want to add to your trading business on occasion.

Swing trading: holding for days

Swing trading involves holding a position for several days. Some swing traders hold overnight, whereas others hold for days or even months. The longer time period gives more time for a position to work out, which is especially important if it is based on news events or if it requires taking a position contrary to the current market sentiment. Although swing trading gives traders more options for making a profit, it carries some risks because the position could turn against you while you are away from the markets.

There's always a tradeoff between risk and return. When you take more risk, you do so in the hopes of getting a greater return. But when you look for a way to increase return, remember that you will have to take on more risk to do it.

Swing trading requires paying attention to some basic fundamentals and news flow. (Fundamental research is discussed in Chapter 12.) It's also a good choice for people who have the discipline to go to bed at night instead of waiting up and watching their position in hopes that nothing goes wrong.

Position trading: holding for weeks

A *position trader* holds a stake in a stock or a commodity for several weeks and possibly even for months. This person is attracted to the short-term price opportunities, but he also believes that he can make more money holding the stake for a long enough period of time to see business fundamentals play out. This increases the risk and the potential return, because a lot more can happen over months than minutes.

Investing: holding for months or years

An *investor* is not a trader. Investors do careful research and buy a stake in an asset in the hopes of building a profit over the long term. It's not unusual for investors to hold assets for decades, although good ones sell quickly if they realize that they have made a mistake. (They want to cut their losses early, just as any good trader should.)

Investors are concerned about the prospects of the underlying business. Will it make money? Will it pay off its debts? Will it hold its value? They view short-term price fluctuations as noise rather than as profit opportunities.

Many traders pull out some of their profits to invest for the long term (or to give to someone else, such as a mutual fund manager or hedge fund, to invest). It's a way of building financial security in the pursuit of longer goals. This money is usually kept separate from the trading account.

Maxims and Clichés that Guide and Mislead Traders

In this chapter, I cover a few of the many maxims traders use to think about their trading, such as

- ✔ The stock doesn't know you own it.
- ✔ Failing to plan is planning to fail.
- ✔ Your first loss is your best loss.

A lot more are out there.

Clichés are useful shorthand for important rules that can help you plan your trading. But they can also mislead you because some are really obvious — too obvious to act on effectively. (Yes, we all know that you make money by buying low and selling high, but how do you tell what low is and high is?) Here's a run-through of some that you'll come across in your trading career, along with my take on what they mean.

Pigs get fat, hogs get slaughtered

Trading is pure capitalism, and people do it for one primary reason: to make money. Sure, a ton of economic benefits come from having well-functioning capital markets, such as better price prediction, risk management, and capital formation. But a day trader just wants to make money.

However, get too greedy, and you're likely to get stupid. You start taking too much risk, deviating too much from your strategy, and getting careless about dealing with your losses. Good traders know when it's time to take a profit and move on to the next trade.

This is also a good example of an obvious but tough-to-follow maxim. When are you crossing from being a happy little piggy to a big fat greedy hog that's about to be turned into a pork belly? Just know that if you are deviating from your trading plan because things are going so great, you might be headed for some trouble.

In a bear market, the money returns to its rightful owners

A *bull* market is one that charges ahead; a *bear* market is one that does poorly. Many people think they are trading geniuses because they make money when the entire market is going up. It was easy to make money day trading Internet stocks in 1999, but it wasn't so easy in 2000 when the bubble burst. And when the markets turn negative, those people who really understand trading and who know how to manage risk will be able to stay in until things get better, possibly even making nice profits along the way.

The corollary cliché for this is "Don't confuse brains with a bull market." When things are going well, watch out for overconfidence. It might be time to update your business and trading plans, but it's not to time to cast them aside.

The trend is your friend

When you day trade, you need to make money fast. You do not have the luxury of waiting for your unique, contrary theory to play out. An investor may be buying a stock in the hopes of holding it for decades, but a trader needs things to work now.

Given the short-term nature of the market, the short-term sentiment is going to trump long-term fundamentals. People trading today may be wrong about the direction of foreign exchange, interest rates, or stock prices, but if you are closing out your positions tonight, you need to work with the information in the market *today*.

In the short run, traders who fight the market lose money.

There are two problems with *The trend is your friend*. The first is that by the time you identify a trend, it may be over. Second, there are times when it makes sense to go against the herd, because you can collect when everyone else realizes their mistakes. This is where the psychology of trading comes into play. Are you a good enough judge of human behavior to know when the trend is right and when it's not?

Buy the rumor, sell the news

Markets react to information. That's ultimately what drives supply and demand. Although the market tends to react quickly to information, it can overreact, too. Lots of gossip gets traded in the markets as everyone looks to get the information they need in order to gain an advantage in the markets. And despite such things as confidentiality agreements and insider-trading laws, many rumors turn out to be true.

These rumors are often attached to such news events as corporate earnings. For whatever reason — good news, analyst research, a popular product — traders might believe that the company will report good quarterly earnings per share. That's the rumor. If you buy on the rumor, you can take advantage of the price appreciation as the story gets more play.

When the earnings are actually announced, one of two things will happen:

✔ They will be as good as or better than rumored, and the price will go up. The trader can sell into that and make a profit.

✔ They will be worse than rumored, everyone will sell on the bad news, and the trader will want to sell to get out of the loss.

Of course, if the rumor is *bad*, you want to do the opposite: sell on the rumor, and buy on the news. For more information on *short selling* — selling securities in hopes that they fall in price — turn to Chapter 14.

The problem with *Buy the rumor, sell the news* is that rumors are often wrong, and there may be more opportunities to buy on bad news when other traders are panicking, thus driving prices down for a few minutes before sanity sets in. But it's one of those rules that everyone talks about, whether or not they actually follow it.

Cut your losses and ride your winners

I mentioned already in this chapter that you need to cut your losses before they drag you down. No matter how much it hurts and no matter how much you believe that you are right, you need to close out a losing position and move on.

But the opposite is not necessarily true. Although good traders tend to be disciplined about selling winning positions, they don't use stops and limits as rigorously on the upside as they might on the downside. They're likely to stick with a profit and see how high it goes before closing out a position.

Note that this conflicts a little with *Pigs get fat, hogs get slaughtered.* Trading maxims can be so contradictory! To prevent overconfidence and sloppiness from greed, ride your winners *within reason*. If your general discipline is to risk three ticks on a futures contract in order to make five, and a contract goes up six ticks before you can close it out, you might want to stick with it. But if you also close out at the end of every day, don't give in to the temptation of keeping that position open just because it's still going up. Keep to your overall discipline.

You're only as good as your last trade

The markets churn on every day with little regard for why everyone trading right now is there. Prices go up and down to match the supply and the demand at any given moment, which may have nothing to do with the actual long-term worth of an item being traded. And it certainly has nothing to do with how much you really, really want the trade to work out.

One of the biggest enemies of good traders is overconfidence. Especially after a nice run of winning trades, a trader can get caught up in the euphoria and believe that he finally has the secret to successful trading under control.

While he's checking the real estate listings for that beachfront estate in Maui, BAM! The next trade is a disaster.

Does that mean that the trader is a disaster, too? No, it just means that the markets won this time around.

Most day traders are working in zero-sum markets, which mean that for every winner, there is a loser. Hence, not everyone can make money every day. The challenge is to maintain an even keel so as not to be distracted by confidence when the trading is going well or by fear when the trading is going poorly. The next trade is a new trade.

A Day in the Life of a Trader

What's it like being a day trader? James Okada Lee, a day trader in Tokyo and proprietor of the Traders Laboratory (www.traderslaboratory.com) answered a few questions about what he does and why he does it. "I trade the U.S. markets from Tokyo, which means I work from 11 p.m. to 6 a.m. every day. Most people think I am insane, but I got used to it after two years," he says.

Q: What do you trade, and how long have you been trading?

I currently specialize in Chicago Mercantile Exchange eMini futures contracts, especially the eMini Dow and Russell contracts. I have been trading for four years now. Before that, I was a professional poker player, which has helped me tremendously in the mental aspects of trading.

I was introduced to trading through a poker buddy of mine when I was 20. He had a friend who was a full-time day trader at 22. I visited his office (he was a prop trader) and that day was the day my life made a complete 360. I remember clearly walking in to the office and seeing a 12-monitor setup with charts, Level 2 quotations, and blinking lights. It was then I decided that I was going to be a day trader and do whatever it takes to be good at it.

One of the biggest reasons why I decided to become a trader was because I felt I had a psychological edge over other people. I spent hours analyzing my poker game for why I was able to consistently win. The biggest reason was player psychology. I kept winning because my psychological makeup was stronger than that of the other players on the table. I understood that poker was a game of patience and discipline. I was also good in reading people and questioning every single move they make. I would constantly ask myself: Why did he spend an extra 20 seconds to bet? Does he look nervous? Why did he take a deeper drag from his cigarette? Did his pupils get wider? Why is he betting smaller than usual? Why is he betting bigger than usual? And so on. These questions help me analyze a player for clues of weakness or strength.

Now, these questions are related when it comes to trading. As a day trader I constantly ask myself: What is the market trying to do now? Is there price acceptance or rejection outside of value? Is the market running out of momentum? Is the market being supported only by small buyers? Are we likely to test the overnight high or the previous day high? Is there selling volume at a key pivot level? What is the tape telling me? And so on. These questions help me understand the language of the markets. What I'm trying to do is follow the big buyers and sellers and decide what they are trying to do, which is similar to reading my opponents in poker.

Q: How did you get started trading?

I never had an opportunity to learn directly from a trader or trading mentor, so 90 percent of my trading was self-taught through trial and error. I committed every amateur mistake in my first year of trading: selling lows, buying highs, using lagging indicators, trading without a plan, not understanding significant support and resistance levels, not understanding the basic concept of supply and demand. As an amateur I thought I had to short because the price was too high or buy because price was too low. How foolish I was! I blew my first trading account in six months.

To get back in, I built a stake through poker and took an office job with an IT company. I was in Tokyo then, and my job had night hours, 9 p.m. to 9 a.m. local time (7 a.m. to 7 p.m. EST). My boss worked daytime hours, so I was alone. I wasn't able to install my trading software on the office computers, so what I did was watch a simple bar chart on a browser (www.futuresource.com) with 15-minute delayed data. I would refresh my browser every 15 minutes to see how the price changed while I worked. This weird method of observation helped build my trading style today.

What I did was use simple Support and Resistance levels on my charts. Since all I could see was a bar chart (no volume, no indicators) the only thing I could do was imagine what price would do in the next 15 minutes when I would refresh my browser. I focused on confluence areas: in other words cluster points of various support and resistance levels, such as pivot points lined up with previous day high/low, weekly pivots lined up with daily pivots, 50-percent range lined up with pivots, and so on. This became the foundation of my trading. I was getting good at identifying these levels of support and resistance, and more often I saw price move the way I had anticipated. This went on for 10 months, 12 hours a day, 24–26 working days a month.

After 10 months I went back to trading full time. I started reading the time of sales tape and created my edge by looking at support and resistance levels and deciding whether the price was going to hold or break according to the tape. Very simple, but it took quite a while to reach this level of simplicity.

Q: Do you close out trades every day, or do you carry some over?

I never hold any overnight positions. I'm based in Tokyo — a 13-hour time difference with New York. So I trade the morning session only 70 percent of the time. I prefer to start each day fresh. It's like getting dealt a new hand.

Q: What piece of equipment or software could you not do without?

Day traders need to be techies. I use four 17-inch LCD monitors and have two Internet providers in case one goes down. In my opinion, day traders need at least two monitors (I recommend more), a fast Internet connection, and a decent computer with at least 1 GB of RAM. I also have several whiteboards on my wall to post notes of various price levels for the day. I currently use TradeStation (www.tradestation.com) for my charting software — definitely something I cannot live without. My job only exists because of advancement in technology. I couldn't possibly do what I do now 20 years ago.

So execution is very important. There are various platforms day traders can use to execute orders. But it is very important that the execution platform allows advanced orders, such as OCO (one cancels the other), bracket orders, and OSO (order sends order) If a platform has the ability to place an automatic stop or target, it makes the life of a day trader much easier. Energy is wasted in manually putting a stop. It can also affect the trader psychologically.

Day traders need a good charting package and good execution software. Software fees can be costly but it's all a part of the expense in this business.

Q: What is a typical day like? How easy is it to quit at the end of the day?

I tend to be a workaholic, so a typical day is pretty intense. I wake up around 1 p.m. Tokyo time (12 a.m. EST). The first thing I do is to check my charts, my Web site (www.traderslaboratory.com), and my trades from the day before. I have a poker habit in that I tend to think about my trades (hands for poker) all throughout the day. Analyzing yourself is very important in both trading and poker. I may decide to go to the gym during this time, but by 9 p.m. Tokyo time (7 a.m. EST) I am back at my desk, concentrating on the upcoming session. From 1 p.m. to 9 p.m., I work about 5–6 hours. I do not have a TV or a phone in my office space, which allows me to concentrate 100 percent on my work. (I tend to get extremely carried away with work and time flies without even noticing.) Once the markets open, I am trading until 1 a.m. Tokyo time (11 a.m. EST). If I choose to come back for the afternoon, I will take a break until 4 a.m. Tokyo time (2 p.m. EST) and then resume trading. If I met my daily in the morning, I am usually done by 1 a.m. Tokyo time (11 a.m. EST).

It is relatively easy for me to quit trading during the day whenever I want. I am very aware of my own mental level in terms of fatigue and do not trade when I am tired. I learned this habit from poker when I used to play 12-hour sessions daily. Fatigue turns into mistakes. And mistakes are very costly in this game. It is quite contrary to what people may assume, since I trade during the night hours. While U.S. traders have the luxury of calling it a day and playing golf, the city is pretty much dead here during my working hours.

Q: What is your secret to managing the stress of trading?

I use several methods to handle stress. I am a student of neuro-linguistic programming, and I use a lot of visualization techniques to ease my mind. Meditation and self-hypnosis also work to clear my mind from any thoughts, positive and negative. Another weird method I use is watching bad movies with Chuck Norris, Arnold Schwarzenegger, Sylvester Stallone, or Jean-Claude Van Damme. Almost any movie with those actors in it is horrible, and for a full two hours I don't have to use my head. Very relaxing in my opinion!

As much as I work, I always take a regular weekly break. Every Saturday I am out partying with friends. I find these moments necessary to eliminate a lot of the work stress. Other than that, I do not have break times and I have not gone on vacation in over six years.

Q: What's your best piece of advice for someone considering day trading?

It is important to know yourself. Without understanding who you are and what kind of trader you are, you are doomed to fail. You have to know your time frame and style as a trader. Once you find your style of trading, you must become an expert in it and have an edge. New traders tend to jump from one style to the next in search for the Holy Grail. There is no Holy Grail in trading. One needs to understand that trading is a game of probabilities and psychology. The futures market is a zero-sum game. One person's mistake is another man's profit. Do not treat trading as a hobby. Hobbies cost money. Trading should be treated as a full-time job and business.

Second, specialize in one market first. Know the market inside out instead of jumping around. A trader must find a market that fits his style also. This is why the trader needs to know who he is first before engaging in the markets. It is also important to be in sync with the markets. A trader who is completely absorbed with his or her market of choice is able to read the language of the markets. Whenever I feel out of sync and unclear about market direction, I will spend the time to observe until I have a clearer understanding.

Third, learn the psychology of the markets. There are the short-term market participants and the long-term market participants. The short-term trader may be looking to make money in the next 5 to 30 minutes. The long-term trader may be looking to make money in the next 3–5 weeks. Both traders are trying to profit under the same rules of the market. In the futures market, for every buyer there must be a seller. Under the same exact information, they have a difference in opinion. Now, if Trader A buys from Trader B, Trader A must sell in order to profit or to cut losses short. If the market goes against Trader A, where will he sell? It's the simple law of supply versus Demand, combined with trader psychology. Understand what the losing traders are doing and learn to exploit their mistakes. If the majority of the traders are short, who is left to sell? Supply has run out. The markets must reverse, which will cause shorts to cover and price to rally.

We are not trading the markets. We are trading other traders. Traders trade their own belief systems. Last, patience and discipline are your best friends. Trading is not gambling. Hold a professional mindset and not a gambler's mentality. Most of the trading day is spent sitting tight and waiting for opportunities. If you lack patience, trading is not right for you.

Chapter 3

Signing Up for Asset Classes

*I*t's one thing to day trade, but *what* are you going to trade? Stocks, pork bellies, or baseball cards? You have myriad choices, but you have to choose so that you can learn the market, know what changes to expect, and make your trades accordingly. And, to avoid of the devilment of the wash-sale rule, which can limit the tax deductibility of short-term losses (and which you can read all about in Chapter 10), you'll probably want to make your universe of trading assets as broad as possible.

Still, you can't trade everything. There are only so many hours in a day and only so many ideas you can hold in your head at any one time. Furthermore, some trading strategies (see Chapter 7) lend themselves better to certain types of assets than others. By learning more about all the various invest-ment assets available to a day trader, you can make better decisions about what you want to trade and how you want to trade it.

What Makes a Good Day Trading Asset

In academic terms, the universe of investable assets includes just about any-thing you can buy at one price and sell at another, potentially higher price. That means artwork and collectibles, real estate, and private companies would all be considered to be investable assets.

Day traders have a much smaller group of assets to work with. It's not realistic to expect a quick one-day profit on price changes in real estate. Online auctions for collectible items take place over days, not minutes. If you're going to day trade, you want to find assets that trade easily, several times a day, in recognized markets. In other words, you want *liquidity*. As an individual trading your own account, you want assets that can be purchased with relatively low capital commitments. And finally, you may want to use *leverage* — borrowed money — to improve your return (discussed in more detail in Chapter 14), so you want to look for assets that can be purchased using other people's money.

Liquidity

Liquidity is the ability to buy or sell an asset in large quantity without affecting the price levels. Day traders look for *liquid assets* so they can move in and out of the market quickly without disrupting price levels. Otherwise, they may not be able to buy at a good price or sell when they want.

At the most basic level, financial markets are driven by supply and demand. The more of an asset supplied in the market, the lower the price; the more of an asset that people demand, the higher the price. In a perfect market, the amount of supply and demand is matched so that prices don't change. This happens if there is a high volume of people trading, so that their supply and demand is constantly matched, or if there is a very low frequency of trades, so that the price never changes.

You may be thinking, wait, don't I want big price changes so that I can make money quickly? Yes, you want price changes in the market, but you don't want to be the one causing them. The less liquid a market is, the more likely your buying and selling is going to affect market prices, and the smaller your profit will be.

Volume

Volume is the total amount of a security that trades in a given time period. The greater the volume, the more buyers and sellers are interested in the security, and the easier it is to get in there and buy and sell without affecting the price.

Day traders also look at the relationship between volume and price. This is an important technical indicator, discussed in more detail in Chapter 12. The simple version is this:

- ✔ High volume with no change in price levels means that there is an equal match between buyers and sellers.

- ✔ High volume with rising prices means that there are more buyers than sellers, so the price will continue going up.

- ✔ High volume with falling prices means that there are more sellers than buyers, so the price will keep going down.

Frequency

Another measure of liquidity is *frequency*, or how often a security trades. Some assets, like stock market futures, trade constantly, from the moment the market opens until the very last trade of the day, and then continue into overnight trading. Others, like agricultural commodities, trade only during market hours or only during certain times of the year. Other securities, like stocks, trade frequently, but the volume rises and falls are regular intervals related to such things as *options expiration* (the date at which options on the stock expire).

The more frequently a security trades, the more opportunities you'll have to identify the short-term profit opportunities that make day trading possible.

Volatility, standard deviation, and variance

The *volatility* of a security is how much the price varies over a period of time. It tells you how much prices fluctuate and thus how likely you are to be able to take advantage of that. For example, if a security has an average price of $5 but trades anywhere between $1 and $14, it will be more volatile than one with an average price of $5 that trades between $4 and $6.

One standard measure of volatility and risk is *standard deviation*, which is how much any given price quote varies from a security's average price. If you are dying to see it, the math is shown in Figure 3-1, but you can calculate it with most spreadsheet programs and many trading platforms.

Figure 3-1:
N is the number of price quotes, x_i is any one price quote, and the funky "X" with the line over it is the average of all the prices over time.

$$\sigma = \sqrt{\frac{1}{N}\sum_{i=1}^{N}\left(x_i - \overline{x}\right)^2}$$

For each of the prices, you'd calculate the difference between it and the average value. So if the average price is $5, and the closing price today is $8, the difference would be $3. (More likely, the research service that you use would calculate the difference for you, and you can learn more about research services in Chapter 7.)

After you have all the differences between the prices and the average, you'd find the square of these differences. If the difference for one day's price is $8, then the square would be $64. You'd add up all the squared differences over the period of time that you are looking at and then find the average of them. That number is called the *variance*, or σ^2. Finally, calculate the square root of the variance, and you have the standard deviation.

The higher the standard deviation, the higher the volatility, the higher the volatility, the more a security's price is going to fluctuate, and the more profit — and loss — opportunities there are for a day trader.

Standard deviation is also a measure of risk that can be used to evaluate your trading performance. That use of the measure is discussed in Chapter 11.

Capital requirements

You don't necessarily need a lot of money to begin day trading, but you do need a lot of money to buy certain securities. Stocks generally trade in *round lots*, which are orders of at least 100 shares. If you want to buy a stock worth $40 per share, you need $4,000 in your account. Your broker will probably let you borrow half of that money, but you still need to come up with the other $2,000.

Options and futures trade by contract, and one contract represents some unit of the underlying security. For example, in the options market, one contract is good for 100 shares of the stock. These contracts also trade in round lots of 100 contracts per order.

No one will stop you from buying a smaller amount than the usual round lot in any given security, but you'll probably pay a high commission and get worse execution for your order. Because the returns on each trade tend to be small anyway, don't take up day trading until you have enough money to trade your target asset effectively. Otherwise, you'll pay too much to your broker without getting much for yourself.

Bonds do not trade in fractional amounts; they trade on a per-bond basis, and each bond has a face value of $1,000. Some trade for more or less than that, depending on how the bond's interest rate differs from the market rate of interest, but the $1,000 is a good number to keep in mind when thinking about capital requirements. Many dealers have a minimum order of 10 bonds, though, so a minimum order would be $10,000.

Marginability

Most day traders make money through a large volume of small profits. One way to increase the profit per trade is to use borrowed money in order to buy more shares, more contracts, or more bonds. *Margin* is money in your account that you borrow against, and almost all brokers will be happy to arrange a margin loan for you, especially if you're going to use the money to make more trades and generate more commissions for the brokerage firm. In Chapter 14, I discuss how margin is used within an investment strategy. Here, though, you want to think about how margin affects your choice of assets for day trading.

Generally, a stock or bond account must hold 50 percent of the purchase price of securities when you borrow the money. So if you want to buy $100 worth of something on margin, you need to have $50 in your account. The price of those securities can go down, but if they go down so much that the account now holds only 25 percent of the value of the loan, you'll get a margin call.

Margin requirements aren't set by the brokerage firms. Instead, the minimum amount in your account — and thus the maximum amount you can borrow — is set by the Federal Reserve Board. That's because of concerns that if too much borrowing takes place, the borrowers will panic in a financial downturn and drag the market down even further. (Excessive trading on margin was a contributing factor to the stock market crash of 1929, in which the Dow Jones Industrial Average fell 13 percent in one day, and the market did not fully recover until 1954.) The Fed limits the amount that can be borrowed, and the different exchanges monitor how member brokerage firms comply. Some brokerage firms set margin limits that are higher than those of the Federal Reserve Board and the exchanges.

You probably think that the 1929 crash was responsible for the Great Depression of the 1930s, right? Think again. Most economic historians believe that the crash was a distraction. Instead, the real problem was that interest rates fell so rapidly that banks refused to lend money, while prices fell so low that companies had no incentive to produce. It's a situation known as *deflation*, and it's relatively rare, but it is devastating when it occurs.

Most stocks and bonds are marginable (able to be purchased on margin), and the Federal Reserve Board allows traders to borrow up to 50 percent of their value. But not all securities are marginable. Stocks priced below $5 per share, those traded on the OTC Bulletin Board or Pink Sheets (discussed later in this chapter), and those in newly public companies often cannot be borrowed against or purchased on margin. Your brokerage firm should have a list of securities that are not eligible for margin.

If leverage is going to be part of your day-trading strategy, be sure that the assets you plan to trade are marginable.

Securities and How They Trade

In the financial markets, people buy and sell securities every day, but just what are they buying or selling? *Securities* are financial instruments. In the olden days, they were pieces of paper, but now they are electronic entries that represent a legal claim on some type of underlying asset. This asset may be a business, if the security is a stock, or it may be a loan to a government or a corporation, if the security is a bond. In this section, I cover different types of securities that day traders are likely to run across and tell you what you need to jump into the fray.

In practice, *asset* and *security* are synonyms, and *derivative* is considered to be a type of asset or security. But to be precise, these three are not the same:

- An asset is a physical item. Examples include a company, a house, gold bullion, or a loan.

- A security is a contract that gives someone the right of ownership of the asset, such as a share of stock, a bond, a promissory note.

- A derivative is a contract that draws its value from the price of a security.

Stocks

A *stock*, also called an *equity*, is a security that represents a fractional interest in the ownership of a company. Buy one share of Microsoft, and you are an owner of the company, just as Bill Gates is. He may own a much larger share of the total business, but you both have a stake in it. Stockholders elect a board of directors to represent their interests in how the company is managed. Each share is a vote, so good luck getting Bill Gates kicked off of Microsoft's board.

A share of stock has *limited liability*. That means that you can lose all of your investment, but no more than that. If the company files for bankruptcy, the creditors cannot come after the shareholders for the money that they are owed.

Some companies pay their shareholders a dividend, which is a small cash payment made out of firm profits. Because day traders hold stock for really short periods of time, they don't normally collect dividends.

How U.S. stocks trade

Stocks are priced based on a single share, and most brokerage firms charge commissions on a per-share basis. Despite this per-share pricing, stocks are almost always traded in round lots of 100 shares. The supply and demand for a given stock is driven by the company's expected performance.

A stock's price is quoted with a *bid* and an *ask*.

- ✔ The bid is the price that the broker will buy the stock from you if you are selling.
- ✔ The ask is the price that the broker will charge you if you are the one buying.

I remember the difference between the bid and the ask this way: the *broker buys* on the *bid*. Let alliteration be your friend!

The difference between the bid and the ask is the *spread*, and that represents the dealer's profit.

Here is an example of a price quote:

```
MSFT $27.70 $27.71
```

That is a quote for Microsoft (ticker symbol: MSFT). The bid is listed first: $27.70; and the ask is $27.71. That's the smallest spread you'll ever see! The spread here is so small because Microsoft is a liquid stock, and there are no big news events going on that might change the balance of buyers and sellers.

The brokerage firm makes money from the commission *and* from the spread. Many novice day traders focus on the amount of the commission and forget that some brokerage firms can execute the order better than others, thus keeping the spread narrower. You need to consider the total cost of trading when you design a trading strategy and choose a brokerage firm.

I tend to use the words *broker* and *dealer* interchangeably, but there is a difference. A broker simply matches buyers and sellers of securities, whereas a dealer buys and sells securities out of its own account. Almost all brokerage firms are both brokers and dealers.

Where U.S. stocks trade

U.S. stocks trade mostly on organized *exchanges* such as the New York Stock Exchange and NASDAQ, but more and more they trade on electronic communications networks, some of which are operated by the exchanges themselves. Brokerage firms either belong to the exchanges themselves or work with a correspondent firm that handles the trading for them, turning over the order in exchange for a cut of the commission.

When you place an order with your brokerage firm, the broker's trading staff executes that order wherever it can get the best deal. But is that the best deal for you, or for the brokerage firm? It's tough to know the right answer. In general, firms that do more trading and participate in several exchanges and electronic communications networks can get you the best execution. (To learn more about choosing brokerage firms, turn to Chapter 6.)

The financial markets are in a state of flux, with a lot of mergers and acquisitions among the exchanges. The information here might be obsolete when you read it, which I think is fascinating. It wasn't so long ago that these exchanges were staid organizations run like private clubs.

The New York Stock Exchange (NYSE)

The New York Stock Exchange is the Big Kahuna of stock exchanges. Most of the largest U.S. corporations trade on it, and they pay a fee for that privilege. The 2,000 or so companies listed on the exchange are known by their *ticker symbols*, shorthand for the company name. On the New York Stock Exchange, all ticker symbols have three letters or fewer, and many old companies have one-letter symbols, like F for Ford and T for AT&T.

Two of the largest companies in the world, Intel and Microsoft, are not listed on the New York Stock Exchange, and supposedly, exchange officials have told both companies that if they move to the NYSE, they can have the ticker symbols I and M, which were unassigned for decades. In 2007, the NYSE gave the M symbol to Macy's, formerly Federated Stores, but as this book was going to press, Macy's was rumored to be acquired by a private equity firm, so M may be available once again to tantalize Mr. Gates and company.

In order to be listed on the New York Stock Exchange, a company generally needs to have at least 2,200 shareholders, trade at least 100,000 shares a month, carry a *market capitalization* (number of shares outstanding multiplied by price per share) of at least $100 million, and post annual revenues of at least $75 million.

The New York Stock Exchange is more than 200 years old, but it has been going through some big corporate changes in order to stay relevant. It's a *floor-based exchange*. The trading area is a big open space in the building, known as the *floor*. The floor broker, who works for the member firm, receives the order electronically and then takes it over to the trading post, which is the area on the floor where the stock in question trades. At the trading post, the floor broker executes the order at the best available price.

Bringing the NYSE into the 21st century

I've been on the floor of the New York Stock Exchange, and it's exciting, watching all these people in colorful cotton jackets running from post to post, talking in their cell phones the entire time. It's not necessarily the most efficient way to execute orders in the modern era, though. That's why in early 2006, the New York Stock Exchange merged with Archipelago, an electronic communications network (discussed in more detail later in this section), and now offers both electronic and exchange trading. Because Archipelago was already publicly traded, the New York Stock Exchange itself became a publicly traded company when the deal closed (NYSE: NYX).

Archipelago had owned the Pacific Stock Exchange, which was shut down after the merger. The NYSE then announced a merger with Euronext, which operates exchanges in Amsterdam, Brussels, Paris, London, and Lisbon; a 5-percent investment in India's National Stock Exchange; and a strategic partnership with the Tokyo Stock Exchange to develop new products and trading systems. These transactions may make it easier for day traders to do business in international securities and should improve execution, thus making it easier to get a profit.

The American Stock Exchange (AMEX)

The American Stock Exchange is a floor-based exchange also headquartered in New York City. Like the New York Stock Exchange, floor brokers receive orders and take them to trading posts to be filled. AMEX specializes in commodity companies — those that mine metals or pump out oil — but there are some other types of businesses listed on it. Listed companies have two- or three-letter ticker symbols and generally are profitable, have a market capitalization (number of shares outstanding multiplied by price per share) of at least $75 million, and have a price per share of at least $2.00. These companies tend to be smaller and more speculative than New York Stock Exchange companies.

NASDAQ

NASDAQ used to stand for the National Association of Securities Dealers Automated Quotation System, but now it's just a name, not an acronym, pronounced just like it's spelled. When NASDAQ was founded, it was an electronic communication network (more on those below) that handled companies that were too small or too speculative to meet New York Stock Exchange or American Stock Exchange listing requirements. What happened was that brokers liked using the NASDAQ network, while technology companies (Microsoft, Intel, Oracle, Apple) that were once small and speculative became huge international behemoths. But the management teams of these companies saw no reason to change how they were listed.

NASDAQ companies have four-letter ticker symbols. When a customer places an order, the brokerage firm looks to see whether there is a matching order on the network. Sometimes, it can be executed electronically; in other cases, the brokerage firm's trader needs to call other traders at other firms to see whether the price is still good. A key feature of NASDAQ is its *market makers*, who are employees of member brokerage firms who agree to buy and sell minimum levels of specific stocks in order to ensure that there is some basic level of trading taking place.

NASDAQ divides its listed companies into three categories:

- ✔ **The NASDAQ Global Select Market** includes the 1,000 largest companies on the exchange and has high governance and liquidity standards for participating firms.

- ✔ **The NASDAQ Global Market** includes companies that are too small for the Global Select Market, but that in general have a market capitalization of at least $75 million, at least 1.1 million shares outstanding, at least 400 shareholders, and a minimum price per share of $5.00.

- ✔ **The NASDAQ Capital Market** is for companies that do not qualify for the NASDAQ Global Market. To qualify here, companies need a market capitalization of at least $50 million, at least one million shares outstanding, about 300 shareholders, and a minimum price per share of $4.00.

Day traders will find that NASDAQ Global Select Market companies are the most liquid. They may also notice changes in trading patterns when a company is close to being moved between categories. An upgrade is a sign of good news to come and increased market interest. A downgrade means that the company most likely isn't doing well and will be of less interest to investors.

Over-the-Counter Bulletin Board (OTC BB)

The Over-the-Counter Bulletin Board is the market for companies that are reporting their financials to the U.S. Securities and Exchange Commission but that do not qualify for listing in any NASDAQ category. It also includes some foreign issuers that have not received listing in a U.S. market. American Bulletin Board companies have four-letter ticker symbols followed by .OB. For example, Vertical Communication's ticker symbol is VRCC.OB. Foreign issuers trade with five-letter symbols — four letters followed by an F. ACS Motion Control, based in Israel, trades as ACSEF.

Brokerage firms get quotations on OTC BB stocks through their NASDAQ workstation or other quotation services, so that they can find current prices and locate buyers and sellers for any orders that they have.

In many cases, OTC BB companies are those that used to be on NASDAQ but that have lost too much money to maintain their listing. A Bulletin Board listing is often a last hurrah before oblivion.

Pink Sheets

Once upon a time, there were few electronic networks, and there was not room for many companies to trade on them. Smaller companies did not trade daily. To find current prices, brokerage firms subscribed to a price service that sent out a weekly newsletter listing the prices for those companies. The newsletter was printed on pink paper, so it became known as the Pink Sheets.

Over the years, NASDAQ expanded and added more listing opportunities for companies, and the Over-the-Counter Bulletin Board was created for companies that had to file with the Securities and Exchange Commission but that did not qualify for NASDAQ. The universe of companies that did not qualify for one of these quotation systems was very small. The Pink Sheets went online (www.pinksheets.com) so that people could get more regular price information.

Pink Sheet companies do not have listing requirements. Most do not qualify for listing on the NASDAQ or OTC BB, usually because they are not current on their filings with the Securities and Exchange Commission. These companies have four- or five-letter ticker symbols and are sometimes shown with the suffix .PK after the ticker. Orders for Pink Sheet companies are placed through brokerage firms who use the service to find prices and match buyers and sellers.

Not all Pink Sheet companies are legitimate. Because of the minimal listing requirements, the Pink Sheets tend to be the hangout for the penny stock (those trading at less than $1.00 per share), the fraudulent company, and the security that's easily manipulated by a boiler-room operator. It can be a tough crowd, and a lot of people get burned.

Electronic Communication Networks (ECN)

In addition to all the exchanges and listing categories, companies titanic and tiny also trade on various _electronic communication networks_, or ECNs. Brokerage firms and such large institutional investors as mutual fund companies subscribe to them in order to trade securities without having to pay exchange fees or commissions. ECNs are also used to trade when the market is closed. Subscribers look to see whether the ECN has a match for their orders; if so, the orders are executed automatically.

Electronic communication networks can be huge. NASDAQ, for example, is used by almost every brokerage firm in the United States, and the New York Stock Exchange acquired Archipelago, an ECN now known as NYSE Arca. Other ECNs are smaller and may combine only a few brokerage firms. In most cases, day traders can't access these networks directly, but instead will access them through their brokerage firms.

Bonds

A *bond* is a loan. The bond buyer gives the bond issuer money. The bond issuer promises to pay interest on a regular basis. The regular coupon payments are why bonds are often called *fixed income investments*. Bond issuers repay the money borrowed — the principal — on a predetermined date, known as the *maturity*. Bonds generally have a maturity of more than ten years; shorter-term bonds are usually referred to as *notes*, and bonds that will mature within a year of issuance are usually referred to as *bills*. Most bonds in the United States are issued by corporations (corporate bonds) or by the Federal government (Treasury bonds). Some are issued by local governments (municipal bonds).

The interest payments on a bond are called *coupons*. If you look on a bulletin board in a coffee shop or other community space, you'll probably see a "car for sale" or "apartment for rent" sign with little slips of paper carrying a phone number or email address cut into the bottom. If you are interested, you can rip off the slip and contact the advertiser later. Bonds used to look the same. The bond buyer would receive one large certificate good for the principal, with a lot of smaller certificates, called coupons, attached. When a payment was due, the owner would cut off the matching coupon and deposit it in the bank. (Some old novels refer to rich people as "coupon clippers," meaning that their sole labor in life was to cut out their bond coupons and cash them in. Nowadays, bond payments are handled electronically, so the modern coupon clipper is a bargain hunter looking for an extra 50 cents off a jar of peanut butter.)

Over the years, enterprising financiers realized that some investors needed regular payments, but others wanted to receive a single sum at a future date. So they separated the coupons from the principal. The principal payment, known as a *zero-coupon bond*, is sold to one investor, while the coupons, called *strips*, are sold to another investor. The borrower makes the payments just like with a regular bond. (Regular bonds, by the way, are sometimes called *plain vanilla*.)

The borrower who wants to make a series of payments with no lump-sum principal repayment would issue an *amortizing* bond to return principal and interest on a regular basis. If you think about a typical mortgage, the borrower makes a regular payment of both principal and interest. This way, the amount owed gets smaller over time so that the borrower does not have to come up with a large principal repayment at maturity.

Other borrowers would prefer to make a single payment at maturity, so they issue *discount bonds*. The purchase price is the principal reduced by the amount of interest that otherwise would be paid.

If a company goes bankrupt, the bondholders get paid before the shareholders. In some bankruptcies, the bondholders take over the business, leaving the current shareholders with nothing.

How bonds trade

Bonds often trade as single bonds, with a face value of $1000, although some brokers will only take on minimum orders of ten bonds. They do not trade as frequently as stocks do because most bond investors are looking for steady income, so they hold their bonds until maturity. Bonds have less risk than stocks, so they show less price volatility. The value of a bond is mostly determined by the level of interest rates in the economy. As rates go up, bond prices go down; when rates go down, bond prices go up. Bond prices are also affected by how likely the loan is to be repaid. If traders don't think that the bond issuer will pay up, then the bond price will fall.

Generally speaking, only corporate and municipal bonds have repayment risk. It's possible that the U.S. government could default, but that's unlikely as long as it can print money. Most international government bonds have similarly low default risk, but some countries *have* defaulted. The most notable was Russia, which refused to print money to repay its debts in the summer of 1998. This caused huge turmoil in the world's financial markets, including the collapse of a major hedge fund, Long-Term Capital Management.

Investment banks and the Federal government sell new bonds directly to investors. After they are issued, bonds are said to trade in the secondary market — some are listed, some trade over-the-counter, meaning dealers trade them amongst themselves rather than over an organized exchange.

A bond price quote looks like this:

```
3 3/4 Mar 07 n  99:28 99:29
```

This is a U.S. Treasury note maturing in March 2007 carrying an interest rate of 3.75 per cent. Similar to stocks, the numbers right after the "n" (for *note*) list the bid and ask. The first number is the bid, and it's the price that the dealer will buy the bond from you if you are selling. The second number is the ask, and it is the price that the dealer will charge you if you are buying. The difference is the spread, and that's the dealer's profit.

But wait, there's more: corporate bonds trade in eighths of a percentage point, and Treasury bonds trade in 32nds. The bid of 99:28 means that the bond's bid price is 99 28/32 per cent of the face value of $1000, or $998.75.

Why on earth do bonds trade in eighths or fractions of eighths? Do traders just like to show off their math skills? No, it goes back to before the American Revolution. The dominant currency in most of Americas then was the Spanish doubloon, a large gold coin that could be cut into fractions to make trade easier. Like a pie, it would be cut into eight equal pieces, so prices throughout the colonies were often set in eighths. (In Robert Louis Stevenson's book *Treasure Island*, the parrot keeps squawking "Pieces of eight! Pieces of eight!" This is why.)

The fractional pricing convention carried over to American securities markets, and it's persisted because it guarantees dealers a bigger spread than pricing in decimals. After all, 1/32 of a dollar is more than 1/100. U.S. stocks were priced in sixteenths until 2001, and bond markets still maintain the old convention.

Most bonds are not suitable for day traders. Only Treasury bonds, issued by the U.S. government, have enough consistent trading volume to attract a day trader. Because of the capital required to trade and the relatively low liquidity of many types of bonds, many traders prefer to use *futures* to bet on interest rates. I discuss futures in detail later in this chapter.

Are you one of those day traders who wants to buy or sell bonds anyway? Or do you just want to know more about the market? Then read on.

Listed bonds

Some larger corporate bonds are traded on the New York Stock Exchange and the American Stock Exchange. Those wanting to buy or sell them place an order through their brokerage firm, which sends an order to the floor broker. The process is almost identical to the trading of listed stocks.

Over-the-counter trading

Most corporate and municipal bonds trade over-the-counter, meaning there is no organized exchange. Instead, brokerage firms use electronic price services to find out where the buyers and sellers are for different issues. Over-the-counter bonds don't trade much. Buyers often give their quality, interest rate, and maturity requirements to their broker, and the broker waits until a suitable bond comes to market.

Treasury dealers

Unlike the corporate and municipal bond market, the Treasury market is one of the most liquid in the world. The best way to buy a new Treasury bond is directly from the government, because there is no commission involved. You can get more information from the Treasury Department's Web site, www.savingsbonds.gov; despite the name, it has information on all kinds of government bonds for all kinds of purchasers.

After the bonds are issued, they trade on a secondary market of Treasury dealers. These are large brokerage firms registered with the government who agree to buy and sell bonds and maintain a stable market for the bonds If your brokerage firm is not a Treasury dealer, it has a relationship with one that it can send your order to.

Treasury dealers do quite a bit of day trading in Treasury bonds for the firm's own account. After all, the market is liquid enough that day trading is possible. Few individual day traders work the Treasury market, though, because it requires a great deal of capital and leverage to make a high return.

Exchange traded funds (ETFs)

Exchange traded funds are a cross between mutual funds and stocks, and they offer a great way for day traders to get exposure to market segments that might otherwise be difficult to trade. A money management firm buys a group of assets — stocks, bonds, or others — and then lists shares that trade on the market. (One of the largest organizers of exchange traded funds is iShares, www.ishares.com) In most cases, the purchased assets are designed to mimic the performance of an index, and investors know what those assets are before they purchase shares in the fund.

Exchange traded funds are available on the big market indexes, like the Standard & Poor's 500 and the Dow Jones Industrial Average. They are available in a variety of domestic bond indexes, international stock indexes, foreign currencies, and commodities.

How U.S. exchange traded funds trade

For day traders, the advantage of exchange traded funds is that they can be bought and sold just like stocks, discussed earlier in this chapter. Customers place orders, usually in round lots, through their brokerage firms. The price quotes come in decimals and include a spread for the dealer.

Where U.S. exchange traded funds trade

The firm that sets up the exchange traded fund gets to choose the market where it will trade, as long as the fund meets the exchange's requirements for size, liquidity, and financial reporting. Exchange traded funds trade on the NYSE, the AMEX, and NASDAQ.

Cash and Currency

Cash is king, as they say. It's money that's readily available in your day trading account to buy more securities. For the most part, the interest rate on cash is very low, but if you are closing out your positions every night, you'll always have a cash balance in your brokerage account. The firm will probably pay you a little interest on it, so it will contribute to your total return.

Money market accounts are boring. For day trading excitement, cash can be traded as foreign currency. Every day, trillions (yes, that's trillions with a *t*) of dollars are exchanged, creating opportunities to make money as the exchange rates change. Currency is a bigger, more liquid market than the U.S. stock and bond markets combined. It's often referred to as the *forex* market, short for *foreign exchange*.

How currency trades

The exchange rate is the price of money. It tells you how many dollars it takes to buy yen, pounds, or euros. The price that people are willing to pay for a currency depends on the investment opportunities, business opportunities, and perceived safety in each nation. If American businesses see great opportunities in Thailand, for example, they'll have to trade their dollars for baht in order to pay rent, buy supplies, and hire workers there. This will increase the demand for baht relative to the dollar, and it will cause the baht to go up in price relative to the dollar.

Exchange rates are quoted on a bid-ask basis, just as are bonds and stocks. A quote might look like this:

```
USDJPY=X 118.47 118.50
```

This is the exchange rate for converting the U.S. dollar into Japanese yen. The bid price of 118.47 is the amount of yen that a dealer would give you if you wanted to sell a dollar and buy yen. The ask price of 118.50 is the amount of yen the dealer would charge you if you wanted to buy a dollar and sell yen. The difference is the dealer's profit, and naturally, you'll be charged a commission, too.

Note that with currency, you're a buyer and a seller at the same time. This can increase the profit opportunities, but it can also increase your risk.

Day traders can trade currencies directly at current exchange rates, which is known as *trading in the spot market*. They can also use currency exchange traded funds (discussed earlier) or currency futures (discussed later in this chapter) to profit from the changing prices of money.

Where currency trades

Spot currency — the real-time value of money — does not trade on an organized exchange. Instead, banks, brokerage firms, hedge funds, and currency dealers buy and sell amongst themselves all day, every day.

Day traders can open dedicated forex accounts through their broker or a currency dealer (one is GTForex, www.gtforex.com) and then trade as they see opportunities during the day.

Commodities and How They Trade

Commodities are basic, interchangeable goods sold in bulk and used to make other goods. Examples include oil, gold, wheat, and lumber. Commodities are popular with investors as a hedge against inflation and uncertainty. Stock prices can go to zero, but people still need to eat! While commodity prices usually tend to increase at the same rate as in the overall economy, so they maintain their real (inflation-adjusted) value, they can also be susceptible to short-term changes in supply and demand. A cold winter increases demand for oil, a dry summer reduces production of wheat, and a civil war could disrupt access to platinum mines.

Day traders aren't going to buy commodities outright - if you really want to haul bushels of grain around all day, you can do that without taking on the risks of day trading. You'd get more exercise, too. Instead, day traders who want to play with commodities can look to other investments. The most popular way is to buy futures contracts, which change in price with the underlying commodity (discussed later in this chapter). Increasingly, many trade commodities through exchange traded funds (see earlier section) that are based on the value of an underlying basket of commodities.

Derivatives and How They Trade

Derivatives are financial contracts that draw their value from the value of an underlying asset, security, or index. For example, an S&P 500 futures contract would give the buyer a cash payment based on the price of the S&P 500 index on the day that the contract expires. The contract's value thus depends on where the index is trading. You are not trading the index itself, but rather you are trading a contract with a value derived from the price of the index. The index value changes all the time, so day traders have lots of opportunities to buy and sell.

Types of derivatives

Day traders are likely to come across three types of derivatives. Options and futures trade on dedicated derivatives exchanges, whereas warrants trade on stock exchanges.

Options

An *option* is a contract that gives the holder the right, but not the obligation, to buy or sell the underlying asset at an agreed-upon price at an agreed-upon date in the future. An option that gives you the right to buy is a *call*, and one that gives you the right to sell is a *put*. A call is most valuable if the stock price is going up, whereas a put has more value if the stock price is going down.

Here's one way to remember the difference: you *call up* your friend to *put down* your enemy.

For example, a MSFT 2007 Mar 22.50 call gives you the right to buy Microsoft at $22.50 per share at the expiration date on the third Friday in March, 2007. (Did you know that traders refer to Microsoft as "Mr. Softy"? Clever, huh?) If Microsoft is trading above $22.50, you can exercise the option and make a quick profit. If it is selling below $22.50, you could by the stock cheaper in the open market, so the option would be worthless.

You can find great information on options, including online tutorials, at the Chicago Board Options Exchange Web site, www.cboe.com.

Futures

A *futures* contract gives one the obligation to buy a set quantity of the underlying asset at set price and a set future date. These started in the agricultural industry because they allowed farmers and food processors to lock in their prices early in the growing season, reducing the amount of uncertainty in their businesses. Futures have now been applied to many different assets, ranging from pork bellies (which really do trade — they are used to make bacon) to currency values. A simple example is a lock in a home mortgage rate; the borrower knows the rate that will be applied before the sale is closed and the loan is finalized. Day traders use futures to trade commodities without having to handle the actual assets.

Most futures contracts are closed out with cash before the settlement date. Financial contracts — futures on currencies, interest rates, or market index values — can only be closed out with cash. Commodity contracts may be settled with the physical items, but almost all are settled with cash. No one hauls a side of beef onto the floor of the Chicago Board of Trade!

Warrants

A *warrant* is similar to an option, but it's issued by the company rather than sold on an organized exchange. (After they are issued, warrants trade similarly to stocks.) A warrant gives the holder the right to buy more stock in the company at an agreed-upon price in the future.

A cousin of the warrant is the *convertible bond*, which is debt issued by the company. The company pays interest on the bond, and the bondholder has the right to exchange it for stock, depending on where interest rates and the stock price are. Convertibles trade on the stock exchanges.

Buying and selling derivatives

Derivatives trade a little differently than other types of securities because they are based on promises. When someone buys an option on a stock, they aren't trading the stock with someone right now, they are buying the right to buy or sell it in the future. That means that the option buyer needs to know that the person on the other side is going to pay up. Because of that, the derivatives exchanges have systems in place to make sure that those who buy and sell the contracts will be able to perform when they have to. Requirements for trading derivatives are different than in other markets.

How derivatives trade

Remember marginability from early in this chapter? Well, the word *margin* is used differently when discussing derivatives, but that's in part because derivatives are already leveraged — you aren't buying the asset, just exposure to the price change, so you can get a lot of bang for your buck. (The risks and rewards of leverage are covered in detail in Chapter 14.)

Margin in the derivatives market is the money you have to put up to ensure that you'll perform on the contract when it comes time to execute it. In the stock market, margin is collateral against a loan from the brokerage firm. In the derivatives markets, margin is collateral against the amount you might have to pay up on the contract. The more likely it is that you will have to pay the party who bought or sold the contract, the more margin money you will have to put up. Some exchanges use the term *performance bond* instead.

To buy a derivative, you put up the margin with the exchange's clearing house. That way, the exchange knows that you have the money to make good on your side of the deal — if, say, a call option that you sell is executed, or you lose money on a currency forward that you buy. Your brokerage firm will arrange for the deposit.

At the end of each day, derivatives contracts are *marked-to-market*, meaning that they are revalued. Profits are credited to the trader's margin account, and losses are deducted. If the margin falls below the necessary amount, the trader will get a call and have to deposit more money.

By definition, day traders close out at the end of every day, so their options are not marked-to-market. The contracts will be someone else's problem, and the profits or losses on the trade go straight to the margin account, ready for the next day's trading.

Where derivatives trade

Traditionally, derivative trading involves *open-outcry* on physical exchanges. Traders on the floor get orders and execute them amongst themselves, shouting and using hand signals to indicate what they want to do. There is no central trading post or market maker to control the activities or guarantee a market. Most traders are employees of large commodities brokerage firms, but some are independent. No matter who employs them, traders may be executing someone else's orders for a fee, or they may be working for proprietary accounts.

Open-outcry has fewer economies of scale than the electronic trading systems that dominate activity in other assets. That's why there are more derivatives exchanges in the United States than active stock exchanges. Still, all the exchanges offer some electronic trading services, and that has become more and more popular. It's also causing much restructuring and consolidation among the exchanges. As I write this, the Chicago Board of Trade is planning a merger with the Chicago Mercantile Exchange; floor traders at both exchanges have been steadily losing market share to electronic trading.

Sometimes, the people in the pits start messing around with each other, and that can cause unusual volatility in the trading of the securities. Day traders who deal in commodities will often notice short periods of irrational trading for those derivatives that trade primarily in pits. The more human involvement there is, the less efficient a market will be.

Chicago Board Options Exchange (CBOE)

The Chicago Board Options Exchange, often known by the acronym CBOE (pronounced *see-bow*), is the largest options market in the United States. This is where orders for stock options are traded. Brokerage firms use floor brokers in the trading pits or the CBOE's electronic trading system to handle customer orders.

Chicago Board of Trade (CBOT)

At the top of the Chicago Board of Trade's building is a statue of Ceres, the Greek goddess of grain. That's because this is the center of futures trading in corn, wheat, rice, oats, and soybeans. The Board of Trade has branched out over the years and now offers futures contracts on financial commodities like Treasury bonds and the Dow Jones Industrial Average. Recently, it added trading in ethanol futures, an expansion from its history with corn. When a brokerage firm gets a customer order for a future traded on the Board of Trade, it can send it to floor brokers to fill in the trading pits, or it can use the exchange's electronic trading system.

Chicago Mercantile Exchange (CME)

Futures in non-grain agricultural products, such as milk, butter, cattle, pork bellies, and fertilizer, trade at The Chicago Mercantile Exchange, known more colloquially as *the Merc*. Other key futures traded here include foreign exchange, interest rates, and Standard and Poor's and NASDAQ indexes. The Merc has also added some alternative products such as futures in weather and real estate. When brokerage firms receive orders for the Merc's futures, they send it to floor brokers, who can fill it in the trading pits, or they can use the Merc's electronic trading system.

New York Board of Trade (NYBOT)

The New York Board of Trade was founded in 1998, when the Coffee, Sugar, and Cocoa Exchange merged with the New York Cotton Exchange. Here, traders can buy and sell futures and options on those commodities as well as on orange juice, the New York Stock Exchange, the U.S. dollar, and the euro. Orders are filled in the trading pits or through an electronic trading system.

New York Mercantile Exchange (NYMEX)

Fuels and metals trade at the New York Mercantile Exchange, which is the largest physical commodities exchange in the United States. Most trading takes place in open-outcry pits, but an electronic system is available for overnight trading.

Chapter 4

Investing, Trading, and Gambling

Day trading isn't investing, nor is it gambling — at least not if done right. But the lines between the three can be thin, and if you know where they are, you'll be in a better position to follow your trading strategy and make more money. And if you can avoid the trap of gambling, you'll be better able to preserve your trading capital.

The difference between investing and gambling is the *risk and return tradeoff*. In investing, the odds are generally in your favor, but that doesn't mean you're going to make money. Some day traders end up gambling, and then the odds are moving against them. And unlike in the finer establishments in Las Vegas, no one is going to bring the failed day trader free drinks to help ease the pain. A lot comes down to personality; if you are on a casino's "do not admit" list, you probably aren't a great candidate for day trading.

This chapter starts off with a lot of gory details about risk and return. It helps you understand how the securities markets price risk and reward those who willing to take it. Then I explain the differences in risk and reward for investors, traders, and gamblers to give you better information to help you plan your day trading.

Understanding Risk and Return

Investors, traders, and gamblers have this in common: They are putting some of their money at risk and they expect to get a return. Ideally, that return comes in the form of cold, hard cash — but at a casino, you might get your return in the form of tickets to a Celine Dion concert after you lose a lot of money at the tables.

Trading is a business: The more you know about the potential risks and the sources of your potential return, the better off you'll be. Your risk is that you won't get the return you expect, and your reward is that you get fair compensation for the risk you take.

What is risk, anyway?

Risk is the measurable likelihood of loss. The riskier something is, the more frequently a loss will occur, and the larger that loss is likely to be. Playing in traffic is riskier than driving in traffic, and skydiving is riskier than gardening. This doesn't mean that you can't have losses in a low-risk activity or big gains in a high-risk one. It just means that with the low-risk game, losses are less likely to happen, and those that do are likely to be small.

What's the difference between risk and uncertainty? Risk involves the known likelihood of something good or bad happening so that it can be priced. What's the likelihood of your living to be 100? Or of getting into a car accident tonight? Your insurance company knows, and it figures your rates accordingly. What's the likelihood of aliens from outer space arriving and taking over the Earth? Who knows! It could happen, but that event is uncertain, not risky — at least until it happens.

The ability to measure risk made modern business possible. Until mathematicians were able to use statistics to quantify human activities, people assumed that bad things were simply the result of bad luck or, worse, the wrath of the gods. But when they could understand probability, it could be applied and used. If a sailor agreed to join a voyage of exploration, what was the probability that he would return home alive? And what would be fair compensation to him for that risk? What was the probability of a silo of grain going up in flames? And how much should the farmer charge the grain buyers for the risk that he was taking, and how much should someone else charge to insure the farmer against that fire?

Considering the probability of a loss

Whenever you take risk, you take on the probability of loss. If you know what that probability is, you can determine whether the terms you are being offered are fair and you have a reasonable expectation for the size of the loss.

One way to determine whether the terms of your day trading strategy are fair is through *backtesting*, which is discussed in Chapter 11.

Let's say that you are presented with this opportunity: You put up $10. You have an 80-percent chance of getting back $11 and a 20-percent chance of losing everything. Should you take it? To find out, you multiply the expected return by the likelihood and add them together: (80% × $11) + (20% × $0) = $8.80. Your expected return of $8.80 is less than the $10 cost of this contract, so you should pass on it.

Now, suppose you are offered this opportunity: You put up $10. You have a 90-percent chance of getting back $11 and a 10-percent chance of getting back $6. Your expected return is (90% × $11) + (10% × $6) = $10.50. This contract would be in your favor, so you should take it.

Now here's a third proposition: You put up $10. You have a 90-percent chance of getting back $13.89 and a 10-percent chance of losing $20 — even more than you put up. Your expected return is (90% × 13.89) + (10% × –$20) = $10.50. It's the same expected return as the proposition above, but do you like it as much?

When thinking about loss, most people tend to put too much weight on the absolute dollar amount that they can lose, rather than thinking about the likelihood. The problem is that the markets don't trade on your personal preferences. This is one of the psychological hurdles of trading that those who are successful can overcome. Can you? (You can find some tips on this in Chapter 8.)

Working with limited liability (usually)

Securities markets rely on the concept of *limited liability*. That is, you cannot lose any more money than you invested in the first place. If you buy a stock, it can go down to zero, but it can't go any lower. If the company goes bankrupt, no one can come to you and ask you to cover the bills. On the other hand, the most the stock can go up in price is infinity, so the possible return for your risk is huge. (Microsoft has grown more than 500-fold since it came public, which isn't quite infinity, but I sure wish I had taken that proposition.)

Most day trading strategies have the same limited liability: You can lose what you trade, and no more. Some strategies have unlimited liability, however. If you sell a stock short (borrow shares and then sell them in hopes that the stock goes down in price, allowing you to repay the loan with cheaper shares, a strategy discussed in Chapter 14), and if the stock goes up to infinity, you have to repay the loan with those infinitely valued shares! Most likely, you're going to close out your position before that happens, but keep in mind that even if you close out your positions every night like a good day trader should, some strategies have the potential to cost you more money than you have in your trading account.

To protect themselves and to protect you against losing more money than you have, brokerage firms and options exchanges will require you to keep enough funds in your account to cover shortfalls (known as *margin*, discussed in Chapter 3). You will have to be approved before you can trade in certain securities. For example, anyone trading options has to fill out an agreement that the brokerage firm must first approve and then keep on file.

Playing the zero-sum game

Many day trading strategies are *zero-sum games*, meaning that for every winner on a trade, there is a loser. This is especially true in options markets. Now, the person on the other side of the trade might not mind being a loser; she may have entered into a trade to *hedge* (protect against a decline in) another investment and is happy to have a small loss instead of a much larger one.

The problem for you as a day trader is that there is little wiggle room in a zero-sum game. Every trade you make is going to win or lose, and your losses may exactly offset your winners. If your strategy takes place in a market that is a zero-sum game, such as the options market, make sure that you've tested your strategy thoroughly (see Chapter 11 for more on that) so that you know whether your odds are better than even.

Finding the probability of not getting the return you expect

In addition to absolute measures of risk and liability, there's another consideration: *volatility*. That's how much a security's price might go up or down in a given time period.

The math for measuring volatility is based on standard deviation (discussed in Chapters 3 and 11). A standard deviation calculation starts with the average return over a given time period. This is the *expected* return — the return that, on average, you'll get if you stick with your trading strategy. But any given week, month, or year, the return might be very different from what you expect. The more likely you are to get what you expect, the less risk you take in the form of volatility.

Standard deviation shows up many times in trading, and there's a detailed explanation of it in Chapter 11. The key thing to know is this: The higher the standard deviation of the underlying securities, the more risk you take with your trade. However, the same volatility creates trading opportunities for day traders to exploit. A security with a low standard deviation isn't going to offer you many chances to make money over the course of a day.

Standard deviation is used to calculate another statistic: beta. *Beta* tells you how risky a security is relative to the risk of the market itself. If you buy a stock with a beta of more than 1, then that stock is expected to go up in price by a larger percentage than the market when the market is up, and it's expected to go down by a larger percentage than the market when the market is down.

High-beta stocks, and options on high-beta stocks, are riskier than low-beta stocks, but they offer a greater potential for return.

The word *beta* comes from the capital assets pricing model, an academic theory that says that the return on an investment is a function of the risk-free rate of return (discussed in the next section), the extra risk of investing in the market as a whole, and then the volatility — beta — of the security relative to the market. Under the capital assets pricing model, there are no other sources of risk and return. Any other sources would be called *alpha*, but in theory, alpha doesn't exist. Not everyone agrees with that, but the terms alpha and beta have stuck.

Getting rewarded for the risk you take

When you take risk, you expect to get a return. That's fair enough, right? That return comes in a few different forms related to the risk taken. Although you might not really care how you get your return as long as you get it, thinking about the break-down of returns can help you think about your trading strategy and how it works for you.

Opportunity cost

The *opportunity cost* of your money is the return you could get doing something else. Is your choice day trading or staying at your current job? Your opportunity cost is your current salary and benefits. You'd give up that money if you quit to day trade. Is the opportunity cost low enough that it's worth your while? It may be. Just because taking advantage of an opportunity carries a cost doesn't mean that the opportunity isn't worth it.

When you trade, you want to cover your opportunity cost. Your cost will be different than someone else's, but if you know what it is up front, you'll have a better idea of whether your return is worth your risk.

There's another way to think about opportunity cost. When you make one trade, you give up the opportunity to use that money for another trade. That means you only want to trade if you know that the trade is going to work out, more likely than not. That's why you need to plan your trades (see Chapter 2) and backtest (run a simulation using your strategy and historic securities prices) and evaluate your performance (see Chapter 11) so that you know that you are trading for the right reasons, and not just out of boredom.

Risk-free rate of return and the time value of money

The value of money changes over time. In most cases, this is because of *inflation*, which is the general increase in price levels in an economy. But it's also because you give up the use of money for some period of time. That's why any investment or trading opportunity should include compensation for the *time value of your money*.

In day trading, your return from time value is small, because you only hold positions for a short period of time and close them out overnight. Still, there's some time component to the money you make. That smallest return is known as the *risk-free rate of return*. That's what you demand for giving up the use of your money, even if you know with certainty that you'll get your money back. In practice, investors think of the risk-free rate of return as the rate on U.S. government treasury bills, which are bonds that mature in less than one year. This rate is widely quoted in *The Wall Street Journal* and electronic price quote systems.

If you cannot generate a return that's at least equal to the risk-free rate of return, you shouldn't be trading.

Risk-return tradeoff

Economists say that there is no such thing as a free lunch. Whatever return you get, you get because you took some risk and gave up another opportunity for your time and money. In that sense, there is no secret to making money. It's all about work and risk.

This is known as the *risk-reward tradeoff*. The greater the potential reward, the greater the amount of risk you're expected to take, and thus the greater potential you have for loss. But if you understand the risks you are taking up front, you may well find that they are worth taking. That's why you have to think about the risks and rewards up front.

The magic of market efficiency

The reason there's a balance between risk and reward is that markets are reasonably efficient. This efficiency means that prices reflect all known information about the companies and the economy, and it means that all participants understand the relative tradeoffs available to them. Otherwise, you'd have opportunities to make a riskless profit, and that's just won't do according to the average economist. "You can't pluck nickels out of thin air," they like to say. In an efficient market, if there's an opportunity to make money without risk, someone would have taken advantage of that already.

Here's how it works: You have information that says that Company A is going to announce good earnings tomorrow, so you buy the stock. Your increased demand causes the price to go up, and pretty soon, the stock price is where it should be given that the company is doing well. The information advantage is rapidly eliminated. And in most cases, everyone gets the news — or hears the rumor — of the good earnings at the same time, so the price adjustment happens quickly.

The oldest economics joke ever told

So now that you're wise to the ways of risk and return, this joke should make sense to you:

Two economists are walking down the street. One sees a $20 bill on the sidewalk and stops to pick it up. "Don't bother," says the other. "If it were real, someone would have taken it already."

"Don't be so sure," says the first economist. He picks it up, sees that it is real, then turns to his friend and says, "How about if I buy you a free lunch?"

Wouldn't it be great if you could get the news of a good earnings report before everyone else, to make a quick trading profit? Yep. At least until the Feds show up and hauled you off to prison — talk about your opportunity costs. It is illegal to trade on *material inside information* (which would be information that is not generally known that would affect the price of the security). And yes, the Securities and Exchange Commission and the exchanges monitor trading to see whether trading patterns suggest illegal trading based on inside information, because they want all investors and traders to feel confident that the investment business is fair. Be very wary of tips that seem too good to be true.

Now, you'll notice in the example that it was the activity of traders that caused the price of Company A stock to go up to reflect the expected good earnings report. The markets may be more or less efficient, but that doesn't mean they work by magic. Price changes happen because people act on news, and those who act the fastest are day traders.

In economic terms, *arbitrage* is a riskless profit. A hard-core believer in academic theory would say that arbitrage opportunities don't exist. In practice, though, they do. Here's how it works: although Company A is expected to have a good earnings announcement tomorrow, you notice that the stock price has gone up faster than the price of a call option on Company A, even though premium should reflect the stock price. So, you sell Company A (borrowing shares and selling it short if you have to), and then use the proceeds to buy the option. When the option price goes up to reflect the stock price, you can sell it and lock in a riskless profit — at least, before your trading costs are considered. Chapter 15 discusses arbitrage in more detail.

Investing

Investing is the process of putting money at risk in order to get a return. It's the raw material of capitalism. It's the way that businesses get started, roads get built, and explorations get financed. It's how our economy matches people who have too much money, at least during part of their lives, with people who need it in order to grow society's capabilities.

Investing is heady stuff. And it's very much focused on the long term. Good investors do a lot of research before committing their money, because they know that it will take a long time to see a payoff. That's okay with them. Investors often invest in things that are out of favor, because they know that with time, others will recognize the value and respond in kind.

One of the best investors of all time is Warren Buffett, Chief Executive Officer of Berkshire Hathaway. His annual letters to shareholders offer great insight. You can read them at www.berkshirehathaway.com/letters/letters.html.

What's the difference between investing and saving? When you save, you take no risk. Your compensation is low — it's just enough to cover the time value of money. Generally, the return on savings equals inflation and no more. In fact, a lot of banks pay a lot less than the inflation rate on a federally insured savings account, meaning that you're paying the bank to use your money.

In contrast to investing, day trading moves fast. Day traders react only to what's on the screen. There's no time to do research, and the market is always right when you are day trading. You don't have two months or two years to wait for the fundamentals to work out and the rest of Wall Street to see how smart you were. You have today. And if you can't live with that, you shouldn't be day trading.

Trading

Trading is the act of buying and selling securities. All investors trade, because they need to buy and sell their investments. But to investors, trading is a rare transaction, and they get more value from finding a good opportunity, buying it cheap, and selling it at a much higher price sometime in the future. But traders are not investors.

Traders look to take advantage of short-term price discrepancies in the market. In general, they don't take a lot of risk on each trade, so they don't get a lot of return on each trade, either. Traders act quickly. They look at what the market is telling them and then respond. They know that many of their trades will not work out, but as long as more than half work, they'll be okay. They don't do a lot of in-depth research on the securities they trade, but they know the normal price and volume patterns well enough that they can recognize potential profit opportunities.

Trading keeps markets efficient, because it creates the short-term supply and demand that eliminates small price discrepancies. It also creates a lot of stress for traders, who must react in the here and now. Traders give up the luxury of time in exchange for a quick profit.

Speculation is related to trading, in that it often involves short-term transactions. Speculators take risks assuming a much greater return than might be expected, and a lot of what-ifs may have to be satisfied for the transaction to pay off. Many speculators hedge their risks with other securities, such as options or futures.

Gambling

A *gambler* puts up money in the hopes of a payoff if a random event occurs. The odds are always against the gambler and in favor of the house, but people like to gamble because they like to hope that if they hit it lucky, their return will be as large as their loss is likely.

Some gamblers believe that the odds can be beaten, but they are wrong. (Certain card games are more games of skill than gambling, assuming you can find a casino that will play under standard rules. Yeah, you can count cards when playing blackjack with your friends, but it's a lot harder in a professionally run casino.) They get excited about the potential for a big win and get caught up in the glamour of the casino, and soon the odds go to work and drain away their stakes.

There is such a thing as a *fair lottery*, which takes place when the expected payoff is higher than the odds of playing. You won't find it at most casinos, although sometimes the odds in a sports book or horse race favor the bettor, at least in the short term. A more common example takes place in lotteries when the jackpots roll over to astronomical amounts. For example, in March of 2007, the multi-state Mega Millions lottery had a jackpot of $370 million, but the odds of winning were 1 in 175 million. This means that a $1.00 ticket had an expected value of $2.11, making it a fair proposition.

Trading is not gambling, but traders who are not paying attention to their strategy and its performance can cross over into gambling. They can view the blips on their computer screen as a game. They can start making trades without any regard for the risk and return characteristics. They can start believing that how they do things affects the trade. And pretty soon, they are using the securities market as a giant casino, using trading techniques that have odds as bad as any slot machine.

Managing the Risks of Day Trading

Now that you know more about the risks, returns, and related activities of day trading, you can think more about how you're going to run your day trading business. Before you flip through the book to find out how to get started, consider two more kinds for risk that you need to think about:

- ✔ Business risk
- ✔ Personal risk

Business risk

Business risk is the uncertainty of the timing of your cash flow. Not every month of trading is going to be great, but your bills will come due no matter what. You'll have to pay for subscriptions while keeping the lights turned on and the computer connected to the Internet. Taxes come due four times a year, and keyboards hold a mysterious attraction for carbonated beverages, causing them to short out at the most inopportune times.

Regardless of what happens to your trading account, you need cash on hand to pay your bills or you'll be out of business. The best way to protect yourself is to start out with a cash cushion just for covering your operating expenses. Keep it separate from your trading funds. Replenish it during good months.

Personal risk

The *personal risk* of trading is that it becomes an obsession that crowds out everything else in your life. Trading is a stressful business, and the difference between those who succeed and those who fail is psychological. And, in fact, the personal risk is so great that I devote an entire chapter to managing it — Chapter 8. Go there if anything you have read in this chapter alarms you.

Chapter 5

Fun with Regulation

· ·

In This Chapter

▶ Looking at a history of day trading and regulations

▶ Wondering who are all these regulators anyway?

▶ Considering some basic brokerage requirements

▶ Handling hot tips

▶ Trading for other people

· ·

*T*he financial markets are wild and woolly playgrounds for capitalism at its best. Every moment of the trading day, buyers and sellers get together to figure out what the price of a stock, commodity, or currency should be at that moment, given the supply, the demand, and the information out there. It's beautiful.

One reason the markets work so well is that they are regulated. That may seem like an oxymoron: Isn't capitalism all about free trade, unfettered by any rules from nannying bureaucrats? Ah, but for capitalism to work, people on both sides of a trade need to know that the terms will be enforced. They need to know that the money in their accounts is there and is safe from theft. And they need to know that no one has an unfair advantage. *Regulation* creates the trust that makes markets function.

Day traders may not be managing money for other investors, and they may not answer to an employer, but that doesn't mean they don't have rules to follow. They have to comply with applicable securities laws and exchange regulations, some of which specifically address those who make lots of short-term trades. Likewise, brokers and advisors who deal with day traders have regulations that they need to follow, and understanding them can help day traders make better decisions about whom to deal with. In this chapter, you find out who does the regulating, what they look at, and how they affect you.

How Regulations Created Day Trading

With the advent of the telegraph, traders could receive daily price quotes. Many cities had *bucket shops*, which were storefront businesses where traders could bet on changes in stock and commodity prices. They weren't buying the security itself, even for a few minutes, but were instead placing bets against others. These schemes were highly prone to manipulation and fraud, and they were wiped out after the stock market crash of 1929.

After the 1929 crash, small investors could trade off the ticker tape, which was a printout of price changes sent by telegraph, or wire. In most cases, they would do this by going down to their brokerage firm's office, sitting in a conference room, and placing orders based on the changes they saw come across the tape. Really serious traders could get a wire installed in their own office, but the costs were prohibitive for most individual investors. In any event, traders still had to place their orders through a broker rather than having direct access to the market, so they could not count on timely execution.

Another reason there was so little day trading back then is that all brokerage firms charged the same commissions until 1975. That year, the Securities and Exchange Commission ruled that this amounted to price fixing, so brokers could then compete on their commissions. Some brokerage firms, such as Charles Schwab, began to allow customers to trade stock at discount commission rates, which made active trading more profitable. (Some brokerage firms don't even charge commissions anymore, but don't worry; they get money from you in other ways.)

The system of trading off the ticker tape more or less persisted until the stock market crash of 1987. Brokerage firms and market makers were flooded with orders, so they took care of their biggest customers first and pushed the smallest trades to the bottom of the pile. After the crash, the exchanges and the Securities and Exchange Commission called for several changes that would reduce the chances of another crash and improve execution if one were to happen. One of those changes was the Small Order Entry System, often known as SOES, which gave orders of 1000 shares or less priority over larger orders.

Then, in the 1990s, Internet access became widely available, and several electronic communications networks started giving small traders direct access to price quotes and trading activities. This meant that traders could place orders on the same footing as the brokers they once had to work through. In fact, thanks to the SOES, the small traders had an advantage: They could place orders and then sell the stock to the larger firms, locking in a nice profit. Day trading looked like a pretty good way to make a living.

Larger institutional traders and NASDAQ market makers resented the way that traders using SOES exploited their advantage, referring to these people as *SOES bandits*.

Your library and bookstore might have older books talking about how day traders can make easy money exploiting SOES. That loophole is long gone, so stick to newer guides. There's a list in the appendix.

In 2000, the Small Order Execution System (SOES) was changed to eliminate the advantage the small traders had, but few of them cared right away. More and more discount brokerage firms offered Internet trading while Internet stocks became wildly popular. No one needed SOES to make profits when Amazon.com and Webvan were going up in price day after day, at least for a while. But then reality caught up with the technology industry, and the market for those stocks cratered in 2000.

We're now in a new era, with new trading practices and new regulation.

Who Regulates What

In the United States, financial markets get general regulatory oversight from two government bodies: the Securities and Exchange Commission (SEC) and the Commodity Futures Trading Commission (CFTC). Both have similar goals: to ensure that investors and traders have adequate information to make decisions and to prevent fraud and abuse.

Neither body has complete authority over the markets, though. Instead, much of the responsibility for proper behavior has been given to self-regulatory organizations that brokerage firms join, and to the exchanges themselves. It's not straightforward, but the overlap between these organizations seems to ensure that problems are identified early on and that the interests of companies, brokers, and investment managers are fairly represented.

Stock and corporate bond market regulation

The stock and corporate bond markets are the most prominent. Regulators are active and visible because these markets have a relatively large number of relatively small issuers. There's not one government issuing currency — there are a whole bunch of companies issuing shares of stock. When it turns out that one of these companies has fraudulent numbers, the headlines erupt, and suddenly everyone cares about what the SEC is up to. That's just the first layer in regulating this market.

Given the rate at which exchanges are merging and organizations are re-arranging themselves, the following list may well be obsolete by the time you read it. But even if the organizations go away, the regulations won't.

The U.S. Securities and Exchange Commission (SEC)

www.sec.gov

The SEC is a government agency that ensures that markets work efficiently. The Commission has five commissioners, appointed by the President and confirmed by Congress, who serve staggered five-year terms. This structure is designed to keep the SEC nonpartisan. One of the commissioners is designated as the chair.

The SEC has three functions:

✔ To ensure that any companies that have securities listed on exchanges in the United States report their financial information accurately and on time, so that investors can determine whether investing in the company makes sense for them

✔ To provide oversight to the markets by ensuring that the exchanges and self-regulatory organizations have sufficient regulations in place and that those regulations are enforced

✔ To regulate mutual funds, investment advisors, and others who make decisions for other people's money

The National Association of Securities Dealers (NASD)

www.nasd.com

The NASD represents and regulates all stock and bond brokerage firms and their employees. More than 5,000 firms are members, with 660,000 employees registered to sell securities. The NASD administers background checks and licensing exams, regulates securities trading and monitors how firms comply, and provides information for investors so that they are better informed about the investing process.

The NASD also requires brokers to know who their customers are and whether an investment strategy is suitable for them. I discuss suitability later in this chapter, but for now, know that that's an NASD function.

A good first stop for a day trader is the NASD's BrokerCheck service. The Web site address is too unwieldy to reprint here, but you can go to www.nasd.org and click on the link to BrokerCheck from that home page. BrokerCheck allows you to look up brokerage firms and individual brokers to see whether they are in good standing. If there have been any complaints filed, you can see what they are and decide for yourself how you feel about them. It's great information that can help you head off problems early on.

The NASD started as a self-regulatory organization, but in the late 1960s it saw that member firms needed a better way to trade over-the-counter securities (securities that do not trade on an organized exchange like the New York Stock Exchange). In 1971, it formed its own electronic communication network, the National Association of Securities Dealers Automated Quotation system, or NASDAQ, pronounced as one word: "NAZ-dack." In 2000, the NASD divested NASDAQ, which is now known only by that name, and returned to its self-regulatory organization roots. Although the two are now separate, brokerage firms that trade securities on NASDAQ must be members of the National Association of Securities Dealers.

The exchanges

Each of the major stock and bond exchanges — the New York Stock Exchange (NYSE), the American Stock Exchange (ASE), and NASDAQ — has its own regulatory body that makes sure that companies with securities traded on the exchange meet the criteria that have been set for their listing. These criteria include timely financial reporting with the SEC and minimum numbers of shares that are actually traded. (Chapter 3 has a description of the different exchanges and their listing requirements.)

The exchanges also monitor how securities are traded in order to look for patterns that might point to market manipulation or insider trading. Each works with brokerage firms that are allowed to trade on its exchange to make sure they know who their customers are and that they have systems in place to make certain these customers play by the rules.

The NYSE used to oversee and license brokers that worked for member firms. At the time of this writing, it is in the process of merging those functions with the NASD. As all NYSE firms are also members of the NASD, this should reduce much duplication of effort.

Treasury bond market regulation

Treasury bonds are a slightly different animal than corporate bonds. They are issued by the U.S. government, so regulation is handled by the Treasury Department's Bureau of the Public Debt (www.treasurydirect.gov) with additional oversight from the SEC.

Derivatives market regulation

The derivatives markets, where options and futures are traded, don't deal in stocks and bonds directly. Instead, they link buyers and sellers of contracts where the value is linked to the value of an underlying security. Derivatives are popular with day traders, because they give them a way to get exposure to interest rates and market index performance with less capital than would be required to buy treasury bonds or large groups of stocks directly.

Derivatives markets have their own regulatory bodies, but they match the format and hierarchy of stock and bond market regulation. The organizations may not be household names, but their functions will seem familiar.

Commodity Futures Trading Commission (CFTC)

www.cftc.gov

The CFTC is a government agency founded in 1974 to oversee market activities in agricultural and financial commodities. The government realized that these markets needed some regulation but were sufficiently different from traditional stock exchanges that the SEC might not be the best agency to handle it. The CFTC is structured similarly to the SEC, with five commissioners holding staggered five-year terms, appointed by the President and confirmed by Congress. One of the commissioners is designated as the chair. This structure is designed to keep the CFTC nonpartisan.

For decades, futures trading was regulated by the U.S. Department of Agriculture, because it involved nothing but agricultural commodities like grain, pork bellies, and coffee. As traders demanded such new products as futures on interest rates and currencies, it became clear that a new regulatory body was needed, and that was the CFTC.

The CFTC has two main functions:

- ✔ To ensure that the markets are liquid and that both parties on an options or futures transaction are able to clear (that is, to meet their contractual obligations)
- ✔ To provide oversight to the markets by ensuring that the exchanges and self-regulatory organizations have sufficient regulations in place, and that those regulations are enforced

National Futures Association (NFA)

www.nfa.futures.org

The NFA regulates 4,200 firms and has 55,000 employees who work on the different futures exchanges. It administers background checks and licensing exams, regulates futures trading and monitors how firms comply, and provides information for investors so that they are better informed about futures trading and how it differs from more traditional investments.

Firms that handle futures are known as *futures commission merchants*, or FCMs, rather than *brokers*. You can find information on FCMs and their employees through the NFA's Background Affiliation Status Information Center, which has the clever acronym BASIC. You can access it at www.nfa.futures.org/basicnet/ or through the NFA's home page. BASIC allows you to look up futures firms and employees to see whether they are registered and whether any complaints have been filed against them. If there have been any complaints filed, you can see how the problem was resolved. It's like that legendary permanent record that your elementary school teachers said would follow you for the rest of your life.

Trading in options on stocks is regulated by the Securities and Exchange Commission and the National Association of Securities Dealers, but trading on options on futures is regulated by the Commodity Futures Trading Commission and the National Futures Association. As the lines between derivative products get blurrier, you may find a lot of overlap, and many in the industry predict that the SEC and CFTC will merge at some point. Because it's possible to research firms and people through several self-regulatory organizations, you may as well take the time to do it. Don't be alarmed if someone is listed one place and not the other, but do be alarmed if a firm or person isn't listed anywhere.

The exchanges

The Chicago Board Options Exchange (CBOE), Chicago Board of Trade (CBOT), Chicago Mercantile Exchange (CME, also called the Merc), New York Board of Trade (NYBOT), New York Mercantile Exchange (NYMEX), and other derivatives exchanges have their own regulatory groups that ensure that their traders comply with exchange rules and rules of other organizations, especially the CFTC. They also develop new types of trading contracts that satisfy market demands while complying with applicable laws. (Chapter 3 has a description of the different exchanges and what they do.)

The exchanges also monitor how derivatives are traded in order to look for patterns that might point to market manipulation or insider trading. Each works with the futures commission merchants that are allowed to trade on its exchange to make sure that they know who their customers are and that they have systems in place to make sure these customers trade well, if not profitably.

Foreign exchange (forex) regulation

Because it is the largest, most liquid market in the world, many day traders are taking up trading in foreign exchange, also known as *forex*. But here's the tricky thing: These markets are not well regulated. There's nothing to stop someone from exchanging U.S. dollars for Canadian dollars; tourists do it every day, often at a hotel desk or retail shop. There's no paperwork, no hassle — and no oversight.

Oversight isn't necessary for someone at a convenience store buying a tube of Smarties (no, not the horrible dry tablets wrapped in cellophane, but rather a fine chocolate candy not available in the States, so if you cross the border, please pick some up for me!) with bucks and getting loonies in return. Unfortunately, this has allowed some firms to misrepresent forex trading to day traders, and it has allowed some day traders to get badly burned. Forewarned is forearmed, as the cliché goes.

Options and futures on currency

Most currency is traded in the *spot*: Traders exchange one currency for another at the current exchange rate. The spot market is not regulated. But many trade currency using options and futures, to bet on where exchange rates might go and to hedge the risks of unexpected changes. Options and futures on currency are regulated as derivatives, through the CFTC, the NFA, and the relevant futures exchanges. In some cases, though, FCMs get customer referrals from foreign exchange firms that are not themselves registered, which can make it unclear whether customers understand what they are getting into.

If you are participating in an unregulated market like forex, you can protect yourself by doing your research so that you know what the risks and rewards are. For that matter, every market has a few unscrupulous individuals, so you will always be better off if you find your own facts rather than rely on someone else. The exchanges and self-regulatory organizations all have great Web sites with lots of information, and you can see a directory of them in this book's appendix.

Banks and oversight

Banks are responsible for most foreign exchange trading, and banks are heavily regulated. This means that the Federal Reserve Banks and the U.S. Treasury Department are paying attention to forex markets, looking for evidence of manipulation and money laundering (discussed later in the chapter). This keeps the market from being a total free-for-all, even though anyone is allowed to trade currency.

Bank oversight isn't enough to protect your from the outlandish claims from crooked forex trading firms, but it does ensure that your contracts are fulfilled.

Brokerage Basics for Firm and Customer

No matter who regulates them, brokers and futures commission merchants have to know who their customers are and what they are up to. That leads to some basic regulations about suitability, pattern day trading, and money laundering — and extra paperwork for you. Don't get too annoyed by all the paperwork you have to fill out to open an account, because your brokerage firm has even more.

Are you suitable for day trading?

Brokerage firms and FCMs have to make sure that customer activities are appropriate. The firms need to know their customers and be sure that any recommendations are suitable. When it comes to day trading, firms need to be sure that customers are dealing with *risk capital* — money that they can afford to lose. They also need to be sure that the customers understand the risks that they are taking. Depending on the firm and what you are trying to do, you might have to submit financial statements, sign a stack of disclosures, and verify that you have received different guides to trading.

It's no one's business but your own, except of course that the various regulators want to make sure that firm employees aren't talking customers into taking on risks that they should not be taking. Sure, you can lie about it. You can tell the broker you don't need the $25,000 you're putting in your account, even if that's the money paying for your kidney dialysis. But if it's gone, you can't say you didn't know about the risks involved.

Staying out of the money Laundromat

Money laundering is the process of giving a provenance to money acquired from illegal activities. Your average drug dealer, Mafia hit man, or corrupt politician doesn't accept credit cards, but he really doesn't want to keep lots of cash in his house. How can he collect interest on his money if it's locked in a safe in his closet? And besides, his friends are an unsavory sort. Can he trust them to stay away from his cache? If this criminal fellow takes all that cash to the bank, those pesky bankers will start asking a lot of questions, because they know that most people pursuing legitimate business activities get paid through checks or electronic direct deposit.

Hence, the felon with funds will look for a way to make it appear that the money is legitimate. There are all sorts of ways to do this, ranging from making lots of small cash deposits to engaging in complicated series of financial trades and money transfers, especially between countries, that become difficult for investigators to trace. Sometimes these transactions look a lot like day trading, and that means that legitimate brokerage firms opening day trade accounts should be paying attention to who their customers are.

Fighting money laundering took on urgency after the September 11, 2001 attacks, because it was clear that someone somewhere had given some bad people a lot of cash to fund the preparation and execution of their deadly mission. The U.S. and several other nations increased their oversight of financial activities during the aftermath of the strikes on the World Trade Center and

Pentagon. That's why a key piece of paperwork from your broker will be the anti-money laundering disclosure. The U.S. Treasury Department's Financial Crimes Informant Network (www.fincen.gov), which investigates money laundering, requires financial institutions to have enforcement procedures in place to verify that new investments were not made from ill-gotten funds.

In order for your brokerage firm to verify that it knows who its customers are and where their money came from, you'll probably have to provide the following when you open a brokerage account:

- ✓ Your name
- ✓ Date of birth
- ✓ Street address
- ✓ Place of business
- ✓ Social Security number or Taxpayer Identification Number
- ✓ Driver's license and passport
- ✓ Copies of financial statements

Special rules for pattern day traders

Here's the problem for regulators: Many day traders lose money, and those losses can be magnified by the use of *leverage strategies* (trading with borrowed money, meaning that you can lose more money than you have in the quest for large profits, discussed in great detail in Chapter 14). If the customer who lost the money can't pay up, then the broker is on the hook. If too many customers lose money beyond what the broker can absorb, then the losses ripple through the financial system, and that's not good.

The National Association of Securities Dealers has a long list of rules that its member firms have to meet in order to stay in business. One, known as NASD Rule 2520, deals specifically with day traders. It sets the minimum account size and margin requirements for those who fit the definition of day traders, and I'll give you a hint: The requirements are stricter than for other types of accounts, to reflect the greater risk.

The NASD defines day trading as the buying or selling of the same security on the same day in a margin account (that is, using borrowed money). Execute four or more of those day trades within five business days, and you are a *pattern day trader*, unless those four or more trades were 6 percent or less of all the trades you made over those five days.

Money laundering: Al Capone or Watergate?

Although some believe that the term *money laundry* dates back to Al Capone's attempts to evade taxes by owning laundries — businesses that had a large amount of small cash transactions — the Federal Reserve Board says that the term didn't come into use until the Watergate scandal, when Nixon's campaign staff had to hide the money used to pay the people who broke into his opponent's psychiatrist's office.

The National Futures Association does not have a definition of day trading, because futures trades by their very nature are short term.

Here's why it matters: If you are a pattern day trader, you can have margin of 25 percent in your account, which means you can borrow 75 percent of the cost of the securities that you are trading. Most customers are only allowed to borrow 50 percent. That's because pattern day traders almost always close out their positions overnight, so there is less risk to the firm of having the loan outstanding. However, you have to have a margin account if you are a pattern day trader. This means you have to sign an agreement saying that you understand the risks of borrowing money, including that you may have to repay more than is in your account and that your broker can sell securities out from under you to ensure you pay what is owed.

Under Rule 2520, you have to have at least $25,000 in your brokerage account. If you have losses that take your account below that, you have to come up with more money before your broker will allow you to continue day trading. You can't plead your case, because the broker has to comply with the law. In fact, if you don't make the deposits necessary to bring your account up to at least $25,000 and at least 25 percent of the amount of money you've borrowed within five business days, you have to trade on a cash basis (no borrowing), assuming the firm will even let you trade.

The rules set by the NASD and other self-regulatory organizations are minimum requirements. Brokerage firms are free to set higher limits for account size and borrowing, and many do in order to manage their own risks better.

Tax reporting

On top of the identity paperwork, you have forms to fill out for tax reporting. IRS Form W9 keeps your taxpayer information on record. Then, at the end of the year, the brokerage firm sends you a 1099 form listing how much money you made in your account. After all, the taxman always gets his cut. Tax issues are covered in Chapter 10.

Hot Tips and Insider Trading

The regulations are very clear for things about suitability and money laundering. You get a bunch of forms, you read them, you sign them, you present documentation, and everyone is happy. The rules that keep the markets functioning are clear and easy to follow.

There's another set of rules that keep markets functioning — namely, that no one has an unfair information advantage. If you knew about big merger announcements, interest rate decisions by the Federal Reserve, or a new sugar substitute that would eliminate demand for corn syrup, you could make a lot of money in the stock market, trading options on interest rate futures or playing in the grain futures market.

Insider trading is not well defined. Any non-public information that a reasonable person would consider when deciding whether to buy or sell a security would apply, and that's a pretty vague standard — especially because the whole purpose of research is to combine bits of immaterial information together to make investment decisions.

Day traders can be susceptible to hot tips, because they are buying and selling so quickly. If these hot tips are actually inside information, though, the trader can become liable. If you get great information from someone who is in a position to know — an officer, a director, a lawyer, an investment banker — you may be looking at stiff penalties. Civil penalties are usually three times your profits, but the government might decide that your trading was part of a criminal enterprise, making the potential penalties much greater.

Insider trading is difficult to prove, so federal regulators use other tools to punish those it suspects of making improper profits. Martha Stewart wasn't sent to prison on insider trading charges; she was charged with obstructing justice by lying to investigators about what happened.

Whenever a big announcement is made, such as a merger, the exchanges go back and review trading for several days before to see whether there were any unusual activities in relevant securities and derivatives. Then they start tracing it back to the traders involved through the brokerage firms to see if it was coincidence or part of a pattern.

The bottom line is this: You may never come across inside information. But if a tip seems too good to be true, it probably is, so be careful.

Taking in Partners

Once your day trading proves to be wildly successful, you might want to take on partners to give you more trading capital and a slightly more regular income from the management fees. You can do it, but it's a lot of work.

If you are trading options and futures, you need to register with the National Futures Association if you're operating a commodity pool or working as a commodity trading advisor. If you're trading stocks and bonds, you have to register with the Securities and Exchange Commission unless you meet the exemption tests that would let you operate as a hedge fund instead.

Registration is not a do-it-yourself project. An error or omission may have tremendous repercussions, including fines or jail time, down the line. If you want to take on partners for your trading business, spend the money for qualified legal advice. It will protect you and show prospective customers that you are serious about your business.

To qualify as a hedge fund, which is a private investment partnership that does not qualify for registration under the Investment Company Act of 1940, you have to deal only with *accredited investors* (those with at least $1 million in net worth or an annual income of $200,000) or *qualified purchasers* (those with $5 million in investable assets). The idea is that these people should have enough money to lose and be able to understand the risks that they are taking. Hedge funds do not have to register with the SEC, but they may have to register with the NFA. However, prospective investors will want to see proof that you know what you are doing and know how to handle their money. That step is beyond the scope of this book, but it's something for a successful day trader to consider.

Part II
Day Trading Tools

The 5th Wave
By Rich Tennant

"No, day trading hasn't interferred with my regular practice at all. In fact, I'm preparing to make a trade now."

In this part . . .

Day trading is first and foremost a business, and here you'll find out how to get set up for success. This part includes information on how to set up your office and find brokerage services; where to get the support services you need to research trades; and how get through the treacherous days with your sanity intact and your positions under control. Then you'll find how to pay taxes on your gains and figure out how well your time, energy, and trading paid off.

Chapter 6

Setting Up Your Accounts and Office

Day trading is possible only because technology costs have come down dramatically over the years. That makes it feasible to set up shop in the comfort of your home. But remember: This is a home business, so you do need to set up for it.

Sure, some days you can sit and trade from your laptop in a coffee shop, but to end up doing that well, you first need to commit to the space and the equipment at home. If you skimp on your Internet connection, for example, you can't be upset if it's unable to handle the data on a big market day. If your PC goes down, you'd better have a way to get it back up fast if you have open positions. And if the responsibility seems overwhelming, maybe you should look for a *trading arcade* — an office space for traders — and move your operation there.

In this chapter, I list different brokers that handle day traders, go over the basics of your office setup, and give you some advice on finding a trading arcade.

Choosing a Brokerage

If you are going to trade, you need a brokerage account. Chapter 3 covers some of the basics of different types of securities and where they trade. That's the first place to start.

If you're going to trade stocks, you need a full-service broker that belongs to NASDAQ, the New York Stock Exchange, and other major exchanges.

If you'd rather trade the stock market through the Chicago Mercantile Exchange's E-Mini index futures, then you need a futures trading account with a broker holding a seat on the Chicago Mercantile Exchange.

Many day traders pursue two or three strategies, which may require holding different brokerage accounts. That's not unusual. If you are going to trade grain futures and tech stocks both, you might want one account with a futures brokerage that belongs to the Chicago Board of Trade and another account with a stock brokerage that offers fast execution.

Direct access to pricing and trading

All brokerage firms offer *price quotes*: a summary of the current bid and offer prices for selling or buying the security in question. But not all of these price quotes are the same. Some are offered in *real time* — meaning that you see the prices as soon as your modem can transmit the change to you. Others are delayed, sometimes by seconds, sometimes by minutes. If you are buying a bond with plans to hold it for ten years, then the difference in price between now and fifteen minutes ago probably isn't material. But if you are looking to day trade in the bond market using short-term changes in treasury futures, then a delay of even 30 seconds might be the difference between your strategy succeeding or failing.

Direct access brokers allow you to see the price quotes in real time so that you can act on them immediately, and they allow you to work through different electronic communications networks rather than going through the firm's own traders. Almost all day trading strategies need direct access in order to maximize profitability.

A traditional retail brokerage, by contrast, offers customers more research and advice and may even improve order execution by waiting until market conditions are more favorable. That's fine for investors, but not so good for day traders.

In addition to different levels of market access, brokerage firms offer different types of price quotes with different amounts of detail. Read on for descriptions and pictures to see what you need for your strategy.

Faster, detailed price quotes are valuable to traders, so brokerage firms usually charge more them. Don't skimp on price services at the expense of your trading profitability.

Level 1 quotes

Level I quotes give you the current bid and ask, or bid and offer, prices for a given security. The *bid*, of course, is the price at which the broker buys the security from you, and the *ask*, also called *offer* in some markets, is the price at which the broker offers to sell the security to you. A Level I quote also shows the size of the most recent buy and sell orders.

Most brokerage firms offer real-time Level I quotes for free, but these numbers do not have enough detail for day trading.

Level 11 quotes

Level II quotes not only tell you what the current bid and offer prices are, but they also tell you who the market makers are — the brokerage firm traders who are buying and selling the security — and what size orders they have at different prices (Figure 6-1). This information can help you gauge the volatility and direction of trading in the market, and that can help you make more profitable trades. Most brokerage firms that specialize in day trading offer Level II quotes in most markets.

SYMBOL	**AMAT**	Applied Materials (NGS)		
LAST SALE	20.15 q	NASDAQ Bid Tick (+)		
NATIONAL BBO	20.15 q	20.16 q	6900 × 3000	

MPID	Bid	Size	MPID	Ask	Size
NSDQ	20.15	3000	NSDQ	20.16	2000
ARCX	20.15	2600	ARCX	20.16	1900
BEST	20.15	1500	TDCM	20.16	1000
NITE	20.15	1400	OPCO	20.17	2100
CINN	20.15	1200	BARD	20.17	1000
BOFA	20.15	1000	CLYP	20.18	2000
AUTO	20.14	5000	SCHB	20.18	1500
LEHM	20.14	1000	NITE	20.18	1100
ABLE	20.14	1000	DAIN	20.18	100
SCHB	20.14	500	TEJS	20.18	100
GSCO	20.14	100	GSCO	20.18	100
RAJA	20.12	1200	MSCO	20.19	1500
TDCM	20.12	1000	JPMS	20.19	100
MONR	20.12	1000	BEST	20.20	1200
SWST	20.12	1000	NFSC	20.20	1000
NORT	20.12	400	FBRC	20.20	800
JPMS	20.12	100	FACT	20.20	100
PERT	20.11	800	UBSW	20.21	1100
PIPR	20.11	100	GSCO	20.21	1000
PRUS	20.10	500	FBCO	20.21	100
FBCO	20.09	1400	LEHM	20.21	100
COWN	20.09	800	RHCO	20.21	100
HDSN	20.09	400	WCHV	20.22	1200
UBSW	20.09	400	GLBT	20.22	1000

Figure 6-1: A NASDAQ Level II quote looks like this.

TotalView quotes

TotalView quotes show all orders in the market for a given security, both attributed to market makers and anonymous (Figure 6-2). This gives traders the most detailed information about what's happening in the market. It may be overkill for some trading strategies, but vital to the success of most. You'll have a better idea of how much information your trading strategies need after you test them using the advice in Chapter 11.

Type of platform

When you have an account with a brokerage firm, you have a way to get information about the markets and place your orders. The conduit is the Internet, but there has to be a way to get your orders to it. Some brokerage firms have their own software that you can use; others allow you to log in through a Web site.

Software-based platforms

With a software-based platform, you have to download and install the brokerage firm's proprietary system onto your computer. When you are ready to start your trading day, you connect to the Internet first, launch the software to see what's happening, and place your trades. Software systems generally offer more features and analytical tools, but you can only trade on a machine that has the software loaded on it.

Web-based platforms

With a Web-based trading platform, you go to the broker's Web site and log in to trade. This means you can trade from any computer that has Internet access, which is a boon if you travel or work from several different locations. In exchange, you may give up some of the analytic and backtesting tools offered through software-based platforms.

Note that Web-based platforms may be designed to work on specific Web browsers. Given the importance of having a stable connection and full functionality in a fast-moving market, if the firm recommends using Internet Explorer, accept that. Don't cling to a preferred alternative.

What about mobile platforms? Some brokerage firms allow you to get price quotes and place trades through a mobile phone. This may be useful to some people, but it's a bad idea for most day traders. Day trading is a business, and that means you need some discipline about setting regular hours and working from a regular workspace. You will probably need more information to work a trade than will fit on your phone's screen. Finally, you need to take a break from the market in order to maintain balance in your life. If you're making trades at your cousin's wedding, you're probably a little out of balance.

SYMBOL	**AMAT**	Applied Materials (NGS)
LAST SALE	20.15 q	NASDAQ Bid Tick (+)
NATIONAL BBO	20.15 q	20.16 q 6900 × 3000

Bid Price	Total Depth	Ask Price	Total Depth
20.15	10700	20.16	4900
20.14	56100	20.17	9100
20.13	26300	20.18	13400
20.12	9900	20.19	11200
20.11	1700	20.20	8700

MPID	Bid	Size	MPID	Ask	Size
NSDQ	20.15	3000	NSDQ	20.16	2000
ARCX	20.15	2600	ARCX	20.16	1900
BEST	20.15	1500	TDCM	20.16	1000
NITE	20.15	1400	NSDQ	20.17	6000
CINN	20.15	1200	OPCO	20.17	2100
BOFA	20.15	1000	BARD	20.17	1000
NSDQ	20.14	28500	NSDQ	20.18	5000
BEST	20.14	12500	OPCO	20.18	2500
NITE	20.14	7500	CLYP	20.18	2000
AUTO	20.14	5000	SCHB	20.18	1500
LEHM	20.14	1000	NITE	20.18	1100
ABLE	20.14	1000	TDCM	20.18	1000
SCHB	20.14	500	DAIN	20.18	100
GSCO	20.14	100	TEJS	20.18	100
NSDQ	20.13	10000	GSCO	20.18	100
GSCO	20.13	8800	NSDQ	20.19	5500
SCHB	20.13	7500	NITE	20.19	3000
NSDQ	20.12	2200	MSCO	20.19	1500
BEST	20.12	2000	OPCO	20.19	1000
RAJA	20.12	1200	JPMS	20.19	100
LEHM	20.12	1000	SCHB	20.19	100
TDCM	20.12	1000	BAR	20.19	4000
MONR	20.12	1000	BEST	20.20	1200
SWST	20.12	1000	NFSC	20.20	1000
NORT	20.12	400	NSDQ	20.20	1000
JPMS	20.12	100	FBRC	20.20	800
PERT	20.11	800	SCHB	20.20	500
GSCO	20.11	500	NITE	20.20	100
LEHM	20.11	100	FACT	20.20	100
NSDQ	20.11	100	UBSW	20.21	1100
NORT	20.11	100	GSCO	20.21	1000
PIPR	20.11	100	NITE	20.21	1000
NSDQ	20.10	13500	NSDQ	20.21	500
SCHB	20.10	3500	TDCM	20.21	100
TDCM	20.10	2000	FBCO	20.21	100
PRUS	20.10	500	LEHM	20.21	100
GSCO	20.09	100	RHCO	20.21	100
NSDQ	20.09	2500	LEHM	20.22	5000
RAJA	20.09	2200	WCHV	20.22	1200
FBCO	20.09	1400	GLBT	20.22	1000
MONR	20.09	1000	NSDQ	20.22	500
NITE	20.09	1000	FBRC	20.22	500
COWN	20.09	800	DAIN	20.22	100
HDSN	20.09	400	NITE	20.22	100
UBSW	20.09	400	BEST	20.22	100

Figure 6-2:
A NASDAQ
TotalView
quote is
the most
detailed
available.

How to open an account

When you open a brokerage account, you have a lot of paperwork to fill out in order to comply with government and exchange regulations. I explain all the laws behind these in Chapter 5. The firm needs to ensure that you are suitable for day trading; that you understand the risks of options, futures, and margin strategies; and that your trading money did not come from ill-gotten gains.

After you fill out and sign the paperwork, you need to transfer funds. Most brokers require a minimum investment of $25,000 to open a day trading account (some set this lower and some higher). Write a check or set up a wire or Internet transfer from an existing bank, brokerage, or mutual fund account.

Brokers Offering Day Trading Services

Following is a list of brokerage firms with services for day traders. It's arranged by specialty (stocks and general trading, options and futures, foreign exchange) and then alphabetically within each category. It's not exhaustive. Keep in mind that every year, new firms are formed, and existing firms are acquired or merged away, so be sure to do your own research. Also, this list does not imply an endorsement of anyone's services.

Barron's (www.barrons.com), the weekly financial newspaper, has a regular column discussing electronic trading firm issues and concerns, many of which are of interest to day traders. Each winter, *Barron's* conducts a survey of online brokerage firms with updates on the latest features and rankings based on such criteria as technology, usability, additional features, customer service, and trading costs. Check it out when you're ready to research.

Brokers for stocks and a bit of the rest

Day traders almost always work through online brokerage accounts. Many firms offering these accounts handle trading in almost all securities. The firms usually belong to all the exchanges, so you can trade almost anything anywhere in the world through them. They often offer a range of news and charting services to help you plan your trading. In some cases, their offerings may be overkill — you not only might not need all their services, you might find them distracting. Some may not handle your security of choice well.

Brokerage firms don't make money just on the commission charged per trade. Other sources of revenue include monthly service charges, fees for real-time quotes, interest on margin loans to customers, and the *spread*, which is the difference between what you pay for a security and what the firm paid to get it. Don't let the commission be the critical factor in deciding among brokerage firms. Think about the services you will need and the relative cost to you of different account offerings.

Charles Schwab Active Trader

www.schwabat.com

Charles Schwab was one of the first discount retail brokerage firms, and it now offers just about every financial service one could want: financial planning, banking, and mutual funds. The Schwab Active Trader account includes trading demonstrations and education services that are particularly useful for active stock traders. It works directly through an Internet browser.

Many day traders, especially those working in other securities besides stocks prefer Schwab's CyberTrader service (covered later in this section).

ChoiceTrade

www.choicetrade.com

ChoiceTrade offers software-based equity stock and option trading services to individuals and small trading firms. Customers can opt for a basic platform or pay a monthly fee for additional charting, analytic, and money management services.

CyberTrader

www.cybertrader.com

CyberTrader is owned by Charles Schwab and offers trading in stocks, options, and futures during market hours and after. Its software includes lots of charting, backtesting, and simulation features that can help you plan your trades and evaluate their effectiveness.

E*TRADE

www.etrade.com

E*TRADE offers trading in stocks, options, and futures as well as services for active traders through its Web-based trading platform. It also offers a software-based platform, Power E*TRADE Pro, with direct access trading and customization abilities.

Fidelity Active Trader Pro

http://personal.fidelity.com/accounts/activetrader/

Fidelity started life as a mutual fund company and continues to dominate that business. It's also branched out into offering a wide range of financial services, including online trading. Its Fidelity Active Trader Pro is a software-based system with lots of bells and whistles, including systems for analyzing and testing options strategies.

Fimat PreferredTrade

www.fimatpreferred.com

Fimat PreferredTrade is a software-based trading system that can handle stock trading as well as a range of options and futures strategies, during and after market hours. Users can perform lots of analytic tricks using real-time data.

Interactive Brokers

www.interactivebrokers.com

Interactive Brokers offers software-based direct access trading, including trading in international markets. It has options, futures, and foreign exchange trading services as well as trading in stocks. Traders can use a range of order types and order-management features to work complicated strategies.

Just2Trade

www.just2trade.com

Just2Trade targets equity day traders with low commissions. The company's goal is to provide fast execution through its Web-based platform, which is useful to day traders who are looking to move quickly. Its services include real-time Level I and Level II quotes at no extra fee.

Mastertrader.com

www.mastertrader.com

Mastertrader.com gives day traders and small firms Web-based direct access trading services, especially in equities. Customers can choose different levels of services (at different fees, of course) to get what they need. It has some education services, including a partnership with Pristine.com, a day trading training company.

ScottradeELITE

www.scottradeelite.com

Scottrade is an online stock broker that offers additional services for those customers with more than $25,000 in their accounts. Under the name ScottradeELITE, it gives these customers Web-based access to NASDAQ Level II and detailed NASDAQ TotalView quotes as long as they do 15 trades a month.

TD AMERITRADE

www.tdameritrade.com

TD AMERITRADE is a Web-based online broker that offers full investing services. Day traders get access to Level I quotes for free, and they can subscribe to Level II quotes. Customers can also test and analyze trading strategies and set up signals and screens to identify changing market trends.

Terra Nova Financial

www.tnfg.com

Terra Nova provides brokerage services to individual and institutional traders. It enjoys a particular advantage in trading international securities and has trading in equities, options, futures, and foreign exchange. Terra Nova has a range of services with different fee levels so that traders can choose what they need. Customers can receive commission rebates for the cost of enrolling in trading courses offered by MarketWise, www.marketwise.com.

TradeKing

www.tradeking.com

TradeKing has a range of basic trading services in stocks, bonds, and options. The company's most unique feature is the community offerings on its site. Customers can create blogs, track each other's trades (if they want), share commentary, and send messages to each other in hopes that they all make better, smarter trades.

TradeStation

www.tradestation.com

TradeStation offers a huge range of services for people who are day trading stocks, options, futures, and foreign exchange. It's a software-based system that includes a rich set of features, especially for developing and testing trading strategies. Traders who have strong systems will like the automatic trading features that signal — and can even act — when appropriate trading opportunities occur.

Zecco

www.zecco.com

Zecco is a relatively new brokerage firm offering trading in stocks and options. Your first 10 trades per day (up to 40 trades a month) are free; after that, you pay $3.50 per trade. Zecco has few services for traders other than message boards where customers can discuss news and share trading tips.

Brokers for options and futures

To effectively day trade options and futures, you need an account with a broker that has direct access to the exchanges' electronic communications networks. Several of the full-service firms listed above offer that service, as do the brokers listed here, which specialize in these markets.

Infinity Brokerage

www.infinitybrokerage.com

Infinity Brokerage offers software-based trading in the options, futures, and foreign exchange markets. Customers can choose from several platforms, depending on trading needs. The firm particularly supports traders working in the stock index futures offered by the Chicago Mercantile Exchange.

Man Futures

www.manfutures.com

Man Financial is a multinational company that works with hedge funds and major institutional investors, but it makes many of its services available to larger day traders. It has a lot of expertise in agricultural commodities as well as financial futures. Traders can choose from several trading platforms, with free simulated trading for those who want to check out futures trading first.

MB Trading

www.mbtrading.com

MB Trading handles stocks as well as derivatives, but it has lots of services for traders of the latter. It doesn't have a lot of frills, as the company seems to assume its customers either don't want them or will build them in house. And, in fact, MB Trading has a lot of support for developers who want to build software around its platform.

OptionsHouse

`www.optionshouse.com`

OptionsHouse was founded by a major options trading firm and has its offices on the original Chicago Board of Trade trading floor. Between that pedigree and the company's name, it's no surprise that it offers direct access Web-based trading in options and their underlying stocks. Its software tools are designed to help you identify profitable opportunities in the options market.

optionsXpress

`www.optionsxpress.com`

The company optionsXpress is designed for people trading options and the stocks underlying them. One of its nifty features is an automatic execution service for subscribers of participating research services (you can learn more about research services in Chapter 7).

thinkorswim

`www.thinkorswim.com`

Providing its customers with a software-based trading platform used mostly to trade options strategies, thinkorswim also offers a full range of products, including mutual funds. In addition to an auto-execute feature for subscribers of select newsletters, it has a paper-trading feature that lets you practice your trades before you commit real dollars.

Brokers for foreign exchange

The foreign exchange, or forex, market is the largest trading market in the world. It has lots of opportunities for day traders to make (or lose) money. Most forex trades take place between banks, corporations, and hedge funds directly, without the use of a broker. If you want to trade this directly, you need to use a trading firm that is tied in to these networks. Many of the brokers listed above offer forex, and here are a few that do little else.

CMC Markets

`www.cmcmarkets.com`

CMC Markets was the first firm to allow individual investors to trade in foreign exchange. The company has a software-based platform that offers trading in 65 different currency pairs. It also has research and education services for its customers.

Gain Capital Group's FOREX.com

    www.forex.com

Gain Capital Group deals mostly with institutional investors and money managers, but it makes its platform available to individual day traders through
its FOREX.com site. There, you can download software that lets you analyze
markets and place trades. The company offers a lot of educational programs
for those interested in foreign exchange.

GTForex

    www.gtforex.com

GTForex lets day traders work with 21 different currency pairs through the
forex, futures, and *contracts for difference* (CFD, where the parties exchange
only the value of the price change on the currency), as well as spot gold and
spot silver. Trades take place through the company's software-based trading
platform, and prospective customers can try it through a demo version.

InterbankFX

    www.interbankfx.com

Want to try your hand at trading forex? In addition to demo accounts,
InterbankFX allows customers to start trading with as little as $250, making it
an option for day traders who want to trade currency along with other types
of securities. It also offers charting and automatic trading services to help
customers design and adhere to their strategies.

MG Financial Group

    www.mgforex.com

MG Financial gives forex day traders a software platform that allows them to
trade several popular currency pairs. Other features include research, charting, and trading via mobile phone. Interested folks can open a demo account
to try their hands at forex trading before making a commitment.

Equipping Your Trading Laboratory

Twenty years ago, you would have had to pay millions of dollars for the
equipment and telecommunications networks that you can now have in your
own home for just a few thousand bucks or so.

You may be thinking, I can do it for free! I have a PC in a corner of the family room, I have Internet access, what else do I need? Ah, but you need plenty. Remember, successful day traders approach trading as a professional activity. That means starting off with an adequate work space and dedicated equipment. If you can't give up an entire room in your house, find a corner or hallway where you can put a desk and a computer just for day trading. It will clear your mind so that you can focus on the work at hand.

Where to sit, where to work

You need a table and a chair. Don't borrow a chair from the dining room, but instead get a good desk chair that will swivel around and adjust to you as you work. You'll need a shelf and a cabinet of some sort to hold your files and documents, too.

Want to get more comfort for the dollar in a desk chair? Consider shopping for used chairs at office equipment dealers. They may come with a few scuffs, but they will probably have more ergonomic settings than chairs at office supply superstores.

There's no rule on the layout of your equipment, but the more you can see and do without getting up from your chair, the better off you'll be. If you find yourself getting sore at the end of the day, investigate ergonomic products such as special keyboards, contoured mice, wrist pads, and foot rests, all of which are readily available at office supply stores.

Counting on your computer

You can't day trade without one computer, and you might want two or three: one to trade from, one for everything else (such as spreadsheets, email, instant messaging), plus a spare in case the trading computer goes down. (See the section "The department of redundancy department" later in this chapter.)

Almost every personal computer on the market today has the power to handle day trading activities, so you don't need to sweat over the details. In general, faster processing speeds are better than slower ones, and more memory and storage are preferable to less.

What about the manufacturer? Well, you probably don't want an Apple Macintosh for day trading, because it's possible that not all the software packages you'll need will be Mac-compatible. If you are one of those die-hard Mac heads, though, be sure to ask brokers and software vendors about compatibility. Other than that, it doesn't matter much.

See it on the big screen

Do yourself a favor and spend money on a big flat-screen monitor, at least 19 inches on the diagonal, so that you can see what's happening in the markets. If you need to look at more than one window at once, say to see charts and Level II quotes at the same time, consider using two or more monitors hooked to the same PC. That way, you'll have a clear view of necessary data. (Most traders work with at least two monitors, because the information they need is too valuable.)

Connecting to the Internet

If you are day trading, you should hook up to the Internet with as much bandwidth as possible — at least a 1.5/256 DSL line. This means that you can download data at 1500 kilobits per second while uploading at 256 kilobits per second. Your Internet service provider might charge more for faster performance, and most day traders will find the price to be worth it. If prices are changing quickly, a delay of half a second can be costly.

A great source of information about the performance of different broadband Internet providers is Broadband Reports, www.broadbandreports.com.

Invest in a firewall and virus protection for your trading PC, but be careful how you do it. Some software will protect your system at the expense of a slow data feed, which will hurt your trading execution. If you decide to *go naked* — operate without a firewall or virus scanner in order to maintain optimal speed — be sure to have a second computer at the ready. When you set your virus scanner, be sure that any automatic downloads or background scans take place after market hours, so that they can't slow you down.

Strangely enough, a phone is optional these days. You will rarely if ever need to place a trading-related call.

The department of redundancy department

When you're day trading, you are intentionally looking at volatile markets and fast-moving securities, because that's where you'll have the most opportunity to make money in a short time. You may very well be leveraged, either through the use of borrowed money or by trading securities with built-in leverage, such as futures. (I have a lot more to say about leverage in Chapter 14). If you're in a position that moves against you and you can't get out, you're sunk.

It's bad enough if you can't get out because the markets are melting down because of some kind of global catastrophe. But suppose you can't get out because the batteries in your wireless mouse have died and you can't find new ones? What if you spill pop and short out your keyboard — or your PC? What if the developer building a McMansion next door accidentally knocks out your phone line and your DSL service? At a minimum, have a cellular phone charged and ready to go so that you can execute trades by phone. All these little workaday calamities have happened to me — and trust me, they are downright annoying if you aren't trading. If you are, they can be ruinous. If you are serious about making money as a day trader, build in redundant systems as much as possible:

- If it's available in your area, subscribe to two Internet service providers, one cable and one DSL. When one goes out, you can switch.

- Have two computers that are duplicates of each other, so that you can swap them out if one goes down.

- Keep extra supplies on hand: extra batteries, extra keyboard, and extra mouse. You want to be able to react quickly when things go wrong. These are all cheap to keep in inventory, too, because the computer makers give keyboards and mice away with every new PC.

- Consider investing in an uninterruptible power supply (UPS) backup for your PC, so that if the power goes down, your computer will stay up. You don't need a backup generator, though — unless you think that you'd still want to trade after your town was devastated by an earthquake or a hurricane. (Of course, it's those crises that create opportunities!)

- Finally, back up your computer regularly. You can do it online through Mozy (www.mozy.com) or through a backup drive connected to your PC. Most backup systems can be set up to work automatically, but don't do it during trading hours or it will slow you down.

Taking a Trip to a Trading Arcade

Don't want to set up your own office? Not ready to commit to two Internet lines, three PCs, and four monitors? Worried you'll be bored and lonely working alone at home? Consider trying a *trading arcade*. These are offices where day traders rent desk space to trade. Some provide additional services along with the real estate, such as training, coaching, and even loans of trading capital. Some charge a flat weekly or monthly fee, some offer services on an a la carte basis, and others take a share of your trading profits.

Although trading arcades are less popular than they were a decade ago, they still exist in many major cities. To find them, you can do an Internet search on *trading arcade* or *trading room* and your town's name. You are more likely to find one if you live near a city with major exchanges that are phasing out floor trading — namely, New York and Chicago.

Before choosing an arcade, find out about its fees and services. Talk to other traders to see what they like and dislike about the operation. And keep in mind that the firm may want to check *you* out.

Chapter 7

Research and Trading Services

In This Chapter

▶ Figuring out where to get a trading education

▶ Supplementing your trading with research

▶ Checking out vendors before you spend your money

*D*ay trading is big business with big profits, but those profits don't always accrue to the day trader. Instead, many a day trader has spent money on training services, software, newsletters, and coaching, only to find that in the real world, the trader can't make enough money to make a living, let alone cover all these costs.

Why does that happen? It could very well be because the trader isn't cut out for day trading in the first place. Day trading isn't for everyone. In other cases, though, the trader failed to do good research before plunking down the cold cash for training in a system that just wasn't very good.

You've already plunked down $24.99 for *Day Trading For Dummies*. Consider that an investment! In this chapter, I cover some of the different services that day traders might want to buy and give you advice on how to determine which ones are worthwhile and which are not.

The Trade of Trading

As much as I wish that *Day Trading For Dummies* told you everything you'd need to know about trading, it's only a starting point. And let's hope that Wiley's marketing department doesn't see that, because otherwise they'll be mad at me. The fact is that there are so many different assets you can trade and ways to trade them, no one resource can give you all you need. A stock trader following a news-based momentum strategy needs different services than a forex trader looking at interest rate discrepancies. That's why I don't teach you, but rather point you to resources that can help you get started and show you how to get the most value from the money you spend.

Day trading is a career. Every career takes time to master, and practitioners have to work to keep their skills up as the field changes. You'll find you'll need some training to get started, and more training to be successful, whether you are trading futures, building bridges, or doing heart surgery.

Freebies from the exchanges

Before you spend more money, check out what several different exchanges and self-regulatory organizations offer for free to help you get started in trading. They have "Webinars," online courses, and plenty of reading material. After all, the financial industry wants people to trade — that's how they make money — but they want them to be successful, because that keeps the market functioning. (Exchanges are businesses, like any other.) Going through such free material first can give you a great sense of how suitable you are for a given strategy and help you make better decisions about the other training you will need.

In this section I list a few resources that are particularly good for new day traders.

Chicago Board Options Exchange Learning Center

> www.cboe.com/LearnCenter/default.aspx

The Options Institute of the Chicago Board Options Exchange offers a series of online tutorials, classes, and seminars covering exchange-traded options in great depth. It also has a two-day seminar for experienced traders who want to come to Chicago. The site includes online toolboxes and calculators as well as a chance for traders to ask questions of options trading experts.

Chicago Board of Trade Classes/Training

> www.cbot.com/cbot/pub/page/0,3181,1130,00.html

The Chicago Board of Trade has online tutorials on trading futures, agricultural commodities, and the Dow Jones Industrial Average. It also offers online seminars on trading strategies and psychology, papers discussing different trading methods, and downloadable manuals (in English, Spanish, and Chinese) that teach different aspects of specific commodities, whether poultry feed or treasury interest rate futures.

Chicago Mercantile Exchange Education Center

> www.cme.com/edu/

Whether you're an individual who wants to learn about futures or an experienced floor trader who needs to make the transition to electronic trading, the Chicago Mercantile Exchange has information for you. It has online training courses in trading in general and trading futures in particular, live online events in specific trading techniques, and papers that describe and analyze different trading strategies. The site even has links to trading simulators offered by different futures commission merchants (brokerage firms that specialize in futures), so you can apply what you learn without risking real money.

The exchanges have been merging and consolidating, so by the time you get this book, some of these may be combined or operating under different names — and that means the links won't work. No matter what happens, they'll still be offering educational services so that the people participating in their markets can be more effective. You can find up-to-date links by doing simple Web searches using such keywords as *futures exchange* or *options exchange*.

Institute for Financial Markets

www.theifm.org

The Institute for Financial Markets is a nonprofit organization that provides basic training programs for people working on the options and futures exchanges. Many of its courses are inappropriate for day traders, who aren't going to be licensed and who do not have mandatory continuing education requirements to maintain those licenses. But some of them are appropriate, and a few are low-cost or even free. Recent offerings include the basics of derivatives and trading strategies.

NASDAQ

www.nasdaq.com/services/onlineInvesting.stm

Okay, let's be honest here: The stock markets want to promote investing more than trading, because they want companies to issue stock on their exchanges. The kind of high volatility that day traders love puts off some starchy corporate officers. Hence, much of the information on NASDAQ's site is about how to select stocks for the long term. Still, there's some information that might be useful to a prospective day trader.

National Futures Association Investor Learning Center

www.nfa.futures.org/investor/investorLearningCenter.asp

The National Futures Association is the self-regulatory organization for the agricultural and financial futures exchanges. This site includes a lot of good information about trading futures as well as a tutorial on trading foreign exchange.

New York Stock Exchange

www.nyse.com/audience/individualinvestors.html

The New York Stock Exchange, like NASDAQ, wants to court investors rather than traders. Still, the exchange's site has information on trading stocks, bonds, and exchange-traded funds that can make you smarter on those topics without spending a dime.

Hitting the road for conferences

Although day trading is a deskbound pursuit, you might want to get out to learn more about trading and research different companies with products for day traders. Many of the exchanges and larger day trading brokerage firms have their own seminars and conferences, but a few are open to the public.

Brokerage firms offering many seminars and training programs may have higher commissions than firms offering less service, but it may be worth it, especially as you get started. You can learn more about some brokerage firms that work with day traders in Chapter 6.

The Money Show

www.moneyshow.com

The Money Show is a series of investment conferences held in different major cities around the country. Registration is free, which means that once you show up, people will be trying to sell you stuff. This could be distracting to an established trader but helpful for a new trader looking to find out more about all the different software and services out there. The conferences also have high-profile speakers, so you can learn from Wall Street celebrities. The Money Show Web site includes articles, podcasts, and free online courses to help you learn more about trading.

Trading Forum

www.traderslibrary.com/tlforum/registration.asp

The Trading Forum is sponsored by Traders' Library, which sells research materials and investing books. The conference isn't cheap, but it covers specific trading strategies and information. It offers a good introduction to trading, especially if the conference happens to be close to where you live.

Taking training classes

Although it's not necessary, many day traders learn the game by enrolling in a training program, ranging from a graduate-level certificate in options offered jointly by Northwestern University and the Chicago Board Options Exchange to DVDs hawked on late-night infomercials. No program can guarantee success, nor is any one program right for every trader. I list a few bigger and better-known programs here, but check them out to make sure they are right for you — just as you should check out programs that aren't listed here.

The larger brokerage and research firms offer their own training courses, often at little or no cost. Consider those as a first option, but keep in mind that their introductory sessions might be sales pitches for more products and services.

Marketwise

www.marketwise.com

Marketwise has a series of online courses in stocks, options, and futures trading. Clients log on at a specific time, and the instructor uses real market data to show them what they need to know. It also has live seminars and one-on-one mentorship programs.

Pristine

www.pristine.com

Pristine has a range of books and DVDs, online and in person classes, and coaching services in English and Spanish covering trading skills that work in most markets. Its courses operate at different levels, with some requiring extensive trading experience using specific software packages.

Schneider Tradercourse

www.tradercourse.com

Schneider Tradercourse offers training in futures and foreign exchange to both professional and individual investors from its offices in London. Some of its programs are weekend seminars, and the company also offers telephone coaching to help traders solve problems.

Secrets of Traders

www.secretsoftraders.com

One thing I like about this company's Web site is that you are expected to read a disclaimer about the risks of trading before you get to the good stuff. Many of the company's programs are designed for floor traders at the exchanges who need to learn to trade futures electronically in order to stay competitive. The course includes books and DVDs.

TradingSchool.com

www.tradingschool.com

TradingSchool.com, based in Los Angeles, has a series of online and in-person classes covering trading psychology as well as trading in stocks, options, financial futures, and currencies. The firm works with day traders as well as money managers and other long-term investors.

The University of Trading

www.universityoftrading.com

The University of Trading offers courses in options, equities, foreign exchange, and financial and agricultural commodities online and at its offices in Chicago. Students have the opportunity to trade alongside experienced instructors as well as hear lectures on different aspects of the markets. The company trains professional traders, some of whom trade for themselves and some of whom take jobs with others.

There are plenty of great and legitimate training firms out there — as well as a lot of scammers. Run from anyone who guarantees your success. I include some information about due diligence at the end of this chapter.

Learning to play at a trading arcade

Many larger cities have day trading arcades, which are offices where traders can rent desk space and get all the quotes and analytics they need to trade. Traders pay monthly rent and may also share some of their profits with the arcade, especially if it provides any training and coaching services.

Trading arcades were the only way to day trade before the widespread availability of high-speed Internet access. They are seeing resurgence as trading moves off the floor of exchanges and into electronic communications networks. Most new trading arcades are clustered near the exchanges and cater to floor traders who are learning how to trade electronically. However, some will work with people who are completely new to trading.

You can find trading arcades through Internet searches, by contacting the options and futures exchanges to see if they know of any that are members (I have in my possession a 2006 directory of trading arcades in Chicago, put out by the Chicago Mercantile Exchange), or by checking online directories such as www.trade2win.com/traderpedia/Trading_Arcade_Index.

Getting the Research You Need

Day traders need a trading system, and they often rely on subscription research services. That's fine, as long as those systems are adding value over and above their cost. Unfortunately, advising day traders is big business, and there may be more money in that than in day trading. Before you call the 800 number given in the infomercial, here's some advice to help you evaluate the service.

There are three main types of outside services:

- ✔ Price data are detailed, real-time price quotes from different markets.
- ✔ Chart services help traders identify profitable trends.
- ✔ Strategic research helps people develop a system for trading or follow a system designed by someone else.

You may need all three, or none, depending on your knowledge of the financial markets and your trading style.

Many day traders find themselves subscribing to price quote and analytical services. The following section is a listing of a handful of popular ones. It's not a definitive list, and this is not an endorsement. Rather, it's a guide to get you thinking about what you might need and where you might go to get it.

If you know you'll need outside pricing and data services, consider that when you are selecting a brokerage firm. Different firms have different software platforms, and some can handle outside data feeds better than others.

(Price) quote me on that

In Chapter 6, I list some of the many brokerage firms that offer day trading services. They all have services that tell you what the prices are for any security at any time, but this doesn't mean that they have all of the prices that you need for your strategy. For example, if you are day trading common stocks, you may need a system that can signal certain price patterns in any of the thousands of stocks trading at any given day. If you are trading options based on the value of underlying stock, you may need that data as well. If you are day trading international securities, you may need real-time data, and your broker might only offer data with a ten-minute delay in some markets.

Besides needing all the prices and related volume and market-maker data, some strategies involve fast trading. *Scalping*, for example, involves making a large number of quick transactions in search of small price movements. Every second counts, and not all brokers can deliver prices fast enough to make scalping profitable. One solution is to get prices from a separate source offering faster delivery. Other trading strategies don't require real-time prices on huge numbers of securities, but they may involve a detailed analysis of end-of-day prices. To do that, you may need more information than your broker can give you.

The quote service can provide the data in real time only if you have enough bandwidth to receive it. Make sure you have the fastest Internet service and modem available in your area, and consider having a second way to connect to the Internet if your primary service goes down.

CQG

www.cqg.com

CQG pulls data from more than 90 different exchanges, making it popular with people who are trading international securities. Traders can buy historical data for backtesting (see Chapter 11 for more), and they can add charting and order routing capabilities to their CQG package. Data can be linked to Microsoft Excel spreadsheets for people who want to do even more number crunching on their own.

DTN

www.dtn.com

Trading fuel or agricultural products? Then you might need more research than most brokers can give you. DTN provides pricing and research for commodities traders, including meteorological research and hurricane-related energy supply forecasts. Day traders active in stocks or financial futures are more likely to use the company's IQ data feeds, which allow users to track 1,300 prices at once, and ProphetX, software that combines price data with analytics that can track small market movements and can handle displays on several different monitors at once.

eSignal

www.esignal.com

eSignal offers detailed prices, news, and trading alerts in most financial markets. Its charting features are more advanced than those offered by most brokerage firms. Especially useful for traders who are looking at several different stocks, eSignal can help identify trading opportunities using a preferred strategy and scan the market for other stocks that meet specified investment criteria. The company also offers backtesting and real-time strategy testing, end-of-day analysis for traders who don't need real-time data, as well as add-on signals that support different proprietary trading strategies.

InstaQuote

www.dafsoft.com

InstaQuote's data is designed for equity options traders. It gives traders price quotes on options and equities alike so that they can identify price discrepancies and monitor valuation. It then connects to the exchange's electronic communications networks, allowing for direct access trading. InstaQuote's platform can work with several different brokerage firms.

Charting your strategy

Almost all day trading strategies rely on technical analysis, which is the process of identifying buy and sell opportunities based on the supply and demand for a security. Technical analysts look at charts of price and volume changes to look for changes in the trend. (It's discussed in more detail in Chapter 12.) Some technical analysis strategies are complicated and require sophisticated charting. That's why many day traders use software that can turn price data into the information they need to make decisions.

Many users of these services get tripped up by the symbols and data displays. Take the time to learn as much as you can about how they work before you're trading in real time with real money; most of these providers offer seminars or online tutorials that will help. Yeah, many of the features are obvious, but you want to avoid costly mistakes.

MarketDelta

www.marketdelta.com

MarketDelta's software provides detailed charting services that match different strategies over several time periods, in colors that make the data stand out. The company mostly deals with professionals, but it has some products suitable for some day traders.

Metastock

www.equis.com

Metastock has several different charting and analytical packages, including one for foreign exchange trading, another for people who day trade in stocks, and a third for stock investors who are holding for longer than a single day. Traders following specific strategies recommended by different market analysts can purchase add-ons that give them the tools needed to trade effectively.

NinjaTrader

www.ninjatrader.com

NinjaTrader is a trading platform for active traders. It can be used instead of a brokerage firm's trading software, or it can be used on its own. The service is best known for its charting capabilities in the foreign exchange and futures markets, but it can also handle market scanning, automated trade execution, and backtesting, and simulation trading.

OmniTrader

www.omnitrader.com

OmniTrader is designed to automate technical analysis (read all about that in Chapter 12), especially for stock traders. The system also includes money management tools (money management is discussed in Chapter 9) as well as simulated trading and backtesting to help you find new strategies.

RealTick

www.realtick.com

RealTick combines data with charting services and market signals for stocks, options, futures, and foreign exchange, making it useful for traders who are working in several markets. The service includes direct access trading through several different brokerage firms.

Trade-Ideas

http://trade-ideas.com

Trade-Ideas is designed for stock traders. The software scans the incoming price data feed to find trading opportunities based on prespecified indicators, and it can also show how much the market is deviating from a trader's style. For traders watching hundreds or thousands of stocks, this can be a useful addendum to a brokerage firm's offerings.

Newsletters, gurus, and strategic advice

Trading relies on information so that everyone in the market can evaluate what the right price for a security should be. Most of this information can be found from an analysis of the news and the price data, both of which are readily available from brokerage firms and quote services. But many traders follow explicit philosophies or rely on the insight of certain analysts. Here's a list of some of the bigger ones that you will come across, in case you want to find out more. Many of the specific theories will be discussed in more detail in Chapter 12.

Many of these market gurus have good ideas, but don't follow any of them blindly. Their techniques don't work in all markets at all times. Besides, anyone with a truly foolproof plan isn't going to give it away. These newsletters are just part of the ongoing conversation in the markets that help traders make decisions.

Elliott Wave

www.elliottwave.com

The *Elliott Wave* is a theory that markets move in grand cycles over a century or more. Within that, there are subcycles lasting years, months, weeks, days, minutes, and seconds. Given all the layers and analysis required, those who follow the theory usually subscribe to research services to help them. This site is maintained by Robert Prechter, who is one of the leading scholars of the theory.

The Marlin Newsletter

www.marlinletter.com

This newsletter is published by two long-time traders at the Chicago Mercantile Exchange and the Chicago Board of Trade. They give their analysis of the financial futures markets, especially those on the Dow Jones Industrial Average and the treasury markets. The company also offers training and a chat room where instructors and analysts discuss real-time trading opportunities.

School of Gann

www.schoolofgann.com

The Gann method of technical analysis looks at the slopes of the charts to predict changes. It's a complicated system, so traders who follow it usually rely on newsletters and research services to help them. School of Gann is one that specializes in this system.

Trending 123

www.trending123.com

Trending 123 publishes newsletters on technical analysis in the U.S., Canadian, and English stock markets and in foreign exchange. It also offers software and email alerts that point out opportunities in the markets based on their analytical system. The company regularly covers psychological aspects of trading to support its customers.

The power of the printed word

Several books cover specific aspects of trading psychology, trading strategy, and research systems in much more detail than I can in the space that the good folks at Wiley have given me. If you turn to the appendix, you'll see a list of other resources that can help you in your research.

Day trading was a hot topic in the late 1990s, and you may find that a lot of the books and articles on the subject date from that era. Some are lurking in your public library; others are still available for sale or can be found on the Internet. Markets change. Don't rely on a system popularized a decade ago unless you've tested it and ensured that it still works.

Doing Your Due Diligence

Trading software, training, and research can get expensive, and some of it is an outright scam. Most of it is legitimate, but that doesn't mean it's right for you. Before you spend your money, do your research. Start with the free programs offered by the exchanges (listed in the first section of this chapter) so that you have enough knowledge to understand what a trading services purveyor is trying to do. Then, do some research and ask some questions. To find out where to go and what to ask, read on.

Where to start your research

You have a ton of tools available to you to do your due diligence. A good first place is the Internet. Go to your favorite search engine and enter the name of the program you're looking at plus the word *scam* or *rip-off* and then see what turns up. If nothing of much interest turns up, proceed to the regulatory agencies listed here.

It's possible that you'll learn very little about any given research firm from an Internet search or checks with the different regulatory organizations. That doesn't mean the firm in question isn't for real, just that it hasn't caused any concerns so far.

Commodity Futures Trading Commission

www.cftc.gov/cftc/cftccustomer.htm

The Commodity Futures Trading Commission regulates futures markets, which are popular with day traders. At this part of the site, you can check out investor advisories, known scams, and recent enforcement efforts to see whether the vendor you're thinking of working with is legitimate or too good to be true.

National Futures Association BASIC

    www.nfa.futures.org/BasicNet/

Futures are popular with day traders, and they are regulated by the National Futures Association. Its Background Affiliation Status Information Center (BASIC) gives you information on people and firms registered with the National Futures Association.

NASD BrokerCheck

    www.nasd.com/InvestorInformation/InvestorProtection/

The National Association of Securities Dealers (NASD) provides this handy service that lets you check on the current enforcement status of different brokerage firms and their employees, especially in the stock, bond, and options markets. (Click the "Check the Background of Your Investment Professional" link.) Some of these firms and people may be offering research services or newsletters, so check to see whether they've had problems.

Securities and Exchange Commission

    www.sec.gov/investor.shtml

The Securities and Exchange Commission has a ton of great information about every aspect of stock and bond investing, with a special emphasis on problems and scams to avoid. Don't let it scare you away from the market; use it to evaluate any services that you're thinking of paying for.

Questions to ask

Once you do your basic background checks, it's time to ask some questions about the service providers you're considering. This section contains a list of questions to get you started.

Do not trust any promises of performance. Day trading is a difficult business. Many people wash out because it doesn't suit their personality. Others fail because they don't have enough startup capital, they don't take the time to figure out how to do it, or they simply have a run of bad luck. No one can promise that you will succeed.

   ✔ Can I get a free trial to check the service out?

   ✔ What training and support do you offer?

   ✔ How long will it take me to learn the system? Will I need to pay for additional training and coaching, or is your built-in support adequate?

✔ Who will be teaching me or advising me, and what is this person's background?

✔ How long have you been in business? Why was the company formed?

✔ What additional features are available at additional costs? How many customers subscribe to only the basic system?

✔ Will this support my trading style and work with the assets I prefer to trade?

✔ Do you screen traders for your program? Do you ask traders to leave? What are the characteristics of those who do well? Of those who don't do well?

✔ Can I talk to other customers?

✔ Is your software compatible with my broker? With other services I'm using? With my computer's operating system? With my Internet bandwidth?

✔ Are your performance numbers actual, or are they hypothetical and based on backtesting? How were the numbers calculated? (Chapter 11 has more information on performance calculation.)

Hypothetical performance is based on an analysis of what would have happened had the system been in place in the past or of what might happen if market conditions cooperate. It can be subject to data mining, which means that the system was developed to generate good performance in backtesting, not because it has any logical or theoretical basis.

Chapter 8

Managing the Stress of the Markets

Day trading can be a ruthless business. Some days, you don't find any trades worth making. Other days, you find trades, but they don't work out the way you want them to. And some days, there are too many good trades, more than you can possibly make, and so you watch profitable opportunities slip away. When you're working with real money, it can be too much to take.

In a money management or brokerage firm, traders have tremendous camaraderie. They are working for the same employer and need to stick together to blow off the stress. What do you do at home, though? How do *you* keep from panicking, getting depressed, or otherwise letting this business hurt your profits and hurt you?

If you're going to day trade, you need to understand the very real physical and psychological stresses that the market pushes on its participants. In this chapter, I offer some information and advice that can help you avoid a crisis.

First, the Cautionary Tales

Trader lore is loaded with stories of people who flamed out in spectacular and destructive ways. People who work on trading desks or on trading floors tell tales of colleagues who went down, walked off the desk, broke down in the pit, or died at the trading post. They can tick off colleagues who are alcoholics, who suffered bitter divorces, who committed suicide. Even though day traders usually work by themselves, stories of their self-destructive behavior abound.

Sure, many day traders lead pleasant lives and suffer no more problems than any other person. That's because they have perspective, balance, and the right personality for the business. Know what can go wrong, because it can help you keep in the right.

Jesse Livermore

Jesse Livermore is sometimes considered to be the father of day trading. He's the subject of the book *Reminiscences of a Stock Operator* by Edwin LeFevre, a classic book about trading (see the Appendix for more information). Livermore was born in 1877 and started trading stocks when he was in his teens. He claimed to have made $1,000 when he was 15, which may not seem like much, except that he was very young and price levels were a little different in 1892. (That $1,000 would be worth over $20,000 in today's dollars.) He made huge fortunes betting against the market in 1907 and again in 1929, and he managed to lose it all both times. By 1934 he was broke and depressed. He attempted suicide in 1935 and succeeded in 1940.

Mark Barton

Mark Barton lost $105,000 day trading and he snapped. On July 27, 1999, he bludgeoned his wife and two children to death. Then he went to the downtown Atlanta offices of Momentum Securities, a brokerage firm that specialized in working with day traders. He had an appointment to deliver $50,000 so that he could cover his losses and start trading again. Instead, he took out a gun, opened fire, and killed four people. He then went to the offices of All-Tech Investment Group, another day trading firm where he had an account, and killed another five people. Barton killed himself before he was arrested. This case is one of the worst workplace massacres in the United States, and it did as much as the 2000 meltdown in NASDAQ technology stocks to reduce the enthusiasm for day trading.

Anecdotal suicides, divorces, alcoholism

Because not that many people day trade consistently, not a lot of good demographic studies have been conducted on just how many day traders end up abusing drugs and alcohol, getting divorced or becoming estranged from friends, and turning to suicide. The anecdotal evidence is pretty strong, though. People in the securities business face high pressure and real dollar losses every day they go to work. Their performance is constantly judged by the market, and it doesn't grade on a curve. If you spend even a few minutes talking to people in the business, you hear horror stories. I personally know a trader who set fire to his house, killing his 90-year-old mother in the process, to get the insurance proceeds to cover his financial shortfalls. (He's currently doing a 190-year sentence.)

Don't be the person who finally gives researchers enough critical mass to report on day trader self-destruction. Stress is a real part of day trading, and not all day traders handle it well. If you know what you're up against and prepare for it, you'll be better off than many.

Controlling Your Emotions

The key to successful day trading is controlling your emotions. After all, the stock doesn't know that you own it, as equity traders like to say, so it isn't going to perform well just because you want it to. This can be infuriating, especially when you are going through a draw-down of your capital. Those losses look mighty personal.

Traditional financial theory is based on the idea that traders are rational. In practice, however, most of them are not. In fact, traders and investors are often irrational in completely predictable ways, which has given birth to a new area of study called *behavioral finance*. It's a hot area generating Nobel Prize winners, and it may eventually help people incorporate measures of investor behavior into buy and sell decisions.

You have to figure out a way to manage your reactions to the market, or you shouldn't be a day trader. Almost to a one, day traders talk about their enemies being fear and greed. If you panic, you'll no longer be trading to win, but trading not to lose. There's an important distinction: If your goal is not to lose, you won't take appropriate risk, and you won't be able to respond quickly to what the market is telling you.

This is all much easier said than done. Human beings are emotional creatures, constantly reacting (and sometimes overreacting) to everything that is happening in their lives. Knowing the emotions that affect trading and having some ways to manage them can greatly improve your overall performance.

The big five emotions

When it comes to trading, five big emotions can take over and mess up your strategy and your returns. At this point in your life, you may already know whether you have tendencies toward some of them. If so, trading can exacerbate them. If you've never experienced them, you might for the first time. Here's a list and some descriptions so that you know what you're up against and can plan accordingly. I include some tips that can help, but if you are really in the throes of an emotional crisis that affects your trading, you should seek out professional help.

Anxiety

Anxiety is the anticipation of things going wrong, and it often includes a physical response: perspiration, clenched jaws, tense muscles, heart palpitations. Anxious people worry, agonize, overanalyze, and generally stress out. And then they avoid whatever it is that makes them upset. That means that a trader might not make an obvious trade, but instead hesitate and miss a market move. He might hold on to a losing position too long because he's worried about the effect that selling it will have on his portfolio. He becomes too nervous to trade according to his plan, and his performance suffers.

One way to fight trading anxiety is to concentrate on following the trading plan, not on making a set amount of money. That way, following the plan becomes more automatic, and you spend less time worrying about what can go wrong.

Boredom

Here's the ugly truth about day trading: It can be really dull. In an eight-hour trading session, you might spend seven and a half hours waiting for the right opening. A flurry of trades, and it's all over. To keep yourself entertained, you might start making bad trades, spending too much time in chat rooms, or letting your mind wander away from the task at hand. None of those things is conducive to profitable trading.

If you are really bored and tempted to do something stupid, close out your positions and take a break. Going for a walk or quitting early can clear your head and help you focus when you get back. Remember, day traders work for themselves, and one of the benefits of that is that there is no boss to find out that you knocked off early. Take advantage of that!

Depression

Depression is a severe downturn in your mood, especially one that causes you to feel inadequate and lose interest in things you used to like. Although everyone is susceptible to depression, the ups and downs of the market can make traders particularly vulnerable. At best, depression can make it hard for a trader to face a day with the market. At worst, it can lead to alcoholism, alienation, and even suicide.

If you think you might be depressed, check out the handy quiz at www.med. nyu.edu/psych/screens/depres.html. Or better yet, go to your doctor.

Fear

Fear is one of the worst emotional enemies of the day trader. Instead of trying to make money, the fearful trader is trying hard not to lose it. She is so afraid of failing that she limits herself, doesn't take appropriate risk, and questions her trading system so much that she no longer follows it, no matter how well it worked for her in the past.

By the way, it isn't just failure that traders fear. Many fear success, sometimes for deep-seated psychological reasons that I am in no position to address. A trader who fears success may think that if she succeeds, her friends will treat her differently, her relatives will try to take her money, and that she will become someone she doesn't want to be.

One way to limit fear is to have a plan for the trading business. Before you start trading, take some time — maybe half a day — to sit down and think about what you want, what will happen to you if you get it, and what will happen to you if you don't. For example, if you lose your trading capital, then you'll have to live on your walk-away fund (see later in this chapter) until you find another job. If you make a lot of money, then you can pay off your mortgage and your friends will be none the wiser.

Greed

Greed seems like a silly thing to have on this list. After all, isn't the whole purpose of day trading to make money? This isn't charity, this is capitalism at its purest. Ah, but there's a popular saying down at the Chicago Board of Trade: "Pigs get fat, but hogs get slaughtered."

Traders who get greedy start to do stupid things. They don't think through what they are doing and stop following their trading plans. They hold positions too long in the hope of eking out a return and sometimes they make rash trades that look an awful lot like gambling. The greedy trader loses all discipline and eventually loses quite a bit of money.

If your goal is simply to make more and more money, you might have a problem with greed. Sure, everyone wants to make more, but there are also a basic *need-to-make number* (enough to cover your costs and your basic living expenses) and a *want-to-make number* (enough to cover costs, basic expenses, and extras that are important to you). If you know what those numbers are, you're well on your way to preventing the problem.

Limit orders, which automatically close out positions when they hit set prices, are one way to force discipline in the face of greed. You can learn more about limit orders in Chapter 2.

Having an outlet

Successful day traders have a life outside of the markets. They close out their positions, shut off their monitors, and go do something else with the rest of the day. That's the whole idea behind day trading.

The problem is that there is always a market open somewhere. Traders work overnight and after hours through electronic communications networks and sometimes move the action to exchanges in other parts of the world. Without something to mark a beginning and an end to your trading day, and without other things happening in your life, the market can consume you in a way that's simply not healthy.

So as you plan your life as a day trader, think about what else you're going to do with your days. Exercise, meditation, socializing, and having outside interests are key to maintaining balance and staying focused on the market when you have to be.

Exercise

Exercise keeps your body in fighting shape so that you can stand up to market stress and react to trends when you need to. Many times when you're trading, you have huge rushes of adrenalin that you can't do much about. You have to stay in front of your screen until the trade is over, no matter how much you want to run away screaming. But after the trading day, you can hit the track or pool or treadmill and burn off some of that adrenalin. Figuring out a regular exercise routine can pay off for your trading.

If you aren't an exerciser now, call your local YMCA. They have introductory programs that can teach you how to use the equipment and help you design a workout that suits your current fitness levels and goals.

Meditation

You may have closed out your positions and shut down your monitors, but the day's trading may keep playing itself out over and over in your head. When you are trading, you may get upset and start thinking about everything else that has ever gone wrong in your life, instead of staying focused on the task at hand. Trading, therefore, requires mental discipline. Good traders can keep their minds clear of everything but their trading system, at least when the markets are at their hairiest.

One way to develop that discipline is to take up meditation. Yeah, it may seem goofy, being a big tough trader type doing something woo-woo like meditation, but if you have trouble keeping your focus, you really might want to take it up. There are an almost infinite number of meditation styles, many of which are associated with different religious traditions, so you can surely find something that works.

Check out the instructions for the Buddhist mindfulness meditation practice at www.shambhala.org/meditationinstruction.html as a way to get started.

Friends and family

Day trading is a lonely activity. You're working by yourself all day. It's just you, your room, and your screen. It's really isolating, and if you don't get other human contact, you'll personalize the market so that you don't feel so lonely. That's bad, because the market isn't a person; it's an agglomeration of all the financial activity taking place, and it has no interest in you whatsoever.

No matter what you do in life, you want to have the support of the people you know and love. And you need to make time for them, too. Start and end your trading day at regular times, and be sure to make plans to see people who are important to you. Going to your kid's ball game, having dinner with your spouse, and seeing your buddies for a few beers on a regular basis can go a long way to keeping your life in balance — and that will keep your trading in balance.

If you like pets, consider getting one to keep you company during the day. There's nothing like a dog that needs a walk to force you to close up shop for the night.

Hobbies and other interests

A lot of people get into day trading because they have long had a fascination with the market. Trading goes from being a hobby to being a living. In many ways, that's perfect. It's so much easier to go to work if you have a job that you love.

But if the market is your only interest, then you're going to be too susceptible to its gyrations and you're going to have trouble sticking to your trading discipline. Plus, whatever upsets you during the trading day is more likely to carry over. So find a new hobby if you don't have one. Maybe it's a TV show, a sport, or knitting, but whatever it is, you need to have something going on outside of your trading.

Trading is just one part of your life.

Support systems

Exercise and friends and family and hobbies and the like are all well and good, but they don't directly address the mindset of trading. Ah, but there's a veritable industry of support for traders, and it's easy to tap into. Many day traders find that reading books, hiring a coach, or finding other day traders helps them get through the day.

Books

A library-full of books have been written on the psychology of trading itself. In addition, many traders rely on other self-help and history books for inspiration and ideas. (I think every trader I've ever known owns a copy of Sun Tzu's *The Art of War,* which is about military strategies and tactics. They find that it helps them prepare their minds to face the market, or at least gives them something interesting to talk about.) I list several books in the Appendix that might help you organize your mind and keep your enthusiasm for the market.

Counseling and coaching

Because it takes a lot of mental toughness to handle big losses — and big gains — many traders find professional support. They use counselors, psychologists, or life coaches to help them deal with the challenges of the market and understand their reactions to it. You can ask other traders or your doctor for a referral, or check the online directory at *Psychology Today*'s Web site, www. psychologytoday.com, or the International Coach Federation, www.coach federation.org. When interviewing coaches or counselors, ask whether they have experience with traders or others who work in finance.

Many day trading training and brokerage firms also offer coaching services that specialize in helping people learn and follow day trading strategies. Some day traders find these people to be invaluable, whereas others find they are just glorified salespeople.

Some day trading coaches may be more interested in selling you specific trading strategies rather than helping you manage your own system. Check references and find out what other forms of compensation the coach receives before signing up.

Finding other traders

To offset the loneliness of trading alone, many day traders choose to work out of trading rooms operated by brokerage firms (see Chapter 6 for more on this) or join organizations where they will meet other traders. These may be formal or informal groups (I list a few in the Appendix) where traders can socialize, learn new things, or just commiserate.

Many day traders get together through Internet message boards and chat rooms, which I discuss in more detail later in this chapter. These groups are less formal, more anonymous, and sometimes more destructive than supportive.

Most day traders lose money and give up their first year. You may find that spending too much time with other traders is more depressing than supportive.

Watching your walk-away money

A lot of traders have a secret that lets them get through the worst of the markets. It's something called *walk-away money*, although traders sometimes use more colorful language to describe it. It's enough money that they can walk away from trading and do something else.

And just exactly how much is it? Well, it varies from person to person, but having enough money to pay three months' worth of expenses on hand and in cash is a good place to start. If you know that you can pay the mortgage and buy the groceries even if you don't make money trading today, you'll be better able to avoid desperate trading. You won't have to be greedy, and you won't have to live in fear.

The more money in your walk-away fund, the better. Then you have more time to investigate alternative careers should day trading prove not to be your thing, and you can relax more when you face the market every day.

Most day traders quit after a year or so. There's nothing wrong with deciding to move on and try something else. If you have some money saved, then you're in a better position to control when you stop trading and what you do next.

If all your trading capital is gone, you might be tempted to tap your walk-away fund to stay in the game. *Don't.* That's the exactly the time that you should use your walk-away money to *walk away*, if only for a short time to clear your head and rethink your strategies. Otherwise, your trading losses may become financial ruin.

Importance of a Trading Plan

You may have noticed that *trading plans* pop up several times in this book, such as in Chapters 2, 8, 12, and 13. That's because they are so important to maintaining the discipline that leads to trading success. You have to know what you're doing and how to recognize entry and exit points and then go and do it.

In this section, I cover how you can use a trading plan to manage stress and give you a few tips for sticking to your trading plan even as the markets sometimes move against you.

Problems following direction

Was that written on all your report cards? I hope not. A good, tested trading plan sets out market patterns that work often enough that you can make good trading profits. But some people have trouble following their plan, and that leads to stressful mistakes.

Prevent choking!

In sports lingo, an athlete who *chokes* starts playing so carefully that he or she looks like a beginner. This is often caused by over-thinking — by being so afraid of failure that the mind slows down and breaks the play down step by step. It's not pretty to watch a contender break down in a championship game. The fans want to see a good match.

Anyone in a high-performance situation can choke. When a trader chokes, he seems to be following the plan, but it's no longer automatic. Trading becomes so slow and deliberative that obvious trades get missed.

The more you trust your plan, the less likely you are to choke. Has it been tested? Are there parts that you can automate? Chapter 11 has some ideas on how to measure a trading plan's performance before you start to trade with the plan.

Reducing panic

Panic occurs when you just stop thinking. Your most basic survival instincts take over, even when they are totally uncalled for. You're losing money? You start to trade more and more, off-plan, in a desperate gamble to win it back. You're making money? You close out all your trades right now so that you can't possibly lose, even if your plan tells you to hold your positions. When you panic, you can't think straight, and you can't follow your plan.

One problem is that when your positions are down, and you seem to be losing money, you really should be buying and sticking it out so that you can make money later. That's tough to do and requires a lot of discipline. Traders learn to avoid panic with experience.

You're probably going to have more than a few losing trades when you get started. In your trading diary (see Chapter 11), keep notes about how it makes you feel to lose money. Can you handle it emotionally? If losing upsets you too much, you might not be cut out for day trading. You can't trade with a clear head if you're bogged down with negative thoughts.

Confidence versus ego

Day trading requires a lot of confidence, because you *are* going to lose money and you *are* going to get beaten up some days. But you not only have to remain confident in the face of adversity, you also have to be careful that you do not cross from confidence into an inflated ego. The more your trading success and failure become part of your personal identity, the more trouble you are going to have.

What's the difference between confidence and ego? It's "I'm smart enough to figure out what the market is telling me" vs. "I'm smarter than the market." The difference is crucial to your success.

Revising and troubleshooting your trading plan

Strong discipline is key to success in trading, but only if you're disciplined in following the right system. If your trading method is flawed, then sticking to it is going to hurt you. If something isn't working, don't get mad at the system; take some responsibility and make some changes.

How do you figure out whether your trading system is right and what changes to make? Go through your trading diary (see Chapter 11 for how to set one up) and ask yourself some questions:

- ✔ Why did you choose this system? What is the market telling you about it? Is it telling you that the system works if you follow it, or is it telling you that there's something wrong with the underlying assumptions.

    What works for someone else might not work for you. There's no flaw in admitting that you made a mistake and that you need to make a change.

- ✔ Were your mistakes because you followed the plan, or because you didn't?

- ✔ What part of the system is causing the trouble? Are you having trouble identifying entry points or exit points? Or are you stuck when it comes time to enter the trade, causing you to miss a point? Or is it that the trades your system identifies never seem to work out?

    Once you know where the problem is, you can change it.

- ✔ Can you improve your trade efficiency? Is there a way to reduce the number of mistakes? Would automating some or all of your trading help?

One way to get your confidence back while still staying in the market is to trade in very small amounts so that your profits and losses don't really matter. Trade 100 shares, not 1,000 shares. You give up the upside for a time, but you can also get out of the cycle of greed and fear that has destroyed many a trader.

The Follies of Chat Rooms

Spend any time on the Internet researching day trading and you'll come across the chat rooms and message boards that some traders use to exchange information. Or at least you'll come across the chat rooms and message boards that purport to be used by traders to exchange information.

Chat rooms were quite the thing in the first big wave of day trading, in the late 1990s. They don't have quite the influence that they once did, but some day traders still rely on them. Some are excellent, help people learn to trade, and offer good perspectives on market action. Others are a distraction at best. In this part, I cover some of the benefits and risks so that you know what you are getting into before you make that first post.

Support group or group think?

Many day traders turn to chat rooms for the camaraderie and support they offer. It seems so great to find other people who are going through the same things that you are! They understand what's happening!

Or do they? I could make a very strong argument that traders who really know what they are doing don't want anyone else to know who they are or what their plan is. Several successful day traders that I talked to while researching this book refused to have their names in it, because they are happier staying off the radar. Meanwhile, even those day traders who make money have trouble making enough money to stick to the business for a long time.

To compound the problem, the people in a chat room might get so agreeable that they start reinforcing bad advice. Instead of getting support to help you through a rough time, you get dragged down.

 In general, a message board that charges a subscription fee is likely to be of better quality than one that's free, just because the fee wards off the people who aren't serious. I've listed a few in the appendix. But no matter what you pay, spend some time lurking — watching the comments without making any yourself. Proprietors of good message boards usually offer temporary access to prospective subscribers to help them evaluate the service. Check to see how people treat each other, what experiences they have, and how their trading systems match yours. And limit your time and watch your reactions to people's postings.

Getting angry at nothing

From the very early days of newsgroups and Internet Relay Chat, people exchanging ideas on the Internet have managed to misunderstand each other and blow small things out of proportion. That's all well and good if you're talking about the latest season of *American Idol*, but it's not so good if you're day trading. The market is a tough-enough evaluator of your performance. You don't need to waste time, energy, and confidence on someone who, intentionally or not, makes a nasty comment on a message board.

At a minimum, try to limit your message board activities to market hours. And if you're one of those people who are quick to anger (hey, I won't tell), it may be best to avoid online discussions with other day traders all together.

Sabotage

Now, here's one other nasty truth about day trader chat rooms: Sometimes the people posting are trying to manipulate the market and sabotage other traders. They plant false and misleading information, seek to undermine others' confidence, and otherwise try to seek an edge by bringing others down. In other words, there may not be much information value at all, and the value of camaraderie may be quite low, too.

The Internet is a wonderful thing, and it makes it possible for people to trade sophisticated financial instruments in real time from the comfort of home. But it has its limitations, and online interaction with other traders can actually add to the stress of day trading. Tread carefully.

Chapter 9

Managing Your Money and Positions

Much of this book is designed to give you ideas about whether to day trade at all, what you want to trade, and how you want to trade it. That leaves one remaining issue: how much of your money to put on the line each time you trade. Risk too much, and you can be put out of business when you lose your capital. Risk too little, and you can be put of out business because you can't make enough money to cover your costs and time.

Over time, many academic theorists and experienced traders have developed different systems of money management designed to help traders, investors, and even gamblers manage their money in order to maximize return while protecting capital. In this chapter, I explain how some of the better-known systems work so that you can figure out how to best apply them to your own trading.

Some of the material in this chapter is related to *leverage*, which is borrowing money to trade. Leverage can dramatically increase the money that you have available to trade as well as the risk and return profile of the trades that you make, so it affects how you manage your money. Flip to Chapter 14 for more information on leverage and why you might want to use it.

What's Your Expected Return?

Before you can figure out how to manage your money, you need to figure out how much money you can expect to make. This is your *expected return*, although some traders prefer the word *expectancy*. You start by laying out your trading system and testing it (described in Chapter 11). You are looking for four numbers:

✔ How many of your trades are losers?

✔ What's the typical percentage loss on a losing trade?

✔ How many of your trades are winners?

✔ What's the typical percentage gain on a winning trade?

Let's say you determine that 40 percent of the time a trade loses, and it loses 1 percent. Sixty percent of the time, the trade wins, and winning trades are up 1.5 percent. With these numbers, you can calculate your per-trade expected return, like this:

```
% of losing trades × loss on losing trades + % of winning
        trades × gain on winning trades = expected
        return
```

Which in this example, works out to be:

```
.40 × −.01 + .60 × .015 = −.004 + .009 = .005
```

On average, then, you would expect to earn a half a percent on every trade you make. Make enough trades with enough money, and it adds up.

You are more likely to make more money if you have a high expectation of winning trades and if those winners are expected to perform well. As long as there is some probability of loss, you stand to lose money.

The Probability of Ruin

Expected return is the happy number. It's how much money you can expect to make if you stay in the trading game. But it has a counterpart that is not so happy but is at least as important: the *probability of ruin*.

As long as there is some probability of loss, no matter how small, there is some probability that you can lose everything when you are trading. How much you can lose depends on how large each trade is relative to your account, the likelihood of each trade having a loss, and the size of the losses as they occur.

Figure 9-1 shows the math for finding R, the probability of ruin.

Figure 9-1:
How to calculate the probability of ruin.

$$R = \left[\frac{(1 - A)}{1 + A} \right]^{c}$$

A is the advantage on each trade in Figure 9-1. That's the difference between the percentage of winning trades and the percentage of losing trades. In the expected return example discussed earlier, trades win 60 percent of the time and lose 40 percent of the time. In that case, the trader's advantage would be:

```
60% - 40% = 20%
```

C is the number of trades in an account. Let's assume that we're dividing the account into ten equal parts, with the plan of making ten trades today. The probability of ruin today is 1.7 percent (Figure 9-2).

Figure 9-2:
Here's an example of the risk of ruin calculation.

$$1.7\% = \left[\frac{(1 - .20)}{1 + .20} \right]^{10}$$

Now, 1.7 percent isn't a high likelihood of ruin, but it's not zero, either. It could happen. If your advantage is smaller, if the expected loss is larger, or if the number of trades is fewer, then the likelihood becomes even higher.

Figure 9-3 shows you the relationship between the trader's advantage, number of trades, and the corresponding probability of ruin, rounded to the nearest percentage.

Probability of Ruin

Trader's Advantage		**Number of Trades**									
		1	2	3	4	5	6	7	8	9	10
	2%	96%	92%	89%	85%	82%	79%	76%	73%	70%	67%
	4%	92%	85%	79%	73%	67%	62%	57%	53%	49%	45%
	6%	89%	79%	70%	62%	55%	49%	43%	38%	34%	30%
	8%	85%	73%	62%	53%	45%	38%	33%	28%	24%	20%
	10%	82%	67%	55%	45%	37%	30%	25%	20%	16%	13%
	12%	79%	62%	49%	38%	30%	24%	18%	15%	11%	9%
	14%	75%	57%	43%	32%	24%	18%	14%	10%	8%	6%
	16%	72%	52%	38%	27%	20%	14%	10%	8%	5%	4%
	18%	69%	48%	34%	23%	16%	11%	8%	5%	4%	3%
	20%	67%	44%	30%	20%	13%	9%	6%	4%	3%	2%

Figure 9-3:
Adding
trader's
advantage
to the mix.

The bigger the edge and the more trades you can make, the lower your probability of ruin. Now, this model is a simplification in that it assumes that a losing trade goes to zero, and that's not always the case. In fact, if you use stops (automatic buy and sell orders, described in Chapter 2), you should never have a trade go to zero. But you can see steady erosion in your account that will make it harder for you to make money. Hence, probability of ruin is a useful calculation that shows whether you will lose money in the long run.

The more trades you can make with your account, the lower your probability of ruin. That's why money management is a key part of risk management.

Why Size Matters

As long as there is some chance of losing all your money, you want to avoid betting all of it on any one trade. But as long as there is a chance of making money, you want to have enough exposure to a winning trade so that you can post good profits. How do you figure it out?

Later in this chapter, I describe some of the different money management systems that traders use to figure out how much money to risk per trade. But first, I want to explain the logic behind a money management system, so that you understand why you need one. That way, you can better manage your funds and improve the dollar returns to your trading.

Valuing volatility

Expected return gives you an idea of how much you can get from a trade on average, but it doesn't tell you how much that return might vary from trade to trade. The average of 9, 10, and 11 is 10; the average of –100, 10, and 100 is also 10. The first number series is a lot narrower than the second. The wider the range of returns that a strategy has, the more *volatile* it is.

There are several ways to measure volatility. One common one is *standard deviation*, which tells you how much your actual return is likely to differ from what you expect to get. There's a detailed explanation of the standard deviation calculation in Chapter 11. The higher the standard deviation, the more volatile, and riskier, the strategy.

In the derivatives markets, volatility is measured by a group of numbers known as the Greeks: delta, gamma, vega, and theta. They're based on calculus.

- ✔ **Delta** is a ratio that tells you how much the option or future changes in price when the underlying security or market index changes in price. Delta changes over time.

- ✔ **Gamma** is the rate of change on delta. That's because a derivative's delta will be higher when it is close to the expiration date, for example, then when the expiration date is further away.

- ✔ **Vega** is the amount that the derivative would change in price if the underlying security became 1 percent more volatile.

- ✔ **Theta** is the amount that a derivative's price declines as it gets closer to the day of expiration.

Day traders seek out more volatile securities, because they offer more opportunities to make money during any given day. That means they have to have ways to minimize the damage that might occur while being able to capitalize on the upward swings. Money management can help with that.

Staying in the market

You only have a limited amount of money to trade. Whether it's $1,000 or $1,000,000, once it's gone, you're out. The problem is that you can have a long string of losing trades before the markets go in a direction that favors you and your system.

Let's say you trade 100 percent of your account. If you have one trade that goes down 100 percent, then you have nothing. If you divide your account into ten parts, then you can have ten total losers before you are out. If you start with ten equal parts and double each time you lose, you can be out after four losing trades.

The riskier your trading strategy, the more thought you need to put into money management. Otherwise, you can find yourself out of the market in no time.

On the other hand, if you divide your account into 100 portions, then you can endure 100 losing trades. If you trade fractions of your account, then you can keep going infinitely, or at least until you get down to a level that's too low to place a minimum order. (That's the philosophy behind the Kelly Criterion, described later in this chapter.) Money management can keep you in the game longer, and that will give you more opportunities to place winning trades.

Considering opportunity costs

Opportunity cost is the value you give up because you choose to do something else. In trading, each dollar you commit to one trade is a dollar that you cannot commit to another trade. Thus, each dollar you trade carries some opportunity cost, and good traders seek to minimize this cost. During the course of the trading day, you may see several great trades, and some opportunities will show up before you are ready to close out a different trade.

If you have committed all your capital to one trade, you will miss out on the second. That alone is a good reason to keep some money on the table each time you trade.

Money Management Styles

Over the years, traders have developed many different ways to manage their money. Some of these are rooted in superstition, but most are based on different statistical probability theories. The underlying idea is that you should never place all of your money in a single trade, but rather put in an amount that is appropriate given the level of volatility. Otherwise, you risk losing everything too soon.

Calculating position size under many of these formulas is tricky stuff. That's why brokerage firms and trading software packages often include money management calculators. Check Chapter 6 for more information on the brokers and Chapter 7 for more on different software and research services.

This is only a sample of some methods. There are other methods out there, and none is suitable to all markets all the time. Folks trading both options and stocks may want to use one system for option trades and another for stock trades. If that's your situation, you have one big money management decision to make before you begin: how much money to allocate to each market.

Fixed fractional

Fixed fractional trading assumes that you want to limit each trade to a set portion of your total account, often between 2 and 10 percent. Within that range, you'd trade a larger percentage of money in less risky trades and at the smaller end of the scale for more risky trades. (In other words, it's not all that "fixed," but no one asked me to pick a name for the system.)

The fixed fractional equation is shown in Figure 9-4.

Figure 9-4:
Here's the equation for calculating fixed fractional trade proportions.

$$N = f\left(\frac{equity}{|trade\ risk|}\right)$$

N is the number of contracts or shares of stock you should trade, f is the fixed fraction of your account that you have decided to trade, equity is the value of your total account, and trade risk is the amount of money you could lose on the transaction. Because trade risk is a negative number, you need to convert it to a positive number to make the equation work. Those vertical bars in the equation (| |) are the sign for absolute value, and that means that you convert the number between them to a positive number.

This means that if you have decided to limit each trade to 10 percent of your account, if you have a $20,000 account, and if the risk of loss is –$3,500, your trade should be what is shown in Figure 9-5.

Figure 9-5:
An example of a fixed fractional trade calculation.

$$0.57 = .10\left(\frac{20,000}{|-3500|}\right)$$

Of course, you probably can't trade .57 of a contract, so in this case, you would have to round up to one.

Fixed ratio

The *fixed ratio* money management system is used in trading options and futures. It was developed by a trader named Ryan Jones, who wrote a book about it. (Check the Appendix for more information.) In order to find the optimal number of options or futures contracts to trade, N, you use the equation shown in Figure 9-6.

$$N = 0.05\left(\sqrt{1 + 8\left(P/\Delta\right)} + 1\right)$$

N is the number of contracts or shares of stock that you should trade, P is your accumulated profit to date, and the triangle, delta, is the dollar amount that you would need before you could trade a second contract or another lot of stock. (This is *not* the same delta measure discussed previously, which is a measure of volatility.)

For example, the minimum margin for Chicago Mercantile Exchange E-Mini S&P 500 futures contract, which gives you exposure to the Standard & Poor's 500 stock index, is $3,500. Until you have another $3,500 in your account, you can't trade a second contract. If you are using fixed ratio money management to trade this future, your delta will be $3,500.

If your delta is $3,500, and you have $10,000 in account profits, you should trade 1.2 contracts (see Figure 9-7). In reality, that means you can only trade one contract or two contracts, nothing in between. That's one of the imperfections of most money management systems.

$$1.2 = 0.05\left(\sqrt{1 + 8\left(10,000/3500\right)} + 1\right)$$

The idea behind fixed ratio trading is to help you increase your exposure to the market while protecting your accumulated profits.

Gann

William Gann developed a complicated system for identifying securities trades. Part of that was a list of rules for managing money, and many traders follow that if nothing else.

The primary rule is: Divide your money into ten equal parts, and never place more than one 10-percent portion on a single trade. That helps control your risk, whether or not you use Gann. (Gann is discussed a little in Chapter 7.)

Kelly Criterion

The Kelly Criterion emerged from statistical work done at Bell Laboratories in the 1950s. The goal was to figure out the best ways to manage signal-noise issues in long-distance telephone communications. Very quickly, the mathematicians who worked on it saw that there were applications to gambling, and in no time, the formula took off.

To calculate the ideal percentage of your portfolio to put at risk, you need to know what percentage of your trades are expected to win as well as the return from a winning trade and the ratio performance of winning trades to losing trades. The shorthand that many traders use for the Kelly Criterion is *edge divided by odds*, and in practice, the formula looks like this:

```
Kelly % = W - [(1 - W) / R]
```

W is the percentage of winning trades, and R is the ratio of the average gain of the winning trades relative to the average loss of the losing trades.

In the beginning of the chapter, I had an example of a system that loses 40 percent of the time with a loss of 1 percent and that wins 60 percent of the time with a gain of 1.5 percent. Plugging that into the Kelly formula, the right percentage to trade is .60 − [(1−.60)/(.015/.01)], or 33.3 percent.

As long as you limit your trades to no more than 33% of your capital, you should never run out of money. The problem, of course, is that if you have a long string of losses, you could find yourself with too little money to execute a trade. Many traders use a "half-Kelly" strategy, limiting each trade to half the amount indicated by the Kelly Criterion, as a way to keep the trading account from shrinking too quickly. They are especially likely to do this if the Kelly Criterion generates a number greater than about 20 percent, as in this example.

Martingale

The *martingale* style of money management is common with serious casino gamblers, and many traders apply it as well. It's designed to improve the amount of money you can earn in a game that has even odds. Most casino odds favor the house (roulette wheels used to be evenly black and red, but casinos found that they could make more money if they inserted a green slice for zero, thus throwing off the odds). Day trading, on the other hand, is a zero-sum game, especially in the options and futures markets. This means that for every winner, there is a loser, so the odds of any one trade being successful are even. The martingale system is designed to work in any market where the odds are even or in your favor.

Under the martingale strategy, you start with a set amount per trade, say $2,000. If your trade succeeds, you trade another $2,000. If your trade loses, you double your next order (after you close or limit the first trade) so that you can win back your loss. (You may have heard gamblers talk about *doubling down*? Well, this is what they are doing.)

Under the martingale system, you will always come out ahead as long as you have an infinite amount of money to trade. The problem is that you can run out of money before you have a trade that works. The market, on the other hand, has almost infinite resources because of the huge volume of participants coming and going all over the world. That means that you have an enormous disadvantage. As long as you have a disadvantage, thoughtful money management is critical.

Monte Carlo simulation

If you have the programming expertise or buy the right software, you can run what's called a *Monte Carlo simulation*. In this, you enter in your risk and return parameters and your account value, let the program run, and it returns the optimal trade size. The system is not perfect — it is only a model that can't incorporate every market situation that you'll face and it has the fractional trade problem that the other systems do. But it has one big advantage: It can incorporate random changes in the markets in ways that simpler money management models cannot.

Monte Carlo simulation is not a do-it-yourself project, unless you have extensive experience creating these programs. If you are interested, you need to find a suitable program. Two options are offered by AnalyCorp, at www.analycorp.com and Decisioneering, www.decisioneering.com. Others are out there as well.

Optimal F

The *Optimal F* system of money management was devised by Ralph Vince, and he's written several books about this and other money management issues (see the Appendix for more information). The idea is that you determine the ideal fraction of your money to allocate per trade based on past performance. If your Optimal F is 18 percent, then each trade should be 18 percent of your account — no more, no less. The system is similar to the fixed fraction and fixed ratio methods discussed earlier, but with a few differences.

Figure 9-8 shows the equation for finding the number of shares of stock, N, to trade.

Figure 9-8:
Here's the
equation for
finding the
number of
shares to
trade under
Optimal F.

$$N = \frac{\left(F * \frac{equity}{risk} \right)}{price}$$

F is a factor based on the basis of historical data, and the risk is the biggest percentage loss that you experienced in the past. Using these numbers and the current price, you can find the contracts or shares you need to buy. If your account has $25,000, your biggest loss was 40 percent, your F is determined to be 30 percent, and you're looking at a stock trading at $25 per share, then you should buy 750 shares (Figure 9-9).

Figure 9-9:
Here's an
example of
the Optimal F
calculation.

$$750 = \frac{\left(.30 * \frac{25,000}{.40} \right)}{25}$$

The Optimal F number itself is a mean based on historical trade results. The risk number is also based on past returns, and that's one problem with this method: it only kicks in after you have some trade data. A second problem is that you need to set up a spreadsheet to calculate it (so read Ralph Vince's book if you want to try it out; you can find more information in the Appendix.) Some traders only use Optimal F in certain market conditions, in part because the history changes each time a trade is made, and that history doesn't always lead to usable numbers.

How Money Management Affects Your Return

It's one thing to describe why you need money management, but it's more fun to show you how it works. And because I love making spreadsheets (we all need a hobby, right?), I pulled one together to show you how different ways of managing your money might affect your return.

In Figure 9-2, I started with the expected return assumptions that I used in the earlier example: 40 percent of the time a trade loses, and it loses 1 percent. 60 percent of the time, the trade wins, and winning trades are up 1.5 percent. In Figure 9-10, I pick a hypothetical account of $20,000 and set up mock trades using these expected return numbers. Figure 9-10 compares the performance of martingale and Kelly money management to betting the whole account each time.

You may notice in Figure 9-10 that you end up with the most money from trading the entire account. That doesn't mean you always get the most money this way, just that that's how the numbers worked out in this case, given the 60/40 win ratio and a 3/2 winning size/losing size ratio. (Keep in mind that if you were using a Kelly or martingale system, you'd probably be doing something with the rest of the account rather than just letting it sit there.)

Martingale: Starting with 10% and Doubling Losses

	Performance	Intial Account Value	% Traded	Amount Traded	Ending Account Value	% Change
Trade 1	1.5%	$ 20,000	10%	$ 2,000	$ 20,030	
Trade 2	1.5%	$ 20,030		$ 2,000	$ 20,060	
Trade 3	-1.0%	$ 20,060		$ 2,000	$ 20,040	
Trade 4	-1.0%	$ 20,040		$ 4,000	$ 20,000	
Trade 5	1.5%	$ 20,000		$ 8,000	$ 20,120	
Trade 6	1.5%	$ 20,120		$ 2,000	$ 20,150	
Trade 7	-1.0%	$ 20,150		$ 2,000	$ 20,130	
Trade 8	-1.0%	$ 20,130		$ 4,000	$ 20,090	
Trade 9	1.5%	$ 20,090		$ 8,000	$ 20,210	
Trade 10	1.5%	$ 20,210		$ 2,000	$ 20,240	1.20%

Kelly: Trading 33%

	Performance	Intial Account Value	% Traded	Amount Traded	Ending Account Value	
Trade 1	1.5%	$ 20,000	33%	$ 6,660	$ 20,100	
Trade 2	1.5%	$ 20,100	33%	$ 6,693	$ 20,200	
Trade 3	-1.0%	$ 20,200	33%	$ 6,727	$ 20,133	
Trade 4	-1.0%	$ 20,133	33%	$ 6,704	$ 20,066	
Trade 5	1.5%	$ 20,066	33%	$ 6,682	$ 20,166	
Trade 6	1.5%	$ 20,166	33%	$ 6,715	$ 20,267	
Trade 7	-1.0%	$ 20,267	33%	$ 6,749	$ 20,199	
Trade 8	-1.0%	$ 20,199	33%	$ 6,726	$ 20,132	
Trade 9	1.5%	$ 20,132	33%	$ 6,704	$ 20,233	
Trade 10	1.5%	$ 20,233	33%	$ 6,738	$ 20,334	1.67%

Betting Everything

	Performance	Intial Account Value	% Traded	Amount Traded	Ending Account Value	
Trade 1	1.5%	$ 20,000	100%	$ 20,000	$ 20,300	
Trade 2	1.5%	$ 20,300	100%	$ 20,300	$ 20,605	
Trade 3	-1.0%	$ 20,605	100%	$ 20,605	$ 20,398	
Trade 4	-1.0%	$ 20,398	100%	$ 20,398	$ 20,194	
Trade 5	1.5%	$ 20,194	100%	$ 20,194	$ 20,497	
Trade 6	1.5%	$ 20,497	100%	$ 20,497	$ 20,805	
Trade 7	-1.0%	$ 20,805	100%	$ 20,805	$ 20,597	
Trade 8	-1.0%	$ 20,597	100%	$ 20,597	$ 20,391	
Trade 9	1.5%	$ 20,391	100%	$ 20,391	$ 20,697	
Trade 10	1.5%	$ 20,697	100%	$ 20,697	$ 21,007	5.04%

Figure 9-10: How money management affects your return.

This is just an example, applying some different strategies to different hypothetical returns. I'm not recommending any one system over another. The best system for you depends on what assets you are trading, your personal trading style, and how much money you have to trade.

Planning for Your Profits

In addition to determining how much to trade each time you place an order, you need a plan for what to do with the profits that accumulate in your account. That's as much a part of money management as calculating your probability of ruin and determining trade size.

Are you going to add the money to your account and trade it as before? Leverage your profits by trading them more aggressively than your core account? Pull money out and put it into long-term investments? Or a combination of the three?

Compounding interest

Compound interest is a simple concept: Every time you get a return, that return goes into your account. You keep earning a return on it, which increases your account size some more. You keep earning a return on your return, and pretty soon, the numbers get to be pretty big.

In order to benefit from that compounding, many traders add their profits back into their accounts and keep trading them, in order to build account size. Although day traders earn little to no interest (which is compensation for loaning out money — say, by buying bonds), the basic principle holds: By returning profits to the trading account to generate even more profits, the account should grow over time.

This practice of keeping profits in the account to trade makes a lot of sense for smaller traders who want to build their accounts and take more significant positions over time.

Pyramiding power

Pyramiding involves taking trading profits and borrowing heavily against them to generate even more profits. Traders usually do this during the day, using unrealized profits in trades that are not yet closed as collateral for loans used to establish new positions. If the new positions are profitable, the trader can keep borrowing until it's time to close everything at the end of the day.

This works great as long as the markets are moving in the right direction. If all the positions in the pyramid remain profitable, you can make a lot of money during the course of the day. But if one of those positions turns against you, the structure collapses and you end up with a call on your margin. Figure 9-11 starts with an initial trade of $2,000 and assumes a return of 10 percent on each transaction — not realistic, necessarily, but it makes for a nice chart. If the profits from each trade are used as collateral for borrowing, and if that 10 percent return holds all day, then the trader can make 17 percent by pyramiding those gains. If a reversal hits before the end of the trading session and the positions lose 10 percent, then pyramiding magnifies the losses — assuming your broker would let you keep borrowing. After all, the borrowed money has to be repaid regardless of what happens in the market.

Pyramiding magnifies returns

Assume that you need to maintain 25% margin

	Initial Trade Equity	Amount Borrowed	Total Trade Size	Profit at 10% Return
First trade	$ 2,000	$ -	$ 2,000	$ 200
Second trade	$ 200	$ 600	$ 800	$ 80
Third trade	$ 80	$ 240	$ 320	$ 32
Fourth trade	$ 32	$ 96	$ 128	$ 13
Fifth trade	$ 13	$ 38	$ 51	$ 5
Sixth trade	$ 5	$ 15	$ 20	$ 2
Return on initial $2000 trade:	$ 332			
Percentage return:	17%			

... And pyramiding magifies losses

	Initial Trade Equity	Amount Borrowed	Total Trade Size	Profit at 10% Return
First trade	$ 2,000	$ -	$ 2,000	$ (200)
Second trade	$ 200	$ 600	$ 800	$ (80)
Third trade	$ 80	$ 240	$ 320	$ (32)
Fourth trade	$ 32	$ 96	$ 128	$ (13)
Fifth trade	$ 13	$ 38	$ 51	$ (5)
Sixth trade	$ 5	$ 15	$ 20	$ (2)
Return on initial $2000 trade:	$ (332)			
Percentage return:	-17%			

Figure 9-11: Pyramiding magnifies returns and losses.

Pyramiding is not related to a *pyramid scheme*. In trading terms, pyramiding is a way to borrow against your profits to generate even bigger profits. A pyramid scheme is a fraud that requires participants to recruit new members, and fees paid by the new members go to the older ones. Eventually, the pyramid collapses because it gets too difficult to recruit new members, and those at the bottom get nothing.

Some investment frauds have been structured as pyramid schemes, so be wary of deals that sound fabulous and also require you to recruit others.

Pyramiding increases your trading risk, but also your expected return. It's a useful way to grow a portion of your trading account, especially when the market is favoring your trading system. It's a good technique for a medium-sized account that would have enough money left over to stay in the market if a pyramid were to collapse on you.

Regular withdrawals

Because day trading can be so risky, many traders look to diversify their total financial risk. One way to do this is to pull money out of the trading account to put into a less volatile long-term investment. Many traders routinely pull out a percentage of their profits and put that money into government bonds, a low-risk mutual fund, or real estate. None of these investments is as glamorous or exciting as day trading, but that's the point: Trading is hard work, and anyone can lose money any day, no matter how big their account is or how much money they have made so far. By moving some money out, a trader can build a cushion for a bad trading stretch, prepare for retirement, and have some money to walk away for a short period or even forever. That can greatly reduce the stress and the fear that go with trading.

The larger the account, the easier it is to pull money out, but even smaller traders should consider taking 5 or 10 percent of each quarter's profits and moving them into another type of investment. Many brokerage firms can set up automatic withdrawal plans that zap money from your trading account to a stock or bond mutual fund, if you don't trust yourself to do it.

Chapter 10

Taxes for Traders

*T*hink day trade returns come without a catch? Think again, because the IRS has plenty of ways to catch you come April 15. Day trading involves strategies that generate both high returns and high tax liabilities, which can eat away at your total return if you are not careful. Not all of your expenses are deductible, and you might think that you're day trading, but the IRS will have a different definition of your activities.

Taxes themselves aren't necessarily bad, because somehow we have to pay for things like roads and schools and national defense. But taxes can be devastating to your personal finances if you haven't planned for them. You need to consider the tax implications of your trading strategy right from the start and keep careful records so that you're ready.

Tax issues for day traders are complex and change frequently. Check the most recent federal regulations at www.irs.gov and work with an accountant or tax expert who has experience in these matters. This chapter is just a guide. I'm a reasonably social gal and all, but I'm not going on an audit with you.

Are You a Trader or an Investor?

Back in Chapter 4, I cover the differences between investing, trading, and gambling. Day traders aren't investing — they are looking to take advantage of short-term price movements, not to take a stake in a business for the long term. Unless, of course, you're asking the IRS about it. The IRS defines trading much differently than people in financial circles do. To the taxmen, you are a trader only if *all* of the following apply to you:

- ✔ You must seek to profit from daily market movements in the prices of securities, not from dividends, interest, or capital appreciation.

- ✔ Your activity must be *substantial*; the IRS code does not spell out what substantial means, but it probably means you're making at least 3,000 trades per year.

- ✔ You must carry on the activity with *continuity* and *regularity*. Day trading is more or less your full-time job, you've stuck with it for at least six months already, and you plan to keep trading into the next year.

If you trade part-time, have other employment, or are new to the day trading game, the IRS probably won't let you define yourself as a trader. Don't care what an IRS agent calls you, as long she doesn't call you for an audit? Well, understanding the difference between *trader* and *investor* in IRS lingo is important to avoid that audit.

Those who qualify as traders enjoy deductions that regular investors don't.

You might qualify as a trader for some of your activities and as an investor for others. If this looks to be the case, you need to keep detailed records to separate your trades, and you should use different brokerage accounts to make the difference clear from the day you open the position.

In political economics, taxation serves two purposes. The first is to raise money for the government. The second is to encourage people to do things that the elected officials who amend the tax code want them to do. Much of the investing tax code is intended to promote the formation and growth of businesses. Short-term day trading doesn't do that, so the tax law doesn't offer short-term investors the same benefits that it gives to long-term investors and business owners.

Hiring a Tax Adviser

You don't have to hire someone to do your taxes, but you probably should. Day trading generates a lot of separate transactions to track, and the tax laws are tricky. Mistakes can end up costing you your entire trading profit.

Do yourself a favor and find yourself a tax expert. You can talk to other traders, get references from the attorneys and accountants you work with now, or even do Internet searches to find people who understand both IRS regulations and the unique needs of people who frequently buy and sell securities, whether or not the IRS calls them traders.

The many flavors of tax experts

Okay, you're waiting for me to say there's only one flavor, and it's vanilla, right? Wrong. Tax experts fall into several different categories, and knowing which is which can help you determine who is best for you.

Certified public accountants

A *certified public accountant* has studied accounting in college and passed exams that tested her knowledge of a wide range of accounting subjects. Because much of accounting involves income tax preparation, many CPAs specialize in this. CPAs generally have the best combined knowledge of tax laws and tax preparation techniques — but not all of them specialize in or even understand day trading.

Enrolled agents

Enrolled agents specialize in tax preparation. They receive registration from the IRS after passing a two-day, eight-hour exam covering only tax topics. That's what they know best. They may not be so good at helping you with other accounting needs, such as preparing payroll for your office assistants.

Tax attorneys

Tax attorneys usually work with CPAs; they are called in to study the legality of proposed strategies or represent a client in tax litigation. They aren't appropriate for most traders, but there may be situations that call for one.

Storefronts and volunteers: probably not a good idea

Every winter, vacant buildings are turned into tax preparation centers, and the IRS promotes its cadre of volunteers who help people with their taxes. These services can be a boon to the average person who lacks the time or patience to deal with the tax forms. But if you are trader, you're going to run into complex problems that most of these services are not prepared to handle.

Only CPAs, enrolled agents, and tax attorneys are allowed to represent clients before the IRS in audits, collections, or appeals. Other paid preparers can represent clients in an audit, but they can't handle more complex matters.

Questions to ask a prospective adviser

After you identify a few prospective candidates to prepare your taxes, talk to them and ask them questions about their experience. You want someone who understands things such as the *wash-sale rule* (which can limit the deductibility of your losses and is covered in more detail below) and the *mark-to-market election* (which can allow you to deduct more losses and is also covered in more detail in this chapter) and who can help you determine what you owe in taxes and not one penny more.

You'll feel more comfortable with your tax preparer if *you* have an understanding of the issues at stake. Even if you are hiring someone — and you should — keep reading this chapter and check the Appendix for more in-depth references on taxes and trading.

Here some things you should ask a potential tax preparer:

- ✔ What investors and traders have you worked with? For how long?
- ✔ Have you worked with traders or investors in my state? Can you prepare my state return?
- ✔ Have you helped traders make the mark-to-market election?
- ✔ What is your experience with the wash-sale rule? How will my trading style be affected by it?
- ✔ Who will be preparing my return? How involved will you be?
- ✔ Do you offer tax analysis of trading strategies?
- ✔ What's your audit record? Why have your clients been audited? What happened on the audit?
- ✔ What are your fees?

It is illegal for tax preparers to base their fees on the size of your tax refund, and it is illegal for them to guarantee you a refund.

You still want to do it yourself?

It's possible for traders to do their own taxes. If you are comfortable with tax forms, if you are only day trading a little bit, and if I haven't deterred you yet, you might be able to do this yourself. You need a few things: the proper IRS forms and tax preparation software that can handle investment income.

Everything you want to know about taxes is at www.irs.gov

The IRS Web site, www.irs.gov, is a treasure trove of tax information. All the regulations, publications, forms, and explanations are there, and some of it is even in plain English. It's so vast and detailed that you will probably be overwhelmed; I'm not sure there is any page in any IRS publication that does not mention dividends received under the State of Alaska Permanent Fund.

Curious to know about this State of Alaska Permanent Fund? It's an annual payment made to all residents of Alaska every year, based on the profits of oil pumped in that state. To put this into context, Alaska had 663,661 residents in 2005, according to the U.S. Census Bureau. I think there are two pages of IRS publications mentioning the fund for every person who gets a check from it.

The primary publication that covers the tax implications of trading and other investing activities is Publication 550, *Investment Income and Expenses*. It's available at www.irs.gov/publications/p550/.

Tax preparation software

Those who do their own taxes know that tax prep software is a godsend, and it's even more valuable for those do-it-yourselfers who trade a lot. The software fills out the forms, automatically adds and subtracts, and even catches typographical errors. In many cases, it can download data straight from your brokerage account, making data entry really simple.

Most of the big brands, such as TaxCut and TurboTax, publish several editions each year — not all of which are set up to import and manage lots of trading data. Among those that have services for investors are TurboTax Premier Investments (www.turbotax.com), TaxCut Premium (www.taxcut.com), and CompleteTax (www.completetax.com).

What Is Income, Anyway?

Income seems like a straightforward concept, but not much about taxation is straightforward. To the IRS, income falls into different categories, with different tax rates, different allowed deductions, and different forms to fill out. In this section I cover income definitions you'll run into as a day trader.

Earned income

Earned income includes wages, salaries, bonuses, and tips. It's money that you make on the job. But even if day trading is your only occupation, your earnings are not considered to be earned income. This means that day traders, whether classified for tax purposes as investors or traders, don't have to pay the self-employment tax on their trading income. Isn't that great?

Well, maybe, maybe not. The self-employment tax, the bane of many an independent business person, is a contribution to the Social Security fund. (Employees pay half of the contribution, and the employer pays the other half. The self-employed have to pay the whole thing.)

The problem is that if you don't have earned income, you are not paying into Social Security. If you are not paying into Social Security, you might not be eligible to retirement benefits. To collect benefits, you have to have paid in 40 credits, and you can earn a maximum of four credits per year. Most employees do this easily, but if you have taken time off work or have a long history of work as an independent investor, you may not have paid enough in.

Any benefits you do collect are based on the 35 years of highest earned income over your work history. Your years of independent trading show up as years with zero earned income, and that might hurt your ultimate benefit.

The Social Security Administration has a handy online calculator, www.social security.gov/planners/calculators.htm, which can help you determine whether day trading makes sense for you right now, given the possible effect on your Social Security benefits.

Investment income

Investment income is your total income from property held for investment before any deductions. This includes interest, dividends, annuities, and royalties. It does not include net capital gains, unless you choose to include them. Do you want to include them? Well, read the next section.

Other than net capital gains, which you might or might not decided to include, most day traders have very little investment income for tax purposes.

Capital gains and losses

A *capital gain* is the profit you make when you buy low and sell high, and that's the aim of day trading. The opposite of a capital gain is a *capital loss*, which happens when you sell an asset for less than you paid for it. Investors can offset some of their capital gains with some of their capital losses to reduce their tax burden.

Those who trade frequently will have many capital gains and losses, though, and they may very well run afoul of complicated IRS rules about capital gains taxation. Day traders get tripped up by capital gain and loss problems all the time. When designing your trading strategy, think long and hard about how much pain taxes might cause.

The financial world is filled with horror stories of people who thought they found a clever angle on making big profits, only to discover at tax time that their tax liability was greater than their profit. In the real world, taxes matter.

Capital gains come in two flavors: short term and long term. You're charged a low rate on long-term capital gains, which right now is defined as the gain on assets held for more than one year. How low? It's 15 percent right now.

Short-term capital gains, which are those made on any asset held for one year or less, are taxed at the ordinary income rate, probably 28 percent or more.

Covering all your basis

Capital gains and losses are calculated using a security's *basis*, which may or may not be the same as the price that you paid for it or sold it at. Some expenses, such as commissions or disallowed wash-sale losses (both of which are discussed later in this chapter), are added to the cost of the security, and that can reduce the amount of your taxable gain or increase the amount of your deductible loss.

For example, if you bought 100 shares of stock at $50 per share and a $0.03 per share commission, your basis would be $5,003 — the $5,000 you paid for the stock and the $3.00 you paid in commission.

The wash-sale problem

Let's say you love LMNO Company, but the price of the shares is down from what it was when you purchased them. You'd like to get that loss on your taxes, so you sell the stock, and then you buy it back at the lower price. You get your tax deduction and still keep the stock. How excellent is that?

It's too excellent to be true. The IRS does not count the loss. This trick is called a *wash sale*. The wash-sale rule was designed to keep long-term investors from playing cute with their taxes, but it has the effect of creating a ruinous tax situation for naïve day traders.

Under the wash-sale rule, you cannot deduct a loss if you have both a gain and a loss in the same security within a 61-day period. (That's calendar days, not trading days, so weekends and holidays count.) However, you *can* add the disallowed loss to the basis of your security.

Here's an example to show you what I mean. On Tuesday, you bought 100 shares of LMNO at $34.60. LMNO announced terrible earnings, and the stock promptly dropped to $29.32, and you sold all 100 shares for a loss of $528. Later in the afternoon, you noticed that the stock had bottomed and looked like it might trend up, so you bought another 100 shares at $28.75 and resold them an hour later at $29.25, closing out your position for the day. The second trade had a profit of $50. You had a net loss of $478 (the $528 loss plus the $50 profit), but the IRS will disallow the $528 loss and let you show only a profit of $50. However, the IRS will let you add the $528 loss to the basis of your replacement shares, meaning that instead of spending $2,875 (100 shares times $28.75), for tax purposes, you spent $3,403 ($2,875 plus $528), which means that the second trade caused you to lose the $478 that you added back. On a net basis, you get to record your loss. The basis addition lets you work off your wash-sale losses, eventually, assuming that you keep careful records and have more winning trades than losing ones in any one security.

To make the calculations easier, several different tax software packages can download trade data from your brokerage account to keep track of your tax situation. One to check out is TradeLog, `www.armencomp.com/tradelog/`. Even if you hire someone to do your taxes, tracking your potential liabilities as you trade can help you avoid costly mistakes.

The wash-sale rule applies to substantially similar securities. LMNO stock and LMNO options are considered to be substantially similar, so you can't get around the rule by varying securities on the same underlying asset. LMNO shares and shares of its closest competitor, PQRS, would probably not be considered to be substantially similar, so you can trade within a given industry to help avoid wash-sale problems.

At an extreme, the wash-sale rule can mean that traders who are in and out of the same securities over and over may be taxed on all their winning trades, without being able to subtract their losing trades for tax purposes. If your winning trades gained $300,000, and your losing trades cost you $200,000, you cleared $100,000 — but the IRS might tax you on the $300,000. Ouch!

There are ways around the wash-sale rule. The obvious solution is to qualify as a trader for IRS purposes and then take the mark-to-market accounting election (I cover the benefits of that later in this chapter). Other methods for avoiding the wash-sale rule include trading a given security only once every 60 calendar days and doing all your trading within a qualified retirement account such as an IRA (also discussed later in this chapter). Some securities are handled differently. Futures contracts are considered to generate investment income and losses, not capital gains. Profits on options contracts are 60 percent long-term capital gains and 40 percent short-term capital gains, which reduces the wash-sale rule effect. Some traders prefer to work with options and futures simply because it makes tax time easier.

If you have any more clever ideas, be sure to run them through an experienced tax pro first.

Tracking Your Investment Expenses

Day traders have expenses. They buy computer equipment, subscribe to research services, pay trading commissions, and hire accountants to prepare their taxes. It adds up, and the tax code recognizes that. That's why day traders can deduct many of their costs from their income taxes. In this section, I go through some of what you can deduct.

You'll make your life much easier if you keep track of your expenses as you incur them. You can do this in a notebook, in a spreadsheet, or through personal finance software such as Quicken or Microsoft Money.

Qualified and deductible expenses

You can deduct investment expenses as miscellaneous itemized deductions on Schedule A of Form 1040 as long as they are considered to be ordinary, necessary, and used to produce or collect income, manage property held for producing income, and directly related to the taxable income produced.

Clerical, legal, and accounting fees

You might use the services of a lawyer to help you get set up, and you will almost definitely want to use an accountant who understands investment expenses to help you evaluate your trading strategy and prepare your state and federal income tax returns each year. There's good news here: You can deduct attorney and accounting fees related to your investment income. If your trading operation gets big enough that you hire clerical help to keep track of all those trade confirmations, you can deduct that cost, too.

Office expenses

If you do your day trading from an outside office, you can deduct the rent and related expenses. You can deduct the expenses of a home office, too, as long as you use it regularly and exclusively for business. If your trading room is also the guest room, it doesn't count.

Whether or not you deduct your office, you can deduct certain office expenses for equipment and supplies used in your business. You can usually write off roughly $100,000 in computers, desks, chairs, and the like if you use them for trading more than half of the time. (The limits change every year.)

To get the deduction, you have to spend the money first, and your expenses don't reduce your taxes dollar-for-dollar. If you are in the 28-percent tax bracket, then each dollar you spend on qualified expenses reduces your taxes by $0.28. In other words, don't go crazy at the office supply store just because you get a tax deduction. It may be helpful to think of deductible expenses as discounts, because in the end that's more or less what they are.

Investment counsel and advice

The IRS allows you to deduct fees paid for counsel and advice about investments that produce taxable income. This includes books, magazines, newspapers, and research services that help you refine your trading strategy. It also includes anything you might pay for investment advisory services, such as trade coaching or analysis.

Safe deposit box rent

Have a safety box down at the bank? You can deduct the rent on it if you store any investment-related documents. If you also keep jewelry that you inherited and never wear or other personal items in the same box, you can only deduct part of the rent.

Investment interest

If you borrow money as part of your strategy, and most day traders do, you can deduct the interest paid on those loans as long as it is not from a home mortgage (because that interest is already deductible) and as long as you are not subject to other limitations. There's always a catch, isn't there? In most cases, this is *margin interest* (see Chapter 8 for more information on margin), and for most day traders, it is relatively small because few day traders borrow money for more than a few hours at a time.

If you borrow money against your account for anything other than investing or trading, you can't deduct the interest. And yes, most brokerage firms let you take out margin for your own general spending, as a way to let you stay in the market and still get cash.

State income taxes

If you itemize your deductions, you can deduct, as taxes, state income taxes on interest income that is exempt from federal income tax. But you cannot deduct, as either taxes or investment expenses, state income taxes on other exempt income. In most cases, exempt income is related to government bond transactions, and few day traders will work in those markets.

The 50 states all have different rules about taxation of investment income. Some states with little or no income tax handle investments differently. Because there are so many different issues, state taxation is beyond the scope of this book. Check with your state revenue department and a state-savvy tax expert to see what you need to know where you live.

What you can't deduct

While day trading, you will probably incur expenses that can't be deducted from your taxes. It's disappointing, but at least if you know what they are upfront, you can plan accordingly.

What? I can't deduct commissions?

Every time you make a trade, you have to pay a commission to your broker. It may be small, just a few cents per share or a few dollars per trade, but you have to pay it. And you can't deduct that cost.

Before you splutter in outrage, read this: You can't deduct it, but you *can* add it to cost and subtract it from the proceeds of your trade.

Here's an example: You buy 100 shares of Microsoft at $29.40 per share, paying a $6.00 commission on the trade. Your total cost for IRS purposes is ($29.40 × 100) + $6.00, which equals $2,946. Later in the day, you sell all 100 shares for $29.50 per share at a $6.00 commission, so your total proceeds for the deal are ($29.50 × 100) – $6.00, or $2,950. Your total profit for tax purposes is $2,950 – $2946, or $4.00.

Including the commission in the basis of your trade works like a deduction in terms of the amount of tax you pay, but it's better for you that it's not a deduction because it's not subject to the limitations that affect the deductibility of other expenses.

If your state charges *transfer taxes* on securities, they are handled the same way as commissions.

Attending stockholders' meetings

Companies hold annual meetings for their shareholders each year, usually at or near the company headquarters. Sometimes they are deathly dull — the board of directors sits around a conference room in a law office and goes through a boilerplate agenda with nothing to discuss. Others are extravaganzas where the company shows off new products, showcases major accomplishments, and takes questions from anyone in attendance. And a few involve contentious issues that can lead to protests and fighting, which is entertaining to watch if you aren't directly affected. (You can see a fun example in Michael Moore's 1989 documentary *Roger and Me*, in which Moore tries to talk to Roger Smith, then the Chairman of General Motors, at the company's annual meeting.)

For long-term investors, these meetings can offer valuable insights on a company's prospects. Day traders probably wouldn't find them very useful, and it's just as well, because the IRS won't let anyone deduct the costs of transportation, hotel stays, meals, and other expenses that might be involved in attending a stockholders' meeting.

Attending investment seminars

The financial services industry offers all kinds of conventions, cruises, and seminars for day traders. You could spend your days attending training seminars instead of actually trading, if you were so inclined. You're welcome to go to these, and in many cases, you should. You might learn things that would help you trade more effectively. However, you can't deduct the costs. Bummer.

There's some gray area here. You can't deduct the costs of attending seminars, but you can deduct the costs of investment counsel and advisory services. Some seminars might qualify as investment advice. This is why you need an experienced tax adviser to help you out.

Did you notice that two of the nondeductible expense categories have the potential to involve travel? The IRS does not want people buying ten shares of Hawaiian Electric Industries stock and then trying to write off a trip to the company's annual meeting in Honolulu, nor do they consider cruises that happen to include a talk by the author of a book on investing to be bona fide investment counsel. They see these activities as vacations, and vacations are not tax deductible.

(Of course, if an author of an investment book happened to be on such a cruise, that might be a deductible cost for book promotion. Most likely. Um, not like I know any authors of investment books who might have looked into this or anything.)

Naturally, there are limitations!

You didn't think the IRS would let you take all your deductions automatically, did you? Of course not. Your deductions might be limited, especially if you do not meet the IRS definition of *trader*.

At-risk rules

The IRS says that your loss is limited by the amount of property you contribute to your investing activities, including money you borrow. In most cases, day trading losses meet the risk definitions, but if you pursue a naked trading strategy that causes you to lose more than your initial investment, you might fall into this category.

Passive activity losses and credits

The IRS defines a *passive* activity as an investment where the investor does not play an active role but does make money. You can deduct passive activity losses only up to the amount of your passive activity income, and you can use credits from passive activity losses only against tax on the income from passive activities. Day trading is generally considered to be active, because you are materially participating, but if you are generating passive losses from other investment activities, you probably won't be able to use them to offset your day trading gains.

Interest expense limitations

The IRS allows you to deduct investment interest up to the amount of your net investment income, which is your investment income less all your allowable deductible expenses except for interest. If you lost money trading, you can't use the interest deduction to reduce your taxes. What you can do, though, is carry the undeducted investment interest into next year, and use it to reduce your taxes on those profits.

You also can't deduct interest expenses on straddles. A *straddle* is an options strategy that involves buying both a put option and a call option on the same stock with the same strike price and expiration date. In most cases, the non-deductible interest and related carrying charges are added to the basis of the straddle (just as commissions are — see earlier in this chapter).

Two-percent limit

If you do not qualify as a trader to the IRS, then you can only deduct investment expenses and other miscellaneous itemized deductions if they add up to more than 2 percent of your adjusted gross income.

Top Secret Tax Information for IRS-Qualified Traders Only

If you meet the IRS qualifications for being a trader, covered earlier, then you can avoid some of the tax headaches faced by people who trade but are not considered by the taxman to be traders. If you trade as your job, make thousands of trades a year, and rarely hold any position for more than a day, then you can fill out something called Form 3115, *Application for Change in Accounting Method*, and tell the IRS that you want to use the *mark-to-market election* in calculating your capital gains and losses. This is not an easy form to fill out, so you should have a professional do it for you.

The form has to be submitted with your prior year's tax return. If you want to use mark-to-market accounting in 2008, for example, you need to submit Form 3115 when you send in your 2007 tax return in April of 2008.

Notice that you can't use the election in your first year of trading. You first have to prove that you are a trader before you are allowed to get the tax benefits that go with the title. Consider it an apprenticeship.

If you qualify for trader status, you receive two benefits:

- Mark-to-market accounting
- Increased expense deductions

Mark-to-market accounting

Under mark-to-market accounting, you no longer have to track capital gains. Instead, you pretend to sell your portfolio at the end of the year and then pretend to repurchase everything at the beginning of the new year so that all capital gains fall into income.

Because day traders usually close all their positions at the end of the day anyway, mark-to-market accounting may not seem like a big deal, but it is: In effect, converting all capital gains to income means that your trades are no longer subject to the wash-sale rule. For most day traders, this means lower taxes and fewer paperwork hassles.

If you use mark-to-market accounting, you can no longer get the 15-percent rate on any long-term capital gains from your trading activities. Unless a day trader is working with listed options, which are considered to show profits that are 60-percent long-term capital gains and 40-percent short-term capital gains, there may not be any long-term capital gains from trading activities.

Greater deductibility of business expenses

In general, the IRS only allows investors to deduct business expenses if they exceed 2 percent of adjusted gross income. However, anyone who gets to join the charmed circle of IRS-qualified traders gets to deduct 100 percent of expenses, regardless of their adjusted gross income. They get to deduct all their investment interest, too.

One caveat, though — the IRS assumes that people are in the business of trading because they are making money at it. If you lose money for three out of five years, even if it's because your expenses exceeded your investment profits, the IRS will probably kick you out of the club.

Reporting Your Investment Expenses

Many of the differences in income and expenses discussed already in this chapter make more sense when you think about how they are reported on your income tax return. In this section, I give you the highlights of some of the most exciting forms for the modern day trader. Note that they are different for those who qualify as traders than for everyone else who day trades.

Forms for qualified traders

If you make the mark-to-market election on Form 3115, you're considered to be in the business of trading. Business expenses for individual tax filers are put on Schedule C of Form 1040, *Profit or Loss from Business*. Then your trading gains and losses are recorded on Part II of Form 4797. If you have any securities at the end of the year in your trading account, pretend that they were sold on the last business day of the year at current fair market value and then immediately reacquired.

Forms for everyone else

Day traders who are not considered traders by the IRS should itemize business deductions and investment interest expenses on Schedule A of Form 1040. You should attach Form 4952 if you used that to figure your investment interest expense. Capital gains and losses from your trading are reported on Schedule D of Form 1040, subject to all the limits on losses.

Paying Taxes All Year

If you have been an employee for years and years, all of your tax liabilities may have been covered by your payroll tax deductions. The IRS likes it best that way, because then it gets money all year 'round. Let's face it — the easier it is to pay, the more likely you are to do it.

People who are self-employed or who have significant earnings from investments and day trading may generate more income than can be covered from payroll withholding. What you need to do is estimate your tax liability four times a year and then write a check for those amounts. (Otherwise, you could face a penalty at tax time.) Estimated taxes are paid on Form 1040 ES and are due on April 15, June 15, September 15, and January 15.

Estimated taxes are not due on a nice, even, quarterly schedule. No, it's a payment schedule that only a bureaucrat could love.

Using Self-Directed Individual Retirement Accounts

Much of the tax hassle associated with day trading is eliminated if you trade through a self-directed *Individual Retirement Arrangement,* or IRA. Most brokerage firms can set them up for you and handle the necessary paperwork. Although individuals can contribute only $4,000 per year ($5,000 for people older than 50), the money can be substantial for those who have been contributing for a long time. Also, you can roll over money from an employer's retirement plan, such as a 401(k), into an IRA after you leave.

You don't have to pay taxes in an IRA until you retire, and then withdrawals are generally treated as ordinary income. This makes them a great vehicle for day traders: You can post big gains, count all your losses, and avoid wash-sale rules for trading within your IRA. It's a sweet way to let your profits accumulate and compound for years. Of course, there's a catch: You can't sell short, you can't use all options strategies, and your brokerage firm may not want to clear funds through the IRA.

Keep in mind, though, that you can't withdraw money from an IRA account until you turn 59½. If you take money out earlier, you'll pay a 10-percent tax penalty, and that offsets a lot of the advantages. If you'll need income from your trading activities to cover your living expenses before then, an IRA is probably not the best way to set up your day trading account.

Chapter 11

But Did You Make Money? Evaluating Performance

A ny one trade involves a lot of variables: price bought, price sold, commissions charged, volume traded, and amount of leverage used. And each of these affects your overall performance. In the heat of a trading day, it can be hard to juggle all these factors and determine just how well you did or did not do.

Performance calculation starts before you trade. You want to test your strategies and see if they work for you, which requires backtesting and paper trading. You want to keep track of your trades in real time with the help of a trading diary. And then, on a periodic basis (at least monthly), you should review your progress to see how much money you are making and whether you need to change your strategy.

Before You Trade: Testing Your System

Performance measurement starts before the trading does. That's because you want to figure out how you will trade before you start betting real money. Chapter 3 describes some of the different securities that can be traded on a daily basis, whereas Chapters 12–15 cover some of the strategies that day traders use. After you figure out the combinations of securities and strategies you want to use, you'll want to see whether they would have made you money in the past. Then you should try them out to see if they still work now.

The happy news? All this is possible without risking a dime, except of course for the money you might spend on backtesting and simulation software. You knew there had to be a catch, right? Consider it an investment in the success of your business.

Backtesting

In *backtesting*, a trader specifies the strategy that he or she would use and then runs it through a database of historic securities prices to see whether the strategy would have made money. The test includes assumptions about commissions, leverage, and position size. The results give information on returns, volatility, and win-loss ratios that can be used to refine a trading strategy and implement it well.

Starting with a hypothesis

What trades do you want to do? After you figure out what and how to trade, you can start setting forth what your strategy will be. Will you look for high-momentum, small-cap stocks? Seek out price changes related to news events in agricultural commodities? Ride large-cap stocks within their ranges? Arbitrage stock index futures and their options?

Once you have done your research, you can lay out your strategy as a hypothesis. It might be something like this: "High-momentum, small-cap stocks tend to close up for the day, so you can buy them in the morning and make money selling them in the afternoon." Or: "News events take at least half an hour to affect pork belly prices, so you can buy or sell on the news and make a profit." With this statement, you can move on to the test to see if it holds.

One of the most valuable parts about backtesting is that you have to be very specific about what your trading rule is. Computers cannot understand vague instructions, and if you find that your trading strategy is too complicated to write out and set into a backtesting program, it's probably too complicated for you to follow.

Running the test

Let's say you start with something simple: Maybe you have reason to think that pharmaceutical companies that are moving down in price on decreasing volume will turn and close up for the day. The first thing you do is enter that into the software: the industry group and the buy pattern that you're looking for. The results will show whether your hunch is correct, and how often and for what time periods.

If you like what you see, you can add more variables. What happens if you add *leverage* (use borrowed money) in your trades? That increases your risk of loss, but it also increases your potential return. How does that affect your trade? Suppose you increase the size of your trades. Would that help you make more money or less? By playing around with the system, you can get a good sense of the best way to make money with your trade ideas. You can also get a sense of when your rule won't work, to help you avoid problems.

Most backtesting software allows for optimization, which means that it can come up with the leverage, position, holding period, and other parameters that will generate the best risk-adjusted return. You can then compare this to your trading style and your capital position to see if it works.

Backtesting is subject to something that traders call *over-optimization*, mathematicians call *curve-fitting*, and analysts call *data mining*. This means that the person performing the test looks at a past time where the market performed well, then identifies all the variables and specifications that generated that performance. Although it sounds great, what often happens is that the test generates a model that includes unnecessary variables and that makes no logical sense in practice. If you find a strategy that works when the stock closes up one day, down two days, then up a third day, followed by four down days when it hits an intra-day high, you probably haven't made an amazing discovery — you've just fit the curve.

People with iPods and MP3 players have elaborate ideas of how the machines' "random shuffle" feature works. Ask, and they'll give you their own elaborate theory for how certain types of songs show up more often than others, how songs with similar titles seem to be played together, and other patterns that they are sure must be there. Why? Because human beings have evolved to see patterns, even when none is there. It's the same with the market. It's entirely possible that although the results of your test look great, but they only show a random event that happened to work out once. That's why you need to keep testing, even after you start trading.

Comparing the results with market cycles

The markets change every day in response to new regulations, interest rate fluctuations, economic conditions, nasty world events, and run-of-the-mill news events. (It's like the joke about weather: If you don't like it now, wait a minute, and it will change.) Different securities and strategies do better in some market climates than in others.

When you are backtesting, it's important to do it over enough time so that you can see how your strategy would work over different market conditions. Here are some things to check:

- How did the strategy do in periods of inflation? Economic growth? High interest rates? Low interest rates?

- What was happening in the markets during the time that the strategy worked best? What was happening when it worked worst? How likely is either of those to happen again?

✔ How does market volatility affect the strategy? Is the security more volatile than the market, less volatile, or does it seem to be removed from the market?

✔ Have there been major changes in the industry over the period of the test? Does this mean that past performance still applies?

✔ Have there been changes in the way that the security trades? For example, the bulk of trading in most commodities used to take place in open-outcry trading pits. Now, it's mostly electronic. Does that change affect your test results?

In the Capital Assets Pricing Model, which is a key part of academic finance theory, the market risk is known as *beta*. The value that a portfolio manager adds to investment performance is known as *alpha*. In the long run, conventional finance theory says that the return on a diversified portfolio comes from beta; alpha does not exist. In the short run, where day traders play, this relationship might not be so strong.

Past performance is not indicative of future results. A strategy may test perfectly, but that doesn't mean it will continue to work. Backtesting is an important step to successful day trading, but it is only one step.

Simulation trading

With a backtested strategy in hand, you might be tempted to start putting real money on the line. Don't, just yet. Start with what is known variously as *ghost trading*, *paper trading*, and *simulation trading*. Sit down in front of your computer screen and start watching the price quotes. When you see your ideal entry point, write it down. When you see your exit point, write it down. Do exactly what you plan to do with real money, just don't use the money. Then, figure out what your performance would have been.

If your strategy does not generate a lot of trades, you can probably keep track with a pen and paper and then enter the data into a spreadsheet to calculate the effects of commissions and leverage and to analyze the performance on both a percentage and a win-loss basis. For more complex strategies that involve a large number of trades on a large number of securities, you might want to use simulation software. These are trading simulation software packages that mimic trading software (and are usually added features to trading software packages; see Chapters 6 and 7 for more information). They let you enter the size of your order, let you use leverage, and tell you whether your trade can be executed given current market conditions.

Markets are affected by supply and demand, and your trade can affect that. And that's the biggest drawback of simulation trading: It's difficult to take the market effects of your trade into account in any reliable way.

The results of your trading simulation can help you refine your trading strategy further. Does it work in current market conditions? Are you able to identify entry and exit points? Can you make enough trades to make money to make your day trading efforts worth while? Do you want to refine your strategy some more, or are you ready to go with it?

It may take a long time to find a suitable strategy. Some traders report spending months finding a strategy they felt comfortable using. Day trading is a business like any other. Consider this part of the market research and education process that you need to go through, just as you would have to spend time doing research before opening a store or training for a new career. Stay patient. It's better to do good simulation for months than to lose thousands of real dollars in hours.

Backtesting and simulation software

Several vendors have risen to meet the challenge of backtesting. The list in this section is by no means exhaustive, nor is it an endorsement of their services. It's just a good place for you to start your research.

If you are just getting started with trading, you may want to work with a cheaper package just to see how it works. If you already have an account with a brokerage firm, check to see if backtesting and simulation are among the services offered. You can always move up as your needs change or if you start pursing exotic strategies with unusual securities.

AmiBroker

AmiBroker (www.amibroker.com) offers a robust backtesting service at a relatively low price. This makes it a popular choice with people who are getting started in day trading and who don't have more expensive services. It also allows users to make sophisticated technical charts that they can use to monitor the markets. One drawback is that you might have to pay extra for the market price quote data, depending on what securities and time periods you want to test.

Cybertrader

Cybertrader (www.cybertrader.com) is Charles Schwab's product for active traders. Its Strategy Tester feature lets you test your trading idea. Then you can set it into a Strategy Ticker that follows your strategy while the market is open, so that you can see how it performs in real time. This isn't quite the same as paper trading, as it isn't testing how well you would pull the trigger, although presumably you would buy or sell whenever your system told you to — right?

Tradecision

Tradecision's (www.tradecision.com) trade analysis software package is a little pricier than most retail trading alternatives, but it offers more advanced capabilities, including an analysis of the strengths and weaknesses of different trading rules. It can incorporate advanced money management techniques and artificial intelligence to develop more predictions about performance in different market conditions. The system may be overkill for most new day traders, but it could come in handy for some.

TradeStation

TradeStation (www.tradestation.com) is an online broker that specializes in services for day traders. Its strategy testing service lets you specify different trading parameters and then it shows you where these trades would have taken place in the past using price charts. That way, you can see what would have happened, which is helpful if you are good at technical analysis. It also generates a report of the strategy, showing dollar, percentage, and win-loss performance over different time periods. It does not have a trade simulation feature.

 If you have the programming expertise, or if your strategy is not well represented in current backtesting programs, you might want to create your own system. Many software-savvy day traders write programs using Excel's Visual Basic functions, allowing them to create custom tests that they then run against price databases.

During the Day: Tracking Your Trades

Once you put your strategy to work during the trading day, it's easy to let the energy and emotion overtake you. You get sloppy and you stop keeping track of what's happening. And that's not good. Day trading is not a video game, it's a job. Keeping careful records helps you identify how well you follow your strategy and helps you identify ways to refine it. It can also show you how successful your trading is, and it makes your life a lot easier when it's time to do your taxes. (You can see Chapter 10 for more information on what the friendly folks at the IRS expect from traders, besides a cut of their profits.)

Setting up your spreadsheet

The easiest way to get started is with a spreadsheet software program such as Microsoft Excel. Set up columns for the asset being purchased, the time of the trade, the price, the quantity purchased, and the commission. Then set up similar columns to show what happens when the position is closed out. Finally, calculate your performance based on the change in the security's price and the dollars and percentage return on your trade. Figure 11-1 gives you an example.

Trade Tracker
2/1/07

POSITIONS Symbol	Description	Purchase Date	Purchase Time	Purchase Price	Lot Attempted	Lot Filled	Comm.	Total Cost	Sale Time	Sale Price	Sale Quantity	Comm.	Total Proceeds	Gain/Loss in Points	Gain/Loss in Dollars	Gain/Loss in Percent
INTC	Intel	2/1/07	9:31	20.98	1000	1,000	6.00	(20,986.00)	9:52	21.10	1000	6.00	21,094.00	12	108.00	0.51%
NVDA	Nvidia	2/1/07	9:33	30.38	1000	1,000	6.00	(30,374.00)	9:58	30.87	1000	6.00	30,864.00	49	490.00	1.61%
AKAM	Akamai	2/1/07	9:46	57.44	500	500	3.00	(28,717.00)	10:36	56.60	500	3.00	28,297.00	-84	(420.00)	-1.46%
INTC	Intel	2/1/07	10:18	21.08	1000	1,000	6.00	(21,074.00)	10:40	20.95	1000	6.00	20,944.00	-13	(130.00)	-0.62%
AKAM	Akamai	2/1/07	11:08	55.09	500	200	1.20	(11,016.80)	12:08	55.39	200	1.20	11,076.80	30	60.00	0.54%
NVDA	Nvidia	2/1/07	11:08	30.38	1000	1,000	6.00	(30,374.00)	11:28	30.31	1000	6.00	30,304.00	-7	(70.00)	-0.23%
INTC	Intel	2/1/07	11:11	20.91	1000	1,000	6.00	(20,904.00)	11:45	21.03	1000	6.00	21,024.00	12	120.00	0.57%
NVDA	Nvidia	2/1/07	11:55	30.38	1000	1,000	6.00	(30,374.00)	12:15	30.72	1000	6.00	30,714.00	34	340.00	1.12%
INTC	Intel	2/1/07	12:23	20.93	1000	1,000	6.00	(20,924.00)	12:56	21.07	1000	6.00	21,064.00	14	140.00	0.67%
INTC	Intel	2/1/07	13:08	21.05	1000	1,000	6.00	(21,044.00)	13:52	21.04	1000	6.00	21,034.00	-1	(10.00)	-0.05%
AKAM	Akamai	2/1/07	13:22	55.43	500	500	3.00	(27,712.00)	13:41	55.48	500	3.00	27,737.00	5	25.00	0.09%
INTC	Intel	2/1/07	14:05	21.03	1000	1,000	6.00	(21,024.00)	14:26	21.09	1000	6.00	21,084.00	6	60.00	0.29%
NVDA	Nvidia	2/1/07	14:09	30.52	1000	1,000	6.00	(30,514.00)	15:09	30.54	1000	6.00	30,534.00	2	20.00	0.07%
INTC	Intel	2/1/07	15:05	21.10	1000	1,000	6.00	(21,094.00)	15:59	21.11	1000	6.00	21,104.00	1	10.00	0.05%

Starting Capital: $ 165,239.00
Day's Profit: $ 743.00
Percent Change: 0.45%
Ending Capital: $ 165,982.00
Ratio of winning to losing trades: 10 : 4
Hourly Wage: $ 92.88

Total commissions paid: $ 146.40

Figure 11-1: You can use this sample to make your own trade-tracking spreadsheet.

Some brokerage firms and trading platforms automatically store your trade data for analysis. You can then download the data into your own spreadsheet or work with it in your trading software. If you make too many trades to keep track of manually, then this feature will be especially important to you.

Profit and loss statement

If you look at the bottom of Figure 11-1, you'll see some quick summary statistics on how the day's trading went: trading profits net of commissions, trading profits as a percentage of trading capital, and the ratio of winning to losing transactions. This information should be transferred into another spreadsheet so that you can track your ongoing success.

Figure 11-2 shows an example of a profit and loss spreadsheet.

Calculate your hourly wage for each day that you trade. Simply take each day's profit and divide it by the number of hours that you worked. That number, more than any other, will help you see whether it makes sense for you to keep trading or if you'd be better off pursuing a different line of work.If you find that calculating the number daily is too stressful, try doing it monthly.

The trading diary

As part of your trading spreadsheet, or in addition to it, you should track the reasons for making every trade. Was it because of a signal from your system?

Because of a hunch? Because you saw an opportunity that was too good to pass up? Then you can keep track of how the trade worked out. Is your trading system giving off good signals? Are you following them? Are your hunches so good that maybe your system needs to be refined? Are you missing good trades because you are following your gut and not the data in front of you?

A *trading diary* gives you information to systematically assess your trading. Start by writing down why you are making a particular trade and do it when you make the trade. Trust me, if you wait until later, you'll forget and you'll change your logic to suit your needs. You can enter the information in a spreadsheet, jot something quick on a piece of scratch paper, or keep a notebook dedicated to your trading. It doesn't have to be fancy, as long as you take the time to make the notes so that you can refer back to it.

Some traders create a form, make copies of it, and keep a stack of them on hand so that they can fill them out easily during the day. They even create predetermined indicators that match their strategies and that they can check off or circle. At the end of the day, they collect their diary sheets into a three-ring binder in order to refer back to the data when it's time to evaluate their trading strategy and their performance against it.

Profit and Loss

	Initial Capital	Net Profit (Loss)	Ending Capital	Percentage Change	Hourly Wage
1/3/07	$ 161,298	$ 134	$ 161,432	0.08%	$ 16.75
1/4/07	$ 161,432	$ (268)	$ 161,164	-0.17%	$ (33.50)
1/5/07	$ 161,164	$ 450	$ 161,614	0.28%	$ 56.25
1/8/07	$ 161,614	$ (183)	$ 161,431	-0.1 1%	$ (22.88)
1/9/07	$ 161,431	$ 192	$ 161,623	0.12%	$ 24.00
1/10/07	$ 161,623	$ 598	$ 162,221	0.37%	$ 74.75
1/11/07	$ 162,221	$ (168)	$ 162,053	-0.10%	$ (21.00)
1/12/07	$ 162,053	$ 987	$ 163,040	0.61%	$ 123.38
1/16/07	$ 163,040	$ (196)	$ 162,844	-0.12%	$ (24.50)
1/17/07	$ 162,844	$ 59	$ 162,903	0.04%	$ 7.38
1/18/07	$ 162,903	$ (273)	$ 162,630	-0.17%	$ (34.13)
1/19/07	$ 162,630	$ (124)	$ 162,506	-0.08%	$ (15.50)
1/22/07	$ 162,506	$ 689	$ 163,195	0.42%	$ 86.13
1/23/07	$ 163,195	$ (397)	$ 162,798	-0.24%	$ (49.63)
1/24/07	$ 162,798	$ 967	$ 163,765	0.59%	$ 120.88
1/25/07	$ 163,765	$ (387)	$ 163,378	-0.24%	$ (48.38)
1/26/07	$ 163,378	$ 469	$ 163,847	0.29%	$ 58.63
1/29/07	$ 163,847	$ 798	$ 164,645	0.49%	$ 99.75
1/30/07	$ 164,645	$ (129)	$ 164,516	-0.08%	$ (16.13)
1/31/07	$ 164,516	$ 723	$ 165,239	0.44%	$ 90.38
January:	$ 161,298	$ 3,941	$ 165,239	2.44%	$ 24.63
2/1/07	$ 165,239	$ 743	$ 165,982	0.45%	$ 92.88

Figure 11-2: A sample profit and loss spreadsheet.

Figure 11-3 offers an example of a trading diary. You can customize it for your own trading strategy, including those indicators that matter most to you.

The trading diary form in Figure 11-3 is just an example. If your trading style is so fast that you don't have time to fill it out, don't fret — come up with some kind of shorthand so that you can keep a running tally of trades made based on a signal from your system, trades based on your own hunches, and trades based on other interpretations of market conditions. Then match your notes against the trader confirmations from your broker to see how you did.

Trading Diary

Date: _____
Time: _____
Security Name: _____   **Symbol:** _____   **Market:** _____

Price entered: _____   **Long/short?**   long   short
Quantity: _____   **Leverage used?**   yes   no

Indicators:
Price trend is	rising	falling	rangebound
Volume is	rising	falling	steady
Sector is	rising	falling	rangebound
Market is	rising	falling	rangebound

Technical Pattern: _____

Price closed: _____
Quantity: _____
Time: _____

Indicators:
Price trend is	rising	falling	rangebound
Volume is	rising	falling	steady
Sector is	rising	falling	rangebound
Market is	rising	falling	rangebound

Technical Pattern: _____

I initiated this trade because (check one):
_____ The trading system signalled it
_____ I had a hunch (explain below)
_____ The market looked right, even though the signal didn't go of f (explain below)
_____ Other (explain below)

I closed out this trade because (check one):
_____ The trading system signalled it
_____ I needed to cut my losses
_____ I had a hunch (explain below)
_____ The market looked right, even though the signal didn't go of f (explain below)
_____ Other (explain below)

Explanation and lessons learned:

_____
_____
_____
_____
_____
_____

Figure 11-3:
A trading diary should be customized to your own preferences.

After You Trade: Calculating Overall Performance

Calculating performance seems easy: Simply use the balance at the end of the year and the balance at the start of the year to find the percentage change. But what if you added to your investment in the middle of the year? What if you took cash out in the middle of the year to buy a new computer? Quickly you're left with algebra unlike any you've seen since high school, but you need to solve it to see how you are doing.

In addition to the increase in your assets, you want to track your *volatility*, which is how much your gains and losses can fluctuate. It's an important measure of risk, especially if your trading strategy relies on leverage (see Chapter 14 for more information on that).

Types of return

The investment performance calculation starts by dividing returns into different categories: income, short-term capital gains, and long-term capital gains. Although almost all a day trader's gains will come from short-term capital gains, I go over the definitions of each so that you know the differences.

Income

When investors talk about *income returns*, they mean regular payments from their investments, usually in the form of dividends from stock or interest payments on bonds. As a day trader, you may earn income on the cash balance in your brokerage account, but probably not from your trading activities.

Capital gains

A *capital gain* is the price appreciation in an asset — a stock, a bond, a house, whatever it is that you're investing in. You buy it at one price, sell it at another, and the difference is a capital gain. (Unless, of course, you sell the asset for less than you paid, and then you have a capital loss.)

For tax purposes, capital gains are classified as either long-term or short-term. Under the current tax law, any capital gain on an asset held for less than one year is considered to be a short-term gain, and if the asset is owned for one year or more before it's sold, then it's considered to be a long-term capital gain. The difference isn't semantic — long-term capital gains are taxed at lower rates than short-term capital gains. You can read all about it Chapter 10.

Income in tax terms is different from income in financial terms. Much of what an investor would consider to be a capital gain, such as the short-term capital gains that day traders generate, the IRS considers to be income.

Calculating returns

Give someone with a numerical bent a list of numbers and a calculator, and she can some up with several different relationships between the numbers. Once the asset values for each time period have been determined, rates of return can be calculated. But how? And over how long a time period? The process gets a little more complicated.

Percentage change

The most common way to calculate investment returns is to use a time-weighted average. It's perfect for traders who start with one pool of money and do not add to it or take money out. This is also called the *Compound Average Rate of Return* (CAGR). If you are looking at only one month or one year, it's a simple percentage, as shown in Figure 11-4.

Figure 11-4: Calculating performance on a percentage basis.

$$\frac{EOY - BOY}{BOY}$$

EOY stands for *end of year asset value* and BOY is *beginning of year value*. The result is the percentage return for one year, and it's simple arithmetic.

Now, if you want to look at your return over a period of several years, you need to look at the *compound* return rather than the simple return for each year. The compound return shows you how your investment is growing. You are getting returns on top of returns, and that is a good thing. But the math gets a little complicated, because now you have to use the root function on your calculator. The equation looks like Figure 11-5.

EOP stands for *end of the total time period*, BOP stands for *beginning of the total time period*, and that N is the *number of years* that we're looking at.

Figure 11-5:
Here's the
equation for
compound
annual
growth rate.

$$\sqrt[N]{\frac{EOP - BOP}{BOP}}$$

The basic percentage rate of return is great; it's an accurate, intuitive measure of how much gain you're generating from your trading activities. As long as you don't take any money out of your trading account or put any money into it, you're set.

However, you may be putting money into your account. Maybe you have a salaried job and are day trading on the side, or maybe your spouse gives you a percentage of his income to add to your trading account. You might also be taking money out of your day trading account to cover your living expenses or to put into other investment opportunities. All that money flowing into and out of your account can really screw up your performance calculation. You need a way to calculate the performance of your trading system without considering the deposits and withdrawals to your trading account.

Here's an example: You start day trading on January 1 with $100,000 in your account. On May 1, your income tax refund from last year arrives, and you add $1,000 of the money to your account and start trading with it. On December 1, you take out $5,000 to buy holiday presents. At the end of the year, your account is worth $115,000. How did you do?

As a day trader, you have a few methods at your disposal for calculating your performance when you make withdrawals and deposits:

- ✔ **The Modified Dietz method** loses a little accuracy but makes up for it with simplicity.

- ✔ **The time-weighted rate of return** isolates investment and trading performance from the rest of the account.

- ✔ **The dollar-weighted rate of return** has many flaws but gives a sense of what the account holder has.

Read on to see the return that would be calculated using each of these methods.

Modified Dietz method

The *Modified Dietz method* is related to the simple percent change formula, but it adjusts the beginning and ending period amounts for the cash inflows and cash outflows. The equation is shown in Figure 11-6.

Figure 11-6:
Here's the equation for the Modified Dietz method.

$$\frac{EOY - BOY - deposits + withdrawals}{BOY + deposits - withdrawals}$$

So with the numbers in our example, it would look like Figure 11-7.

Figure 11-7:
Calculating using the Modified Dietz method.

$$\frac{115,000 - 100,000 - 1,000 + 5,000}{100,000 + 1,000 - 5,000}$$

And that equals 19.8 percent.

The advantage of the Modified Dietz method is that it so easy to do. You can calculate it to give you a rough idea of how you are doing with your trading when you don't have the time to run a more detailed analysis. The key disadvantage is that it doesn't consider the timing of the deposits and withdrawals. It would generate the same answer if you took out $5,000 in May and put in $1,000 in December, even though the amount of money you would have to trade between May 1 and December 1 would be very different.

Time-weighted rate of return

The *time-weighted rate of return* shows the investment performance as a percentage of the assets at hand to trade. It's the standard of trader evaluation, but the math is much more complicated than with the basic percentage change or the Modified Dietz method. You need to calculate the CAGR for each time period and then do a second calculation to incorporate each of those over a longer period. Using our example, you'd calculate one return for the first four months of the year, another for the next seven months, and then a third return for the month of December. These three returns would be then be multiplied to generate a return for the year.

The general equation looks like Figure 11-8.

Figure 11-8:
Figuring
the time-
weighted
rate of
return.

$$\sqrt[N]{\left(1 + r_{p1}\right)\left(1 + r_{p2}\right)\left(1 + r_{p3}\right)\dots\left(1 + r_{pn}\right)} - 1$$

N is the total number of time periods that you are looking at, and r_{pn} is the return for that particular time period. To make it easy, you can do the calculation in a spreadsheet. Figure 11-9 shows the time-weighted return for this example.

Figure 11-9:
Here's an
example of
the time-
weighted
rate of
return
calculation.

	January	May	December
Beginning of Period Account Value	$ 100,000	$ 109,000	$ 123,000
Deposit/(Withdrawal)	$ -	$ 1,000	$ (5,000)
Adjusted Beginning Account Value	$ 100,000	$ 110,000	$ 118,000
Trading Earnings	$ 9,000	$ 13,000	$ (3,000)
End-of-Period Account Value	$ 109,000	$ 123,000	$ 115,000
Period Percentage Return:	9.00%	11.82%	-2.54%
Annual Return:			18.78%

The result is 18.78 percent, a little below the Modified Dietz return.

If you plan on adding to or taking money out of your account, you can make your return calculations much easier by setting a regular schedule and sticking to it. Otherwise, you'll have to do calculations for fractional time periods. It's not impossible, but it's kind of a hassle.

The time-weighted rate of return gives you the best sense of your trading performance, and its precision for this use more than offsets the complexity of the calculation. You want to look at this number when you are deciding whether to change or refine your strategy.

Dollar-weighted returns

The *dollar-weighted return*, also called the *money-weighted return*, is the rate that makes the net present value of a stream of numbers equal to zero. That calculation is also called the *internal rate of return* or *IRR*, and it is used for other things than just return calculations. It's a way of determining what the return is for a stream of numbers over time, and it's useful for calculating returns when you're putting money into or taking money out of your trading account. And if you have a financial calculator such as the Hewlett-Packard HP12C or the Texas Instruments BA2+, it's pretty easy to calculate.

Ah, but there's a catch! Although it's useful, the dollar-weighted method can misstate returns and can occasionally show nonsensical results if there are too many negative returns in a series. And yes, day traders often have negative returns. Figure 11-10 shows the dollar-weighted rate of return using the same data used in the two examples.

	January	May	December
Beginning of Period Account Value	$ 100,000	$ 109,000	$ 123,000
Deposit/(Withdrawal)	$ -	$ 1,000	$ (5,000)
Adjusted Beginning Account Value	$ 100,000	$ 110,000	$ 118,000
Trading Earnings	$ 9,000	$ 13,000	$ (3,000)
End-of-Period Account Value	$ 109,000	$ 123,000	$ 115,000
Period Percentage Return:	9.00%	11.82%	-2.54%
Annual Return:			12.10%

Figure 11-10: Calculating the dollar-weighted rate of return.

The result is 12.1 percent, lower than the other two examples because the dollar-weighted return overstates the withdrawal and the loss in the last month of the year. The withdrawals affect the account's spending power, offsetting the investment performance. But the overall account balance is up more than 12.1 percent, even considering the deposit at the beginning of May — the weight of the cash flows threw off this calculation.

Because of the problems with dollar-weighted returns, professional investors who analyze investment returns usually prefer the time-weighted, compound average approach. Still, the dollar-weighted return has some value, especially for an investor who wants to know how the asset value has changed over time. Because a day trader is usually both an investor and an account owner, the dollar-weighted rate of return can show whether the investment performance is affecting spending power. This measure is particularly useful if you are trying to decide whether to continue day trading

Just as you have alternatives in calculating your performance, so too does anyone trying to sell you a trading system or training course. Ask questions about the performance calculation method and how cash flows and expenses are handled. The numbers might not look so great once you grade the math behind them.

The risk to your return

Now that you have return numbers from your profit and loss statements and your return calculations, it's time to perform black-belt performance jujitsu and determine your risk levels. I'm not going to go into all of the many risk and volatility measures out there, because believe me, the good editors of the *...For Dummies* books don't want to proofread all the math.

Batting average

Baseball players are judged by how often they hit the ball. After all, they can't score until they get on base, and they can't get on base without a hit or a walk. The number of hits relative to the number of times at bat is the batting average. It's a simple, beautiful number.

Day traders often calculate their batting average, too, although they might call it their *win-loss percentage* or *win ratio*. It's the same: the number of successful trades to the total number of trades. Not all trades have to work out for you to make money, but the more often the trades work for you, the better your overall performance is likely to be. If you have both good performance and a high batting average, then your strategy may have less risk than one that relies on just a handful of home run trades amidst a bunch of strikeouts.

Standard deviation

Want something harder than your batting average? Turn to *standard deviation*, which is tricky to calculate without a spreadsheet but forms the core of many risk measures out there.

The standard deviation calculation starts with the average return over a given time period. This is the *expected* return, the return that, on average, you get if you stick with your trading strategy. But any given week, month, or year, the return might be very different from what you expect. The more likely you are to get what you expect, the less risk you take. Insured bank savings accounts pay a low interest rate, but the rate is guaranteed. Day trading offers the potential for much higher returns, but also the possibility that you could lose everything any one month — especially if you can't stick to your trading discipline.

The explanation is a lot easier to understand once you take a gander at Figure 11-11.

In Step One, you take every return over the time period and then find the average. A simple mean will do. Here, there are 12 months, so I added all 12 returns and then divided by 12.

In Step Two, you take each of the 12 returns and then subtract the average from it. This shows how much any one return differs from the average, to give you a sense of how much the returns can go back and forth.

In Step Three, you take each of those differences and then square them (multiply them by themselves). This gets rid of the negative numbers. When you add those up, you get a number known in statistics as the *sum of the squares*.

Now you have enough for Step Four: taking the average of the sum of the squares.

Calculating Standard Deviation

	Step One: Find the expected return		Step Two: Subtract expected return from each reported return	Step Three: Calculate the square of each difference
	Percentage Return		R-E(R)	(R-E(R))^2
January	(0.02)		(0.0211)	0.0004
February	0.01		0.0079	0.0001
March	(0.00)		(0.0040)	0.0000
April	0.09		0.0849	0.0072
May	0.01		0.0082	0.0001
June	0.01		0.0082	0.0001
July	(0.08)		(0.0818)	0.0067
August	0.02		0.0182	0.0003
September	0.03		0.0282	0.0008
October	(0.04)		(0.0418)	0.0017
November	(0.01)		(0.0118)	0.0001
December	0.01		0.0049	0.0000
Total	0.02		Sum of the squares:	0.0176
E(R)	0.0018	Step Four:	Average of the sum of the squares	0.0015
		Step Five:	Square root of the average of the sum of the squares, also known as standard deviation	0.0383

Figure 11-11: Calculating standard deviation.

And for Step Five: the square root of the average of the sum of the squares. That square root from Step Five is the *standard deviation*, the magic number we're looking for.

Of course, you don't have to do all of this math. Almost all trading software calculates standard deviation automatically, but at least you now know where the calculation comes from.

The higher the standard deviation, the riskier the strategy. This number can help you determine how comfortable you are with different trading techniques you might be backtesting, as well as whether you want to stick with your current strategy.

In academic terms, *risk* is the likelihood of getting any return other than the return you expect. To most normal human beings, there's no risk in getting more than you expect — the problem is in getting less of a return than you were counting on. This is a key limitation of risk evaluation.

Past performance is no indicator of future results. That truism applies to risk as well as to return.

Using benchmarks to evaluate your performance

To understand your performance numbers, you need one more step: what your performance is relative to what else you could be doing with your money.

Performance relative to an index

The most common way to think about investment performance is relative to a *market index*. These are the measures of the overall market that are quoted all the time in the news, such as the Standard & Poor's 500 and the Dow Jones Industrial Average. Not only are these widely watched, but many mutual funds and futures contracts are designed to mimic their performance. That means investors can always do at least as well as the index itself, if their investment objectives call for exposure to that part of the broad investment market.

Indexes aren't perfect. One big problem is that day traders often look at the wrong index for the type of investment that they have. They'll compare the performance of trading in agricultural commodities to the Standard & Poor's 500 when a commodities index would be a better measure.

If you aren't sure what to use, pick up a copy of *Barron's*, a weekly financial publication put out by Dow Jones & Company, the same people who publish *The Wall Street Journal* and the Dow Jones Industrial Average. In the Market Lab section there is a long list of different stock, bond, and commodity indexes for the United States and the world. You can find the one that best matches your strategy and use it to compare your performance.

In some cases, your trading practices may overlap more than one index. If so, pick the indexes that are appropriate and compare them only to those trades that match. If you trade 40 percent currencies and 60 percent metals, then you should create your own hybrid index that's 40 percent currencies and 60 percent metals.

Performance relative to your time

A few pages back when I talk about tracking your trades and doing a profit and loss statement, I say that you should calculate your hourly wage. There's a reason for that. Instead of day trading, you could put your money in a nice, simple, index mutual fund and take a regular job. If your hourly wage is less than what you can earn elsewhere, you might want to consider doing just that.

Of course, there are benefits to working on your own that don't often show up in your bank account. I say this as someone who left finance to be a financial writer. If you enjoy day trading and if you make enough money to suit your lifestyle, by all means, don't let the relative numbers stop you.

Part III
Day Trading Strategies

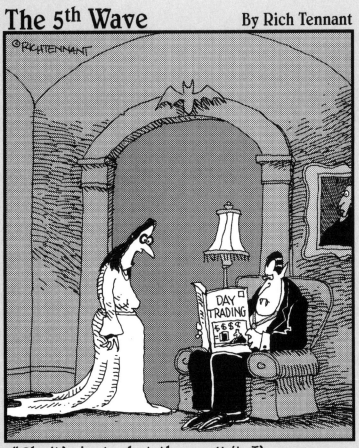

The 5th Wave   By Rich Tennant

"Oh, it's just what they call it. I'm sure you can do it at night, too."

In this part . . .

Good day traders don't just rush in and buy and sell willy-nilly. They use research and follow strategies to help them determine where and when to buy and sell their positions. Some of the strategies and tools include selling short to profit from securities that are declining in price and using leverage to make bigger trades in hopes of bigger returns. This part includes information that can help you make better portfolio decisions, even if you decide not to become a day trader. Of course, the markets are the best teacher — and the harshest. The more you understand the information that traders want to see, the better you'll understand what the markets are telling you.

Chapter 12

Using Fundamental and Technical Analysis

*I*n some ways, day trading is easy. Open up an account with a brokerage firm and off you go, buying and selling securities! But how are you going to know when to buy and when to sell? That's not a simple matter. Most day traders fail, because it's easy to place the order, but hard to know if the order is the right one.

Traders use different research systems to evaluate the market. They have access to tools that can help them figure out when a security is likely to go up in price and when it is likely to go down.

Research systems fall into two categories: fundamental and technical. *Fundamental* research looks at the specific factors that affect a security's value. What's the relationship between the trade deficit and futures on two-year treasury notes? What's the prediction for summer rainfall in Iowa, and how will that affect December corn futures? How dependent is a company on new products to generate earnings growth?

Technical research, on the other hand, looks at the supply and demand for the security itself. Are people buying more and more shares? Is the price going up as they buy more, or does the price go up just a little bit? Does it seem like everyone who is likely to buy has already bought, and what does that mean for the future price?

Anyone with a surefire system has already made a fortune and retired to a private island in a tropical climate. He or she is too busy enjoying drinks with umbrellas in them to share that surefire trading system with you.

Research Techniques Used in Day Trading

Day traders need to make decisions fast, and they need to have a framework for doing so. That's why they rely on research. But what kind? Most day traders rely heavily on *technical* research, which is an analysis of charts formed by price patterns to measure the relative supply and demand for the security. But some use fundamental analysis to help inform their decisions, too.

What direction is your research?

Securities are affected by matters specific to each type and by huge global macroeconomic factors that affect every security in different ways. Some traders prefer to think of the big picture first, whereas others start small. And some use a combination of the two approaches. Neither is better; each is simply a different perspective on what's happening in the markets.

Top-down research

With a *top-down* approach, the trader looks at the big economic factors: interest rates, exchange rates, government policies, and the like. How will these things affect a particular sector or security? Is this a good time to buy stocks or short interest rate futures? The top-down approach can help evaluate the prices in big market sectors, and it can also help determine what factors are affecting trading in a subsector. You don't have to trade stock market index futures to know that the outlook for the overall stock market will have an effect on the trading of any specific company's stock.

Bottom-up research

Bottom-up analysis looks at the specific performance of the asset. It looks at the company's prospects and then works backward to figure out how it will get there. What has to happen for a company's stock price to go up 20 percent? What earnings does it have to report, what types of buyers have to materialize, and what else has to happen in the economy?

Fundamental research

Day traders do very little fundamental research. Sure, they know that demand for ethanol affects corn prices, but they really want to know what the price will do right now relative to where the price was a few minutes ago. How a proposed farm bill might affect ethanol prices in six years doesn't figure into day trade, though. Knowing a little bit about the fundamentals — those basic facts that affect the supply and demand for a security in all markets — can help the day trader respond better to news events. It can also give you a better feel for when *swing trading* (holding a position for several days) will generate a better profit than closing out every night. But knowing a lot can drag a day trader down.

Fundamental analysis can actually *hurt* you in day trading, because you may start making decisions for the wrong reasons. If you know too much about the fundamentals, you might start considering long-term outlooks instead of short-term activity. For example, many people buy Standard & Poor's (S&P) 500 Index mutual funds for their retirement accounts because they believe that in the long run, the market will go up. That does not mean that people should trade eMini S&P futures or an S&P exchange-traded fund today, because there can be a lot of zigzagging between right now and the arrival of the long-run price appreciation.

Fundamental research falls into two main categories: top-down and bottom-up. As I mentioned earlier, top-down starts with broad economic considerations and then looks at how those will affect a specific security. Bottom-up looks at specific securities and then determines whether those are good buys or sells right now.

If you love the very idea of fundamental research, then day trading is probably not for you. Day trading requires quick responses to price changes, not a careful understanding of accounting methods and business trends. A little fundamental analysis can be helpful in day trading, but a lot can slow you down.

Technical analysis

Information about the price, time, and volume of a security's trading can be plotted on a chart. The plots form patterns that can be analyzed to show what happened. How did the supply and demand for a security change, and why? And what does that mean for future supply and demand? Technical analysis is based on the premise that securities prices move in trends, and that those trends repeat themselves over time. Therefore, a trader who can recognize a trend on the charts can determine where prices are most likely to go until some unforeseen event comes along that creates a new trend.

The basic element of technical analysis is a *bar*, which shows you the high, low, open, and closing price of a security for a given day. It looks like Figure 12-1.

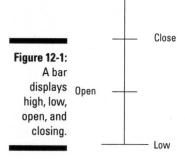

Figure 12-1:
A bar displays high, low, open, and closing.

In most markets, every day generates a new *bar* (many traders talk about bars instead of days, and they aren't talking about where they go after work). A collection of bars, with all their different high, low, open, and close points, is put together into a larger *chart*. Often, a plot of the volume for each bar runs underneath, with the result looking like Figure 12-2.

Figure 12-2:
Here's a plot of volume underneath a year's worth of bars.

Many patterns formed in the charts are associated with future price moves. Technical analysts thus spend a lot of time looking at the charts to see if they can predict what will happen. Many software packages (some of which are discussed in Chapter 7) send traders signals when certain technical patterns occur, so that the traders can place orders accordingly.

Bulls and bears and pork bellies, oh my!

Traders work cattle and hogs at the Chicago Mercantile Exchange, but bulls and bears are in every market. What do those mythical animals symbolize?

Bulls believe that the market is going up, and bullish news and bullish patterns are good.

Bears believe that the market is going down, so bearish news and bearish patterns are bad.

No one is exactly sure why the words came into use, but the best guess for the symbolism is that when attacked, bulls charge and bears retreat.

Technical analysis is a way to measure the supply and demand in the market. It's a tool for analyzing the markets, not predicting them. If it were that easy, everyone would be able to make money in the markets.

Price changes

Market observers debate *market efficiency* all the time. In an efficient market, all information about a security is already included in the security's price, so there's no point to doing any research at all. Few market participants are willing to go that far, but they concede the point that the price is the single most important summary of information about a company. That means that technical analysis, looking at how the price changes over time, is a way of learning about whether a security's prospects are improving or getting worse.

Volume changes

The basic bar shows how price changed during the day, but adding *volume* information tells the other part of the story: how much of a security was demanded at that price. If demand is going up, then more people want the security, so they are willing to pay more for it. The price tells traders what the market knows; the volume tells them how many people in the market know it.

How to Use Technical Analysis

Technical analysis helps day traders identify changes in the supply and demand for a security that may lead to profitable price changes ahead. It gives traders a way to talk about and think about the market so that they can be more effective.

Charts are generated by most brokerage firm quote systems, sometimes with the help of additional software that automatically marks the chart with trendlines. That's because a technical trader is looking for those trendlines. Is the security going up in price, and is that trend going to continue? That's the information that a trader needs before placing an order to buy or sell.

One interesting aspect of technical analysis is that the basics hold no matter what market you are looking at. Technical analysis can help you monitor trends in the stock market, the bond market, the commodity market, and the currency market. Anywhere people try to match their supply and their demand to make a market, technical analysis can be used to show how well they're doing it.

Finding trends

A technical analyst usually starts off by looking at a chart and drawing lines that show the overall direction of the price bars for the period in question. Rather than plot the graph on paper or print out the screen, she probably uses software to draw the lines. Figure 12-3 shows what this basic analysis looks like.

Figure 12-3:
Basic analysis of trends in price bar changes draws lines showing the general movement.

With the basic trendlines in place, the trader can start thinking about how the trends have played out so far and what might happen next.

Here's the thing about trends: Sometimes it's good to follow, and sometimes it's good to deviate. Remember when you were a kid, and you wanted to do something that all your friends were doing? And your mother would invariably say, "If all your friends jumped off of a bridge, would you have to jump off, too?"

Well, Mom, guess what? If the bridge was on fire, if the escape routes were blocked by angry mobs, if the water were just a few feet down, yes, I just might jump off the bridge like everyone else. Likewise, if someone was paying us good money to jump, and I knew I wasn't likely to get hurt on the way down, I'd be over the railing in a flash. Sometimes it's good to be a follower.

But if my friends were idiots, if there were no fire and no angry mob, and if I couldn't swim, I might not be so hasty.

Trend following is like those mythical childhood friends on that mythical hometown bridge. Sometimes, you should join the crowd. Other times, it's best to deviate.

Draw those trendlines!

The most basic *trendline* is a line that shows the general direction of the trend. And that's a good start, but it doesn't tell you all you need to know. The next step is to take out your ruler, or set your software, to find the trendlines that connect the highs and the lows. That will create a channel that tells you the *support level* — the trendline for the lows — and the *resistance level* — the trendline for the highs. Unless something happens to change the trend, securities tend to move within the channel, so extending the line into the future can give you a sense of where the security is likely to trade. Figure 12-4 shows you an example.

Figure 12-4:
Drawing
trendlines
to identify
channels.

Resistance Line

Support Line

When a security hits its support level, it is usually seen as relatively cheap — so that's a good time to buy. When a security hits its resistance level, it is usually seen as relatively expensive, so that's a good time to sell. Some day traders find that simply moving between buying at the support and selling at the resistance can be a profitable strategy, at least until something happens that changes those two levels.

Calculating indicators

In addition to drawing lines, technical analysts use their calculators — or have their software make calculations — to come up with different *indicators*. These are numbers that are used to gauge performance. The following is a list of some common indicators, with definitions.

Pivot points

A *pivot point* is the average of the high, low, and close price for the day. If the next day's price closes above the pivot point, that sets a new support level, and if the next day's price is below the pivot point, that sets a new resistance level. Hence, calculating pivot points and how they change might indicate new upper and lower stops for your trading. (You can learn more about using stops in Chapter 2.)

For markets that are open more or less continuously, such as foreign exchange, the close price is set arbitrarily. The usual custom in the United States is to use the price at 4:00 p.m. Eastern time, which is the closing time for the New York Stock Exchange.

Moving averages

Looking at all those little high-low-open-close lines on a chart will give your bifocals a workout. To make the trend easier to spot, traders calculate a *moving average*. It's calculated by averaging the closing prices for a given time period. Some traders prefer to look at the last 5 days, some at the last 60 days. Every day, the latest price is added, and the oldest price is dropped to make that day's calculation. Given the wonders of modern computing technology, it's easy to pull up moving averages for almost any time period you want. The average for each day is then plotted against the price chart to show how the trend is changing over time. Figure 12-5 shows an example of a 10-day moving average chart.

Figure 12-5: This price chart shows a 10-day moving average.

Traders use the moving average line to look for crossovers, convergences, and divergences. A *crossover* occurs whenever the price crosses the moving average line. Usually, it's a good idea to buy when the price crosses above the moving average line and to sell when the price crosses below it.

To use *convergence* and *divergence* in analysis, the trader looks at moving averages from different time periods, such as 5 days, 10 days, and 20 days. Figure 12-6 shows what it looks like.

Figure 12-6:
This figure shows moving average convergence and divergence.

When two or three of the moving average lines converge (come together), that means that the trend may be ending. That often makes it a good time to buy if the trend has been down — and a good time to sell if the trend has been up. If two or three of the moving average lines split up and diverge, that means that the trend is likely to continue. That means that it's probably a good time to buy if the trend is up and sell if the trend is down.

A moving average is a lagging indicator. It sums up trading activity in the last 5, 10, 30, or 60 days. That means that the line will smooth out changes in the trend that may affect future prices.

Trends move in phases

Price trends tend to move in cycles that can be seen on the charts or observed in market behavior. Knowing the phases of a trend can help you better evaluate what's happening. Here is a summary of some phases of a trend:

- **Accumulation:** This is the first part of the trend, where traders get excited about a security and its prospects. They start new positions or add to existing ones.

- **Main phase (also called continuation):** Here, the trend moves along nicely, with no unusual price action. The highs get higher on an uptrend, and the lows get lower on a downtrend. A trader might make money, but not big money, following the trend here.

- **Consolidation (also called congestion):** This is a sideways market. The security stays within the trend, but without hitting higher highs or lower lows. It just stays within the trading range. A consolidation phase is good for scalpers, who make a large volume of trades in search of very small profits. It can be boring for everyone else.

- **Retracement (also called correction or pullback):** This is a secondary trend, a short-term pullback away from the main trend to the support level. Retracements create buying opportunities, but they can also kill day traders who are following the trend.

- **Distribution:** In the distribution phase, traders don't think that the security can go up in price any more. Hence, they tend to sell in large volume.

- **Reversal:** This is the point where the trend changes. It's time to sell if you had been following an uptrend and buy if you had been following a downtrend. Many reversals follow classic patterns, which are discussed later in this chapter.

Those ever-changing trends

Although technical traders look to follow trends, they also look for situations where the trend changes so that they can find new profit opportunities. In general, day traders are going to follow trends, and swing traders — those who hold securities for a few days or even weeks — are going to be more interested in identifying changes that may play out over time.

Momentum

Following the trend is great, but if the trend is moving quickly, you want to know so that you can get ahead of it. If the rate of change on the trend is going up, then rising prices are likely to occur.

To calculate *momentum*, take today's closing price for a security, divide that by the closing price ten days ago, and then multiply by 100. This gives you a *momentum indicator.* If the price didn't go anywhere, the momentum indicator will be 100. If the price went up, the indicator will be greater than 100. And if it went down, it will be less than 100. In technical analysis, trends are usually expected to continue, so a security with a momentum indicator above 100 is expected to keep going up, all else being equal.

But it's that "all else being equal" that's the sticky part. Technical analysts usually track momentum indicators over time to see if the positive momentum is, itself, a trend. In fact, momentum indicators are a good confirmation of the underlying trend.

Momentum is a leading technical indicator. It tells you what is likely to happen in the future, not what has happened in the past.

Momentum trading is usually done with some attention to the fundamentals. When key business fundamentals such as sales or profits are accelerating at the same time that the security is going up in price, the momentum is likely to continue for some time. You can learn more about momentum trading and investing in Chapter 16.

Finding breakouts

A *breakout* occurs when a security price passes through and stays above — or below — the resistance or support line, which creates a new trend with new support and resistance levels. A one-time breakout may just be an anomaly, what technicians sometimes call a *false breakout*, but pay attention to two or more breakouts. Figure 12-7 shows what breakouts look like.

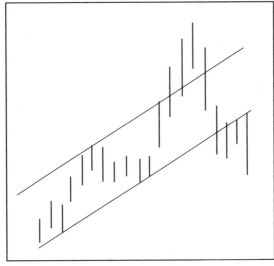

Figure 12-7:
A breakout
indicates a
new trend.

When a true breakout occurs, a new trend starts. That means an upward breakout will be accompanied by rising prices, and a downward breakout will be accompanied by falling prices.

With a false breakout, some traders buy or sell thinking that the trend will continue, see that it doesn't, and then turn around and reverse their positions at a loss.

A false breakout can cause those misled traders to wreak havoc for a day or two of trading. This is where the ability to size up the intelligence of the other traders in the market can come in handy.

Good technical analysts look at several different indicators in order to see whether a change in trend is real or just one of those things that goes away quickly as the old trend resumes.

Reading the Charts

How long does it take to find the trend? How long does it take for the trend to play out? When do you act on it? Do you have minutes, hours, or days to act?

Because markets tend to move in cycles, technical analysts look for patterns in the price charts that give them an indication of how long any particular trend may last. In this section, I show you some of the common patterns that day traders look for when they do technical analysis. Alas, some are only obvious in hindsight, but knowing what the patterns mean can help you make better forecasts of where a security price should go.

This is just an introduction to some of the better-known (and cleverly named) patterns. Technical analysts look for many others, and you really need a book on the subject to understand them all. Check out the appendix for more information on technical analysis so that you can get a feel for how you can apply it to your trading style.

Waving your pennants and flags

Pennants and *flags* are chart patterns that show retracements, which are short-term deviations from the main trend. With a retracement, there's no breakout from the support or resistance level, but the security isn't following the trend, either.

Figure 12-8 shows a pennant. Notice how the support and resistance lines of the pennant (which occur within the support and resistance lines of a much larger trend) converge almost to a point.

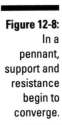

Figure 12-8:
In a
pennant,
support and
resistance
begin to
converge.

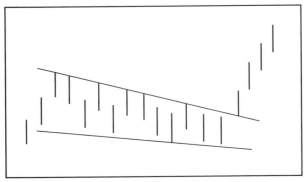

Figure 12-9, by contrast, is a flag. The main difference between a flag and a pennant is that the flag's support and resistance lines are parallel.

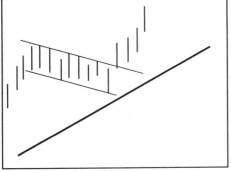

Figure 12-9:
A flag, like a
pennant,
usually
indicates
falling
volume.

Pennants and flags are usually found in the middle of the main phase of a trend, and they seem to last for two weeks before going back to the trendline. They are almost always accompanied by falling volume. In fact, if the trading volume isn't falling, you are probably looking at a *reversal* — a change in trend — rather than a retracement.

Not just for the shower: head and shoulders

The *head and shoulders* formation is a series of three peaks within a price chart. The peaks on the left and right (the shoulders) should be relatively smaller than the peak in the center (the head). The shoulders connect at a price known as the neckline, and once the right shoulder formation is reached, the price plunges down.

The head and shoulders is one of the most bearish technical patterns, and it looks like Figure 12-10.

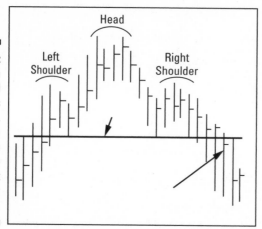

Figure 12-10: In a head and shoulders formation, the price goes down after the right shoulder formation.

The head and shoulders formation seems to result from traders holding out for a last high after a security has had a long price run. At some point, though, the trend changes, because nothing grows forever. And when the trend changes, the prices fall.

An upside-down head and shoulders sometimes appears at the end of a downtrend, and it signals that the security is about to increase in price.

Drinking from a cup and handle

When a security hits a peak in price and falls, sometimes because of bad news, it can stay low for a while. But eventually, the bad news works itself out, the underlying fundamentals improve, and it becomes time to buy again. The technical analyst sees this play out in a *cup and handle* formation, and Figure 12-11 shows you what it looks like.

The handle forms as those who bought at the old high and who felt burned by the decline take their money and get out. But other traders, who do not have the same history with the security, recognize that the price will proba-bly resume going up now that those old sellers are out of the market.

A cup and handle formation generally shows up over a long period of trading — sometimes as long as a year — so, many subtrends will occur during that time. A day trader will likely care more about those day-to-day changes than the underlying trend taking place. Still, if you see that cup formation and the hint of a handle, it's a sign that the security will probably start to rise in price.

Figure 12-11:
A cup and
handle
formation is
a long-term
trend.

Handle

Cup

Mind the gap

Gaps are breaks in prices that show up all the time, usually when some news event takes place between trading sessions that causes an adjustment in prices and volume. Whether it's an acquisition, a product line disappointment, or a war that broke out overnight, the news is significant enough to change the trend, and that's why traders pay attention when they see gaps.

A gap is a break between two bars, and Figure 12-12 shows what one looks like:

Gap

Figure 12-12:
A gap down
often means
it's time to
sell.

Gaps are usually great signals. If a security gaps up at the open, that usually means that a strong uptrend is beginning, so it's time to buy. Likewise, if it gaps down, that's often the start of a downtrend, so it's better to sell.

Day traders can get sucked into a gap, a situation known as a *gap and crap* (or *gap and trap*, if you prefer more genteel language). When the security goes up in price, many traders view that as a great time to sell, so the day trader who buys on the gap up immediately gets slammed by all the selling pressure. Some day traders prefer to wait at least 30 minutes before trading on an opening gap, while others rely on their knowledge of the buyers and sellers in a given market to decide what to do.

Grab your pitchforks!

A *pitchfork* is sometimes called an *Andrews pitchfork* after Alan Andrews, the technical analyst who popularized it. It identifies long-run support and resistance levels for subtrends by creating a channel around the main trendline. Figure 12-13 shows what it looks like.

Figure 12-13:
A pitchfork makes a channel around the main trendline.

Point 2

Point 3

Point 1

The upper fork shows the resistance level for upward subtrends, and the lower fork shows the support level for lower subtrends. The middle line forms a support and a resistance line, depending on which side of it trading takes place. If the price crosses above the mid-line, it can be expected to go no higher than the highest line. Likewise, if it crosses below the mid-line, it can be expected to go no lower than the lowest line.

Different Approaches to Technical Analysis

Technical analysts tend to group themselves under different schools of thought. Each approaches the charts differently and uses them to glean different information about how securities prices are likely to perform. In this section, I offer an introduction to a few of these approaches. If one strikes your fancy, you can look in the Appendix for resources to help you learn more.

Dow Theory

The *Dow Theory* was developed by Charles Dow, the founder of *The Wall Street Journal*. The theory and the market indexes that are part of it helped sell newspapers; they also helped people make money in the markets. It's the basis for the traditional technical analysis described in this chapter. Dow believed that securities move in trends; that the trends form patterns that traders can identify; and that those trends remain in place until some major event takes place that changes them. Further, trends in the Dow Jones Industrial Average and the Dow Jones Transportation Average can predict overall market performance.

Not all technicians believe that the Dow Jones Industrial Average and Dow Jones Transportation Average are primary indicators in the modern economy, but they rely on the Dow Theory for their analysis, and they still read the *Journal*.

Fibonacci numbers and the Elliott Wave

Remember back when you had to take standardized tests, you'd often have to figure the next number in a series? Well, here's such a test. What's the next number in this series? (Hint: this is not a phone number in Chad.)

```
0, 1, 1, 2, 3, 5, 8, 13, 21
```

If you answered 34, you're right! The series is known as the *Fibonacci numbers*, sometimes called the Fibonacci series or just the Fibs. It's found by adding together the preceding two numbers in the series, starting with the first two digits on the number line. 0 + 1 = 1; 1 + 1 = 2; 1 + 2 = 3; and so on into infinity. Furthermore, once the series gets well into the double digits, the ratio of one number to the one next to it settles at .618, a number known as the *Golden Proportion*; this means that the ratio of the smaller and the larger of two numbers is the same as the ratio of the larger number to the sum of the two numbers. In nature, this is the proportion of a perfect spiral, like that found on a pinecone and a pineapple.

Ralph Elliott was a trader who believed that over the long run, the market moved in waves described by the Fibonacci series. For example, Elliott believed that a bull market would be characterized by three down waves and five up waves. Furthermore, he believed that support and resistance levels would be found 61.8 percent above lows and below highs. If a security falls 61.8 percent from a high, that would be good time to buy, under the Elliott Wave system.

Elliott believed that these waves ranged from centuries to minutes, so traders and investors both use the system to identify the market trends that suit their timeframes. Others — including me — think it's highly unlikely that the human activity in the stock market would follow the same natural order as the ratio of the spiral on a mollusk shell.

Japanese Candlestick charting

Candlestick charts were developed by traders in the Japanese rice futures markets in the 18th century, and they've carried through into the present. The basic charts are similar to the high-low-close-open bars that I talk about earlier in this chapter, but they are shaped a little differently to carry more information. Figure 12-14 shows an example:

High

Open or close

Figure 12-14: Candlesticks are like slightly more sophisticated bars.

Open or close

Low

The length of the rectangle (the so-called *candle*, also known as the body) between the open and the close price gives a sense of how much volatility the security has, especially relative to the high and low prices above and below the rectangle (the so-called *wick*, also known as the shadow). The shapes and colors create different patterns that traders can use to discern the direction of future prices. (Most technical analysis packages will color the candlesticks green on up days and red on down days, to make finding trends even easier.)

The Gann system

William Gann supposedly made 50 million dollars in the stock and commodities markets in the first half of the 20th century using a system that he may or may not have taught to others before his death. There's a lot of mystery and mythology about the Gann system; some traders rely on what they perceive to be his method, whereas others dismiss it, in part because Gann relied on astrology to build his forecasts.

The *Gann system*, as it is defined nowadays, looks at the relationship between price and time. If a security moves one point in one day, that's a 1×1 Gann angle, and that's normal trading. If a security moves two points in one day, it would be said to create a 2×1 Gann angle, which is bullish. An angle of less than 1×1 would be bearish.

Furthermore, Gann recognized that the market would move back and forth while in a general upward or downward cycle, but some of those fluctuations were more positive than others. Just as the system looks for price movements over time with even proportions (1×1, 2×1, and so on), it also looks for orderly retracements. When a security moves back 50 percent, say from a low of $20 to a high of $40 and then back to $30, it would be a good time to buy under the Gann system.

Many traders swear by the 50 percent retracement guide — even those who think that Gann is otherwise a crazy system. This may be the origin of one hoary trading chestnut: buy whenever a price dips, because it's likely to be heading on its way back up.

Pitfalls of Technical Analysis

As discussed in Chapter 7, a lot of people make a lot of money selling services to day traders. They produce videos, organize seminars, and (ahem) write books to tell you how to be a success. But in the financial world, success is a combination of luck, skill, and smarts.

Before you commit wholeheartedly to any particular school of research, and before you plunk down a lot of money for some "proven" system demonstrated on an infomercial, think about who are you are and what you are trying to do. Despite all the books and all the seminars and all the business-school debates, every form of research has its drawbacks. Keep them in mind as you develop your day-trading business plan.

If it's obvious, there's no opportunity

Many day trading systems work much of the time. For example, a security gaps up, meaning that due to positive news or high demand, the price jumps from one trade to the next (refer to Figure 12.12 for a gap formation). This is good, and the security is likely to keep going up. So you buy the security, you make money. Bingo! But here's the thing: Everyone is looking at that gap, everyone is assuming that the stock will go up, so everyone will buy and that will bid up the security. Double Bingo! The profit opportunity is gone. So maybe you're better off going short? Or avoiding the situation entirely? Who knows! And that's the problem. Looking for obvious patterns like gaps tells you a lot about what is happening in the market, but only your own judgment and experience can tell you what the next move should be.

Reverse-reverse psychology

Sitcoms always revert to tired formulas. The smart kid brags about how he or she will dominate a talent or quiz show and then panics on the big day. The two people who can't stand each other will get a horrible sickness that requires them to be quarantined — in the same hospital ward. The teenage son can't believe what fabulous soup his mother made, and it turns out she was brewing a homemade cleaning solution.

Or there's this one: The kids want to do something that the parents don't approve of. The parents try reverse psychology. "Go to the party, kids, have fun!" they say, thinking that the kids will not want to do anything that parents approve of. The kids, knowing that the parents are trying to pull the reverse psychology, decide to play along with reverse-reverse psychology. "Don't worry, we'll stay home!" they say — and then sneak out. Hilarity ensues.

Technical analysis is a useful way to gauge market psychology. But when trying to determine the mood of the market, it's really easy to start over-analyzing and working yourself into a knot. Should you follow the trend or trade against it? But if everyone trades against it, would you be better off following it?

Instead of puzzling over what's really going on, develop a system that you trust. Do that through backtesting, simulation, and performance analysis. Chapter 11 has plenty of advice on how to do this. The more confident you feel in how you should react given a market situation, the better your trading will be.

The random walk with an upward bias

Under the efficient markets theory, all information is already included in a security's price. Until new information comes into the market, the prices move in a random pattern, so any security is as likely to do as well as any other. In some markets, like the stock market, this random path has an upward bias, meaning that as long as the economy is growing, companies should perform well, too; therefore, the movement is more likely to be upward than downward, but the magnitude of the movement is random.

If price movements are random, some people are going to win and some are going to lose, no matter what systems they use to pick securities. If price movements are random with an upward bias, then more people are going to win than lose, no matter what systems they use to pick securities. Some of those who win are going to tout their system, even though it was really random chance that led to their success.

Technical analysis is a useful way to measure the relative supply and demand in the market, and that in turn is a way to gauge the psychology of those who are trading. But it's not perfect. Before you plunk down a lot of money to learn a complex trading system or to subscribe to a newsletter offering a can't-miss method of trading, ask yourself if the person selling it is smart or just lucky. A good system gives you discipline and a way to think about the market relative to your trading style. A bad system costs a lot of money and may have worked for a brief moment in the past, with no relevance to current conditions.

Chapter 13

Market Indicators and Day Trading Strategies

Day traders put their research to work through a range of different strategies. All strategies have two things in common: They are designed to make money, and they are designed to work in a single day. And the best ones help traders cut through the psychology of the market.

Although some trading is handled through automatic algorithms and other programs that place orders whenever certain conditions take place, the vast majority of trading takes place between human beings, who want to make money, in markets where short-term profit potentials can be very small. As much as they want to be dispassionate, traders are going to get sucked into hope, fear, and greed: the three emotions that ruin people every day. To complicate matters, many markets, such as options and futures, are zero-sum markets, meaning that there is a loser for every winner. Some markets, such as the stock market, have a positive bias, meaning that there are more winners than losers in the long run — but that doesn't mean that will be the case today.

With thin profit potential and so much emotional upheaval, it can be tough to make money in the long run. This chapter might help. In it, I cover some common day trading strategies, and I discuss some of the cold analysis that goes into figuring out the psychology of the markets.

The Psychology of the Markets

For every buyer, there is a seller. There has to be, or no transaction will take place. The price changes to reach the point where the buyer is willing to buy the security and the seller is willing to part with it. This is basic supply and demand. The financial markets are more efficient at matching supply and demand than almost any other market there is. There are no racks of unsold sweaters at the end of the season, no hot model cars that can't be purchased at any price, no long lines to get a table. The prices change to match the demand, and those who want to pay the price — or receive the price — are going to make a trade.

Despite this ruthless capitalistic efficiency underlying trading, the markets are also dominated by human emotion and psychology. All the buyers and all the sellers are looking at the same information, but they are reaching different conclusions. There's a seller out there for every buyer, so the trader looking to buy needs to know why the seller is willing to make a deal.

And why would someone be on the other side of your trade?

- ✔ **The other person may have a different time horizon.**

  For example, long-term investors might sell on bad news that changes a security's outlook. A short-term trader might not care about the long-term outlet, if the selling in the morning is overdone, creating an opportunity to buy now and sell at a higher price in the afternoon.

- ✔ **The other person may have a different risk profile.**

  A conservative investor might not want to own shares in a company that's being acquired by a high-flying technology company. That investor will sell, and someone with more interest in growth will be buying.

- ✔ **The other person may be engaging in wishful thinking, or acting out of fear, or trading from sheer greed.**

- ✔ **You may be engaging in wishful thinking, acting out of fear, or trading from sheer greed.**

It's highly unlikely that you are smarter than everyone else trading, but you might be more rational and disciplined. In the long run, controlling your emotions and sticking to your limits will make you more money than if you are smart but can't control your trading. And if you happen to be both disciplined and smart, you might do very well.

Betting on the buy side

Every market participant has his or her own set of reasons and rationales for placing an order today. In general, though, it's safe to say that although there are many reasons to sell — to pay taxes, generate cash for college tuition, or meet a pension obligation, among many others — there's only one reason to buy: You think the security is going up in price.

For that reason alone, traders often pay more attention to what is happening to buy orders than to sell orders. They look at the number of buy orders coming in, how large they are, and at what price to get a sense of who out there is projecting a profit. I cover volume and price indicators in more detail later in the chapter.

Because there are so many good reasons to sell but only one good reason to buy, it can take a long time for the market to recognize bearish (pessimistic) sentiment indicators. Even if you see that prices should start to go down in the near future, you have to consider that the market today can be very different from what you see coming up. And day traders only have today.

The projection trap

If you took a peek at some of the technical analysis charts in Chapter 12, you may have noticed that it's possible to see what you want to see in some price charts. And if you thought a little about fundamental analysis, you might have seen that it's just as easy to interpret information the way you want to, too. Instead of looking objectively at what the market is telling them, some traders see what they want to see. That's one reason it's so important to know your system and use your limits. Information in Chapters 2 and 11 can help you with both.

The best traders are able to figure out the psychology of the market almost by instinct. They can't necessarily explain what they do — which makes it hard for someone trying to learn from them. But they can tell you this much: If you can rationally determine why the person on the other side of the trade is trading, you can be in a better position to make money and avoid the big mistakes brought on by hope, fear, and greed.

Measuring the Mood of the Market

For decades, most traders were rooted on the floors of the exchanges. They had a good sense of the mood of the market because they could pick up the mood of the people in the pits with them. They often knew their fellow traders well enough to know how good they were or the needs of the people they were working for. It made for a clubby atmosphere, despite all the shouting and arm waving. It wasn't the most efficient way to trade big volume, but it allowed traders to read the minds of those around them.

And now, almost all trading is electronic, and not all those old floor traders have been able to make the transition. Some find that unless they can watch the behavior of other traders and hear the emotions in their voices, they can't gauge what's happening in the markets.

Other professional traders, who work for brokerage firms or fund companies, trade electronically, but along long tables (known as trading desks) where they sit next to colleagues trading similar securities. Even though everyone is trading off a screen, they share a mood and thus a sense of what's happening out there. Some day traders can replicate this by setting up shop at a trading arcade, a business that operates trading desks for day traders (and you can learn more about them in Chapter 6), but most traders are working alone at home, with nothing but the information on their screens to tell them what's happening in the market.

There are ways to figure out what's happening, even just looking at the screen, and some of these may work for you. These include price, volume, and volatility indicators, and you're in the right place to learn more about them.

Some traders rely on Internet chat rooms to help them measure market sentiment. This can be risky. Some chat rooms have smart people who are willing to share their perspectives on the market, but many are dominated by novice traders who have no good information to share, or by people who are trying to manipulate the market in their favor. Check them out carefully before lurking or participating.

Pinpointing with price indicators

In an efficient market, all information about a security is included in its price. If the price is high and going up, then the fundamentals are doing well. If the price is low and going lower, then something's not good. And everything in between means something else.

The change in a security's price gives you a first cut of information. Price changes can be analyzed in other ways to help you know when to buy or when to sell.

Momentum

Momentum, which is also discussed in Chapter 12, is the rate at which a security's price is increasing (or decreasing). If momentum is strong and positive, then the security will show both higher highs and higher lows. People want to buy it for whatever reason, and the price reflects that. Likewise, momentum can be strong and negative, and negative momentum is marked with lower highs and lower lows. No one seems interested in buying, and that keeps dragging the price down.

The exact amount of momentum that a security has can be measured with indicators known as *momentum oscillators*. A classic momentum oscillator starts with the moving average, which is the average of the closing prices for a past time period, say the last ten trading days. Then the change in each day's moving average is plotted below the price line. When the oscillator is positive, traders say that the security is *overbought*; when it is negative, they say that the security is oversold. Figure 13-1 shows a momentum oscillator plotted below a price line.

If a momentum oscillator shows that a security is overbought (when it's above the center line), that means that too many people own it relative to the remaining demand in the market, and some of them will start selling. Remember, some of these people have perfectly good reasons for selling that may have nothing to do with the underlying fundamentals of the security, but they are going to sell anyway, and that will bring the price down. Traders who see that a security is overbought will want to sell in advance of those people.

Figure 13-1:
A momen-
tum
oscillator
indicates
(no surprise
here)
momentum.

If a momentum oscillator shows that a security is oversold (when the line is below the center line), that means that the security is probably too cheap. Everyone who wanted to get out has gotten out, and now it may be a bargain. When the buyers who see the profit opportunity jump in, the price will go up.

The trend is your friend . . . until the end. Although there are great reasons to follow price trends, remember that they all end, so you still need to pay attention to your money management and your stops, no matter how strong a trend seems to be.

Given that most trends end, or at least zig and zag along the way, some traders look for securities that fit what they call the *1-2-3-4 criterion*. If a security goes up in price for three consecutive days, then it's likely to go down on the fourth day. Likewise, if a security has fallen in price for three days in a row, it's likely to be up on day four. Be sure to run some simulations (see Chapter 11) to see if this works for a market that interests you.

Trading on the tick

A *tick* is an upward or downward price change. For some securities, such as futures contracts, the tick size is defined as part of the contract. For others, such as stocks, a tick can be anywhere from a penny to infinity (at least in theory).

You can also calculate the tick indicator for the market as a whole. (In fact, most quotation systems calculate the market tick for you.) This is the total number of securities in that market that traded up on the last trade, minus the number that traded down on the last trade. If the tick is a positive number, that's good — that means that the market as a whole has a lot of buying interest. Although any given security might not do as well, a positive tick shows that most people in the market have a positive perspective right now.

By contrast, a negative tick shows that most people in the market are watching prices fall. Sure, some prices are going up, but there are more unhappy people than happy ones (assuming that most people are trading on the long side, meaning that they make money when prices go up, not down). This shows that there's negative sentiment in the market right now.

Tracking the trin

Trin is short for *trading indicator*, and it's another measure of market sentiment based on how many prices have gone up relative to how many have gone down. Most quotation systems will pull up the trin for a given market, but you can also calculate it on your own. The math looks like Figure 13-2.

Figure 13-2:
Calculating
the trading
indicator
(the trin)
can give you
a measure
of market
sentiment.

$$\frac{\frac{advances}{declines}}{\frac{advance\ volume}{decline\ volume}}$$

The numerator is based on the tick: the number of securities that went up divided by (not less) the number that went down. The denominator includes the volume: the number of shares or contracts that traded for those securities that went up, divided by the number of securities traded for those that went down in price. This tells you just how strongly buyers supported the securities that were going up and just how much selling pressure faced those securities that went down.

If the trin is less than 1.00, that usually means that there are a lot of buyers taking securities up in price, and that's positive. If the trin is above 1.00, then the sellers are acting more strongly, and that indicates that there's a lot of negative sentiment in the market.

Volume

The trin indicator looks at price in conjunction with volume. That makes this a good time to introduce volume indicators.

Volume tells you how much trading is taking place in the market. How excited are people about the current price? Do they see this as great opportunity to buy or to sell? Are they selling fast, to get out now, or are they taking a more leisurely approach to the market these days? This information is carried in the volume of the trading, and it's an important adjunct to the information you see in the prices. Volume tells you whether there's enough support to maintain price trends, or if price trends are likely to change soon.

Force index

The *force index* gives you a sense of the strength of a trend. It starts with information from prices, namely that if the closing price today is higher than the closing price yesterday, that's positive for the security. And that means that if today's closing price is lower than yesterday's, then the force is generally negative. Then that price information is combined with volume information. The more volume that goes with that price change, the stronger that positive or negative force.

Although many quotation systems will calculate force for you, you can do it yourself, too. For each trading day,

```
Force index = volume × (today's moving average –
        yesterday's moving average)
```

In other words, the force index simply scales the moving average momentum oscillator (discussed above) for the amount of volume that accompanies that price change. That way, the trader has a sense of just how overbought or oversold the security is any particular day.

On-balance volume

The *on-balance volume* is a running total of the amount of trading in a security. To calculate it, first look at today's closing price relative to yesterday's. If today's close is higher than yesterday's, then add today's volume to yesterday's on-balance volume. If today's closing price is less than yesterday's, then subtract today's volume from yesterday's total. And if today's close is the same as yesterday's, don't do anything: Today's balance is the same as yesterday's.

Many traders track on-balance volume over time, and here's why: A change in volume signals a change in demand. That might not show up in price right away if there are enough buyers to absorb volume from sellers. But if there are still more buyers out there, then the price is going to go up. Hence, the volume from even small day-to-day increases in price need to be added up over time. If the volume keeps going up, then at some point, prices are going to have to go up to meet the demand.

On the downside, the volume from small price declines will add up over time, too. Over time, it may show that there is very little pent-up interest, indicating that prices could languish for some time.

Many traders look to on-balance volume to gauge the behavior of so-called *smart money*, such as pension funds, hedge funds, and mutual fund companies. Unlike individual investors, these big institutional accounts tend to trade on fundamentals rather than emotion. They tend to start buying a security at the point where the dumb money is tired of owning it, so their early buying may show big volume with little price change. But as the institutions keep buying, the price will have to go up to get the smarter individuals and the early institutions to part with their shares.

Open interest

Open interest has a different meaning in the stock market than in the options and futures markets, but in both cases, it gives traders useful information about demand.

In the stock market, open interest is the number of buy orders submitted before the market opens. If the open interest is high, that means that people are ready to add shares to their positions or initiate new positions, and that in turn means that the stock is likely to go up in price on the demand.

In the options and futures markets, open interest is the number of contracts at the end of every day that have not been exercised, closed out, or allowed to expire. Day traders won't have open interest, because by definition, day traders close out at the end of every day. But some traders will keep open interest, either because they think that their position has the ability to increase in profitability or because they are hedging another transaction and need to keep that options or futures position in place. If open interest in a contract is increasing, then new money is coming into the market and prices are likely to continue to go up. This is especially true if volume is increasing at about the same rate as open interest. On the other hand, if open interest is falling, then people are closing out their positions because they no longer see a profit potential, and prices are likely to fall.

Volatility

The *volatility* of a security is a measure of how much it tends to go up or down in a given time period. The more volatile the security, the more the price will fluctuate. Most day traders prefer volatile securities, because that creates more opportunities to make a profit in a short amount of time. But volatility can make it tougher to gauge market sentiment. If a security is volatile, the mood can change quickly. What looked like a profit opportunity at the market open might be gone by lunchtime — and back again before the close.

Average true range

The *average true range* is a measure of volatility that's commonly used in commodity markets, but some stock traders use it, too. Many quotation systems calculate it automatically, but if you want to do it yourself, start with finding each day's *true range*. This is the greatest of

- ✔ The current high less the current low.
- ✔ The absolute value of the current high less the previous close.
- ✔ The absolute value of the current low less the previous close.

Calculate those three numbers, then take the highest of them and average it with the true range for the past 14 days.

Each day's true range number shows you just how much the security swung between the high and the low, or how much the high or the low that day varied from the previous day's close. It's a measure of how much volatility occurred each day. When averaged over time, it shows how much volatility takes place over time. The higher the average true range, the more volatile a security is.

Beta

Beta is the *covariance* (that is, the statistical measure of how much two variables move together) of a stock relative to the rest of the market. The number comes from the Capital Assets Pricing Model, which is an equation used in academic circles to model the performance of securities. Traders don't use the Capital Assets Pricing Model, but they often talk about beta to evaluate the volatility of stocks and options.

What does beta mean?

- A beta of one means that the security moves at a faster rate than the market. You would buy high betas if you think the market is going up, but not if the market is going down.

- A beta of less than one means that the security moves more slowly than the market. This is good if you want less risk than the market.

- A beta of exactly one means that the security moves at the same rate as the market.

- A negative beta means that the security moves in the opposite direction of the market. The easiest way to get a negative beta security is to *short* (borrow and then sell) a positive beta security.

VIX

VIX is short for the Chicago Board Options Exchange Volatility Index. The calculation of it is complex enough to border on being proprietary, but it is available on many quotation systems and on the exchange's Web site, www.cboe.com/micro/vix/introduction.aspx.

The VIX is based on the implied volatility of options on stocks included in the S&P 500 Index. The greater the volatility, the more uncertainty investors have, and the more options that show great volatility, the more widespread the concern is within the market. Hence, some consider the VIX to be a gauge of market fear. The greater the VIX, the more bearish the outlook for the market in general.

Traders can use the VIX to help them value options and futures on the market indexes. (For that matter, traders who want to take a position on market volatility can use option contracts on the VIX offered by the Chicago Board Options Exchange.) The VIX can also be used to help confirm bullish or bearish sentiment that shows up in other market signals, such as the tick or the on-balance volume measures described earlier.

In addition to the VIX, the exchange also tracks the *VXN* (volatility on the NASDAQ 100 Index) and the *VXD* (volatility on the Dow Jones Industrial Average.)

Volatility ratio

The *volatility ratio* tells traders what the implied volatility of a security is relative to the recent historical volatility. It shows if the security is expected to be more or less volatile right now than it has been in the past, and it's widely used in option markets. The first calculation required is the *implied volatility*, which is backed out using the Black-Scholes model, an academic model for valuing options. When you plug in time until expiration, interest rates, dividends, stock price, and strike price to the model, the implied volatility is the volatility number that then generates the current option price. (You don't have to do this yourself, as most quotation systems generate implied volatility for you.)

Once you have the implied volatility, you can compare it to the historical volatility of the option, which tells you just how much the price changed over the last 20 or 90 days. If the implied volatility is greater than the statistical volatility, the market may be overestimating the uncertainty in the prices, and the options may be overvalued. And, if the implied volatility is much less than the statistical volatility, the market may be underestimating uncertainty, so the options may be undervalued.

Measuring Money Flows

Money flows tell you how much money is going into or out of a market. They are another set of indicators that tell you where the market sentiment is right now and where it might be going soon. They combine features of price and volume indicators to help traders gauge the market. Although amounts spent to buy and sell have to match — otherwise, there would be no market — the enthusiasm of the buyers and the anxiousness of the sellers shows up in the volume traded and the direction of the price change. Just how hard was it for the buyers to get the sellers to part with their positions? And, how hard will it be to get them to part with their positions tomorrow? That's the information contained in money flow indicators.

The most basic money flow indicator is closing price multiplied by the number of shares traded. If the closing price was higher than the closing price yesterday, then the number is positive; if the closing price today was lower than the price yesterday, then the number is negative.

Accumulation/distribution index

In trading terms, *accumulation* is controlled buying, and *distribution* is controlled selling. This is the kind of buying and selling that doesn't lead to big changes in securities prices, and it's usually because the action was planned. No one accumulates or distributes a security in a state of panic.

But even if the buying and selling activity isn't driven by madcap rushes in and out of positions, it's still important to know whether, on balance, the buyers or the sellers have the slight predominance in the market, because that may affect the direction of in the near future. For example, if a security has been in an upward trend, but there are more and more down days with increasing volume, that means that the sellers are starting to dominate the trading and that the price trend is likely to go down.

Here's the equation:

```
Accumulation/distribution = ((Close - Low) - (High -
          Close)) / (High - Low) × Period's volume
```

Some traders look at accumulation/distribution from day to day, whereas others prefer to look at it for a week or even a month's worth of trading.

Money flow ratio and money flow index

Money flow is closing price multiplied by the number of shares traded. That basic statistic can be manipulated in strange and wonderful ways to generate new statistics carrying even more information about whether the markets are likely to have more buying pressure or more selling pressure in the future.

The first is the *money flow ratio*. This is simply the total money flow for those days where prices were up from the prior day (days with positive money flow), divided by the total money flow for those days where prices were down from the prior day (which are the days with negative money flow). Day traders tend to calculate money flow ratios for short time periods, such as a week or ten days, while swing traders and investors tend to care about longer time periods, like a month or even four months of trading.

The money flow ratio is sometimes converted into the *money flow index*, which can be used as a single indicator or tracked relative to prices for a given period of time. This equation looks like Figure 13-3.

Figure 13-3:
This
equation
figures out
the money
flow index.

$$MFI = 100 - \frac{100}{1 + money\ ratio}$$

If the money flow index is more than 80, the security is usually considered to be overbought — meaning that the buyers are done buying, and the sellers will put downward pressure on prices. If the money flow index is less than 20, then the security is usually considered to be oversold, and the buyers will soon take over and drive prices up. In between, the money flow index can help clarify information from other market indicators.

Short interest ratios

Short selling is a way to make money if a security falls in price. In the options and futures markets, one simply agrees to sell a contract to someone else. In the stock and bond markets, it's a little more complicated. The short seller borrows stock or bonds through the brokerage firm, and then sells them. Ideally, the price will fall, and then the trader can buy back the stock or bonds at the lower price to repay the loan. The trader keeps the difference between the price where the security was sold and the price where the security was repurchased. (The process is described in more detail in Chapter 14.)

People take the short side of a position for only one reason: They think that prices are going to go down. They may want to hedge against this, or they may want to make a big profit if it happens. In the stock market in particular, monitoring the rate of short selling can give clues to investor expectations and future market direction.

The New York Stock Exchange and NASDAQ report the short interest in stocks listed with them. The data are updated monthly, as it can take a while for brokerage firms to sort out exactly how many shares have been shorted and then report that data to the exchanges. The resulting number, the *short interest ratio*, tells the number of shares that have been shorted, the percentage change from the month before, the average daily trading volume in the same month, and the number of days of trading at the average volume that it would take to cover the short positions.

The loans that enable short selling have to be repaid. If the lender asks for them back, or if prices go up so that the position starts to lose money, the trader is going to have to buy shares in order to make repayment. The harder it is to get the right number of shares in the market, the more desperate the trader will become, and the higher prices will go.

An increase in short interest shows that investors are becoming nervous about a stock. However, given that short interest is not calculated frequently, the number would probably not give a trader a lot of information about the prospects for the company itself. This doesn't mean short interest doesn't carry a lot of useful information for traders. It does. If the short interest is high, then the security price is likely to go up when all the people who are short need to buy back stock. Likewise, if short interest is low, there will be little buying pressure in the near future.

High short interest, along with other bullish indicators, is a sign that prices are more likely to go up than down in the near future.

Information Cropping up During the Trading Day

Technical analysis (described in Chapter 12) and all the indicators discussed in this chapter offer useful information about what's happening in the markets, but there's one problem: Because so many of those indicators are based on closing prices and closing volume, they aren't much use during the trading day. And in fact, many traders read through the information in the morning before the open to sort out what is likely to happen and what the mood of the market is likely to be, but then they have to recalibrate their gauge of the market as information comes to them during the trading day. That information doesn't show up on charts or in neat numerical indicators until the day ends. But there are several sources of information that are updated while the market is open to give a trader a sense of what's happening at any given time.

Price, time, and sales

The most important information for a trader is the current price of the security, how often and in what volume it has been trading, and how much the price has moved from the last trade. This is the most basic real-time information out there, and it's readily available through a brokerage firm's quotation screens.

In Chapter 6 there is a discussion of the different quotation services that traders can obtain from their brokerage firms. Although your broker may charge you more to get more detailed quotes, it's worth it for most trading strategies. Knowing how the price is moving can give you a sense of whether the general mood of the market is being confirmed or contradicted. That can help you place more profitable trades.

Order book

High-level price quote data, such as that available through NASDAQ Level II or NASDAQ TotalView, include information on who is placing orders and just how large those orders are. (Refer to Chapter 6 to see what this looks like.) The book gives you key data, because it gives you a sense of how smart the other buyers and sellers are. Are they day traders just trying not to be killed? Or are they institutions that have done a lot of research and are under a lot of performance pressure? Sure, day traders are often very right and institutions are often very wrong, but the information you see in the order book can help you sense whether people are trading on information or on emotion.

An additional piece of information from the order book can help you figure out what's happening in the market now — namely, the presence of an *order imbalance*. An order imbalance means that the number of buyers and sellers don't match. This often happens during the open, because some traders prefer to place orders before the market opens, whereas others prefer to wait until after the open. These imbalances tend to be small and clear up quickly. However, if a major news event takes place, or there's a great deal of fear in the market, large imbalances can occur during the trading day. These can be disruptive, and in some cases the exchange stops trading until news is disseminated and enough new orders are placed to balance out the orders.

News flows

Although much of the discussion in this chapter has been about the information contained in price, volume, and other trade data, the actual information that comes from news releases is at least as important.

Much of the news is regularly scheduled and much predicted: corporate earnings, Federal Reserve discount rates, unemployment rates, housing starts, and the like. When this information comes in, traders want to know how the actual results compare with what was expected, and how this fits with the overall bullish or bearish sentiment of the market.

The second type of news is the unscheduled breaking event, such as corporate takeovers, horrible storms, political assassinations, or other happenings that were not expected and that take more time for the market to digest. That's in part because these events have the ability to change trends rather than play out against them. In some cases, the markets will halt trading to allow this information to disseminate; in others, traders have to react quickly based on what they know now and what they suspect will happen in the near future.

What's the difference between risk and uncertainty? *Risk* is something that happens often enough that people can quantify the damage. *Uncertainty* is something that might happen, but no one can figure out the likelihood. A fire that knocks out power to Midtown Manhattan sometime in the next ten years is a risk; the invasion of the planet by aliens from outer space is uncertainty.

News can happen at any time. It can change a trend and throw all your careful analysis into disarray. That's why careful analysis is no substitute for risk management. Watch your position sizes and have stops in place so that you exit when you need to. Chapter 2 has a lot of information on these topics.

Anomalies and Traps

Traders can be superstitious, and that shows up in different anomalies and traps that affect the mood of the market even if there is no logical reason for their existence. You want to be aware of them, because they can affect trading, even if there doesn't seem to be a justification for them.

An *anomaly* is a market condition that occurs regularly, but for no good reason. It can be related to the month of the year, the day of the week, or the size of the company involved.

A *trap* is a situation where the market doesn't perform the way you expect it to given the indicators that you are looking at. You have a choice: Go with what the market is telling you, or go with what your indicators are telling you.

To a long-term investor, perception is perception. When it's different from reality, there's an opportunity to make money. To a short-term trader, perception is reality, because that affects what happens before everyone figures out what's real.

Bear traps and bull traps

Traders talk about getting caught in traps, which neatly fits the language of bulls and bears. When this happens, they are stuck moving against the market, and that causes them big trouble. After all, day trading is about identifying trends and moving with them, because you only have a few hours to work before it's time to close out. In this section, I list a few common traps to help you identify them and, I hope, avoid them.

The best antidote for a trap is to take your loss and move on to the next trade.

Chart traps

If you go back to Chapter 12 and look at some of the sample charts, and if you look at actual price charts created in the market every day, you might notice that sometimes, it's really hard to tell whether a breakout is false or real, whether a trend is changing or just playing out with a smaller subtrend. A ton of subjectivity goes into reading charts, and some days you'll read them wrong. You'll be thinking that you are ahead of the market when you've actually just traded against it. Ouch!

Some traders try to work around this by automating their trading. Several different software packages will scan the market and identify potential trading opportunities (see Chapter 7 for more information.) But even the best software will misread the market on some occasions. That's why you need to monitor your positions and make sure you stick to your loss limits.

Contrarian traps

Way back in Chapter 1, I noted that about 80 percent of day traders lose money. So maybe you're thinking that the way to make money is to just do the opposite of what everyone else is doing. But the reason that they lose money isn't so much that they are wrong about the trend, it's that they are sloppy in their trading and don't limit their losses. (That's why so much of this book is about the business of trading, rather than the actual mechanics of placing buy and sell orders.)

In a *contrarian trap*, the trader has made the decision to trade against the market, and that's exactly what happens: He or she loses money because the market is moving in the opposite direction. Taking a contrary position doesn't work too well in day trading. In most cases, you have to go with the flow, not against it, to make money in a single day's session. The market is always right in the short term.

Calendar effects

Many trading anomalies follow time periods. That's not completely unexpected, as many economic and business trends follow the calendar. Companies report their results quarterly. Most close their books for tax purposes at the end of the year. Investors are also evaluated quarterly. Retail sales follow holiday seasons, demand for commodities follows the growing season, and fuel demand varies with the weather. Whatever you decided to trade, you need to do enough fundamental research (the study of the business and economic factors that affect the security, described in Chapter 12) so that you know how your chosen securities move over time.

But some of the calendar effects make little logical sense, yet they influence trading. Hence, this explanation of the January effect, the Monday effect, and the October effect.

The January effect

Many years, the stock market goes up in the early part of January. Why? No one is entirely sure, but the guess is that people tend to sell at the end of December for tax reasons, and then buy back those securities in January. It may also be that in the new year, everyone is flush with excitement and ready to see the market go up, so they put money to work and start buying.

If stocks go up in January, then you can get a jump on the market by buying in December, right? And that would make prices go up in December. To get a jump on the December rally, you could buy in November. And that's exactly what people started to do, and the once-pronounced January effect is now weak to non-existent. (People still talk about it, though.) In an efficient market, people will eventually figure out these unexplained phenomena, then trade on them until they disappear. Use these anomalies as a way to gauge psychology, not as hard and fast trading rules.

The Monday effect

The market seems to do more poorly on Monday than on the other days of the week. And no matter what the evidence shows (and the research is ambiguous and the findings vary greatly based on the time period and the markets examined), many traders believe this, so it has an effect. Why? There are two thoughts. The first is that everyone is in a bad mood on Monday because they have to go back to work after the weekend. The second is that people spend all weekend analyzing any bad news from the end of the prior week, then sell as soon as they get back to the office.

The October effect

The stock market has had two grand crashes and one smaller but profound one, all in October. On October 29, 1929, a day known as Black Tuesday, the Dow Jones Industrial Average declined 12 percent in one day as market speculators caught up with the less rosy reality of the economy. This crash kicked off a general decline that contributed to the Great Depression of the 1930s. On October 19, 1987, known as Black Monday, the Dow Jones Industrial Average declined 23 percent. No one is really sure why it happened, but it did. Then, on October 13, 1989, the Dow Jones declined 7 percent in the last hour of trading when a leveraged buyout for United Airlines fell through.

Because of these crashes, many traders believe that bad things happen in October, and they act accordingly. Of course, bad things happen in other months. The crash in the NASDAQ market that marked the end of the 1990s tech bubble took place in March of 2000, but no one talks about a March effect.

Chapter 14

Short Selling and Leverage

*I*n a certain sense, day trading isn't risky at all. Day traders close out their positions overnight to minimize the possibility of something going wrong while the trader isn't paying attention. Each trade is based on finding a small price change in the market over a short period of time, so it's unlikely that anything is going to change dramatically. But here's the thing: Trading this way leads to small returns. It's hard to justify trading full time if you aren't making a lot of money when you do it, no matter how low your risk is.

And, of course, some days, there aren't many good trades to make. You can be looking for securities to go up, and they aren't. Zero trades lead to zero risk, and zero return.

That's why savvy traders think about other ways to make money on their trades, even if it involves taking on more risk. It's that risk that generates the return that many traders crave. In this chapter, I cover two techniques for finding trades and increasing returns: *short selling* and *leverage*. Both involve borrowing, also known as leverage, and both increase risk.

Taking Other People's Money to Make Money

The dollars you make from trading depend on two things: your percentage return on your trades and the dollars you have to start out with. If you double your money but only have a $1,000 account, then you are left with $2,000. If you get a 10 percent return but have a $1,000,000 account, then you make $100,000. Which would you rather have? (Yes, I know, you'd rather double your money with the $1,000,000 account. But I didn't give you that choice, alas.)

The point is that the more money you have to trade, the more dollars you can generate, even if the return on the trade itself is small. If you have $500,000 and borrow $500,000 more, then your 10 percent return will give you $100,000 to take home, not $50,000. You have doubled the dollars returned to you by doubling the money you used to place the trades, not by doubling the performance of the trade itself. Clever, huh?

Leverage gives you more money to trade. That helps you generate more dollars for your account — or lose more dollars, if you aren't careful or have a string of reversals.

When you borrow money or shares of stock, you have to pay it back, no matter what happens. That's why borrowing can be risky.

Why leverage is important in short-term trading

Day traders and other short-term traders aren't looking to make big money on any single trade. Instead, the goal is to make small money on a whole bunch of trades. Unfortunately, it can be hard for all those little trades to add up to something big. That's why many day traders turn to leverage. They either borrow money or stock from their brokerage firm, or they trade securities that have built-in leverage, such as futures and foreign exchange.

The fine print on margin agreements

Leverage not only adds risk to your own account, it adds risk to the entire financial system. If everyone borrowed money and then some big market catastrophe happened, then no one would be able to repay their loans, and those who lent the money would go bust, too.

As a result, there's an incredible amount of oversight that goes with leverage strategies. The Securities and Exchange Commission, the Commodity Futures Trading Commission, the different exchanges, and even the U.S. Treasury Department regulate how much money a trader can borrow. Many brokerage firms have even stricter rules in place as part of their risk management, and they are expected to demonstrate to the National Association of Securities Dealers and the National Futures Association that they follow their practices.

This means you have about as much flexibility when you borrow from your broker in order to buy and sell securities as you would have if you borrowed from your friendly neighborhood loan shark to play a high-stakes poker game. Meaning: not much. Margin loans are highly regulated, and you must meet the broker's terms. If you fail to repay the loan, your positions will be sold from underneath you. If you try to borrow too much, you will be cut off. No amount of begging and pleading will help you.

Your brokerage firm makes you sign a margin agreement, which says that you understand the risks and limits of your activities. You probably can't have a margin account unless you meet a minimum account size, maybe $10,000 or more, and the amount you can borrow depends on the size of your account. Generally, a stock or bond account must hold 50 percent of the purchase price of securities when you borrow the money. The price of those securities can go down, but if they go down so much that the account now holds only 25 percent of the value of the loan, you'll get a margin call. (Some brokers will call in loans faster than others; their policies are disclosed in their margin agreements.)

Brokerage firms handle margin trades all the time. You do the paperwork once, when you sign a margin agreement. Each time you place an order, you're asked if you are making the trade with cash or on margin. Click the "Margin" box, and you've just borrowed money. It's that easy.

Managing margin calls

If the value of your account starts falling, and it looks like it is falling below the 25 percent maintenance margin limit, you'll get a *margin call.* Your broker will call you and ask you to deposit more money in your account. If you can't do that, the broker will start selling your securities to close out the loan. And if you don't have enough to pay off the loan, the broker will close your account and put a lien, which is a claim on your assets, against you.

Most brokerage firms have risk-management limits in place, so you'll probably get plenty of warning before you get a margin call or see your account closed out. After all, neither you nor your brokerage firm wants to lose money. Just keep in mind that it's a possibility.

At least one brokerage firm advertises that, as a service to you, it will close out your account as soon as you lose the amount in it, to keep you from losing more money. It's as much a service to the brokerage as it is to you, but it's an example of the built-in risk management that firms have to limit risks to everyone.

The dangers of risk: Long-Term Capital Management

Leverage adds risk to low-risk strategies, which increases returns as long as nothing goes wrong. But sometimes things go horribly wrong, even for the big guys. In 1998, Long-Term Capital Management, a hedge fund formed by several leading traders and academics (including a few Nobel Prize winners), failed.

The fund's basic trading style had very little risk. Its traders looked for small price differences between bonds that were expected to go away. (This is known as *arbitrage* and is discussed in Chapter 15.) To generate big money, the fund borrowed tons of money, which turned that low-risk strategy into a risky one. In the summer of 1998, the Russian government defaulted on its bonds. Investors panicked and traded their European and Japanese bonds for U.S. government bonds.

Long-Term Capital Management had bet that small differences in price between the U.S. bonds and the overseas ones would disappear; instead, the concern over Russia's problems caused the small price differences to get bigger. Much bigger. This made it difficult for Long-Term Capital Management's managers to repay the money that the fund had borrowed, which put pressure on the banks and brokerage firms that had given the loans. The Federal Reserve Bank organized a restructuring plan with the banks that were owed money by Long-Term Capital Management in order to prevent a massive financial catastrophe. In total, Long-Term Capital Management lost $4.6 billion dollars.

Margin bargains for day traders only

Day traders are often able to avoid margin calls because they borrow money for such short periods of time. Good day traders look for small market moves and cut their losses early on, which minimizes the risk of using other people's money. And, by definition, day traders close out their positions every night.

If you qualify as a pattern day trader, you get two benefits. First, your brokerage firm probably won't charge you any interest as long as you do not hold a margin loan balance overnight. Second, you may be allowed to borrow more than 50 percent of the purchase price of securities. Some firms allow pattern day traders to borrow 75 percent or more of their trade value.

The New York Stock Exchange and National Association of Securities Dealers define a *pattern day trader* as one with a margin account holding at least $25,000. This trader must also buy then sell, or sell short then buy, the same security on the same day four or more times in five business days. The number of day trades should be more than six percent of the customer's total trading activity for that same five-day period.

Short Selling

Traditionally, investors and traders want to buy low and sell high. They buy a position in a security and then wait for the price to go up. It's not a bad way to make money, especially because if the country's economy continues to grow even a little bit, then businesses are going to grow and so are their stocks.

But even in a good economy, some securities go down. The company may be mismanaged, it may sell a product that's out of favor, or maybe it's just having a string of bad days. For that matter, maybe it went up a little too much in price, and now investors are coming to their senses. In these situations, you can't make money buying low and selling high. If only there were a way to reverse the situation.

Well, there is a way — selling short. And in short — hah! — _selling short_ means that you borrow a security and then sell it in hopes of repaying the loan of the shares by buying back cheaper shares later on.

In trading lingo, when you own something, you are considered to be _long_. When you sell it, you are considered to be _short_. You don't have to be long before you go short.

How to sell short

Most brokerage firms make it easy to sell short. You simply place an order to sell the stock, and the broker asks whether you are selling shares that you own or selling short. Once you place the order, the brokerage firm goes about borrowing shares for you to sell. It loans the shares to your account and executes the sell order.

You can't sell short unless the brokerage firm is able to borrow the shares. Sometimes, so many people have sold a stock short that there are no shares to borrow. If that's the case, you'll have to find another stock or another strategy this time.

Once the shares are sold, you wait until the security goes down in price, then you buy the shares in the market at a bargain. These purchased shares are then returned to the broker to pay the loan, and you keep the difference between where you sold and where you bought — less interest, of course.

The stock exchanges are in the business of helping companies raise money, so they have rules in place to help maintain an upward bias in the stock market. That can work against the short seller. The key regulation is what's called the *uptick rule*, which means you can only sell a stock short when the last trade was a move up. You can't short a stock that's moving down.

Figure 14-1 shows how short selling works. The trader borrows 400 shares selling at $25 each and then sells them. If the stock goes down, she can buy back the shares at the lower price, making a tidy profit. If the stock stays flat, she loses money because the broker will charge her interest based on the value of the shares she borrowed. And if the stock price goes up, she not only loses money on the interest expense, but she is also out on her investment.

Figure 14-1:
Looking at short selling in the equities market.

The trader borrows 400 shares of SuperCorp shares to sell. The shares are trading at $25 each. She sells them for $10,000. The brokerage firm charges 10% interest

Beginning Price	Shares Borrowed	Proceeds from Sale	Repurchase Price	Repurchase Cost	Loan Value	Net Profit	Interest Expense	Rate of Return	% Change in Stock Price
$ 25	400	$ 10,000	$ 40	$ (16,000)	10,000	$ (6,000)	$ 1,000	-70%	60%
$ 25	400	$ 10,000	$ 25	$ (10,000)	10,000	$ -	$ 1,000	-10%	0%
$ 25	400	$ 10,000	$ 15	$ (6,000)	10,000	$ 4,000	$ 1,000	30%	-40%

The interest and fees that the broker charges those who borrow stock accrue to the broker, not to the person who actually owns the stock. In fact, the stock's owner will probably never know that his shares were loaned out.

Choosing shorts

Investors — those people who do careful research and expect to be in their positions for months or even years — look for companies that have inflated expectations and are possibly fraudulent. Investors who work the short side of the market spend hours, usually doing careful accounting research, looking for companies that are likely to go down in price some day.

Day traders don't care about accounting. They don't have the time to wait for a short to work out. Instead, they are looking for stocks that go down in price for more mundane reasons, like more sellers than buyers in the next ten minutes. Most day traders who sell short simply reverse their long strategy. For example, some day traders like to buy stocks that have gone down for three days in a row, figuring that they'll go up on the fourth day. They'll also short stocks that have gone up three days in a row, figuring that they'll go down on the fourth day. You don't need a CPA to do that!

Trading strategies are covered in more detail in Chapters 12 and 13, if you are looking for some ideas.

Short squeezes and other risks

Shorting stocks carries certain risks, because a short sale is a bet on things going wrong. In theory, there's no limit on how much a stock can go up, so there is no limit on how much money a short seller can lose. Two traps in particular can get a short seller. The first is a short squeeze due to good news, the second is a concerted effort to hurt those who are short.

Squeeze my shorts

With a *short squeeze*, a company that has been popular with a lot of short sellers has some good news that drives the stock price up. When the price goes up, short sellers lose money, and some may even have margin problems. And the original reason for going short may be proven to be wrong. Those who are short start buying the stock back in order to reduce their losses, but their increased demand drives the stock price even higher, causing even bigger losses for those who are still short. Ouch!

Calling back the stock

All is not sweetness and light in the world of short selling. Many market participants distrust those folks who are doing all the careful research, in part because they are often right. Company executives are often optimists who don't like to hear bad news, and they'll blame short sellers for all that is wrong with their stock price.

Meanwhile, some short sellers have been known to get impatient if their sale isn't making money and start spreading ugly rumors. Many companies, brokers, and investors hate short sellers and try tactics to bust them. Sometimes they issue good news or spread rumors of good news to create a squeeze. Other times, they collectively ask holders of the stock to request that their brokerage firm not loan out their shares. This means that those who shorted it have to buy back and return the shares even if it makes no sense to do so.

Lots to Discover About Leverage

Leverage is the use of borrowed money to increase returns. Day traders use it a lot to get bigger returns from relatively small price changes in the underlying securities. And as long as they consistently close their positions out at the end of the day, day traders can borrow more money and pay less interest than people who hold securities for a longer term.

The process of borrowing works differently in different markets. In the stock and bond markets, it's straightforward. You just tell your broker you're borrowing when you place the order. In the options and futures markets, you're buying and selling contracts that have leverage built into them. You don't borrow money outright, but you can control a lot of value in your account for relatively little money down.

In stock and bond markets

Leverage is straightforward for buyers of stocks and bonds: You simply click the box marked "Margin" when you place your order, and the brokerage firm loans you money. (The margin process is defined in more detail earlier in the chapter.) Then, when the security goes up in price, you get a greater percentage return because you've been able to buy more for your money. Of course, that also increases your potential losses.

Figure 14-2 shows how it works. The trader borrows money to buy 400 shares of SuperCorp. If the stock goes up 4 percent, she makes 8 percent. Whoohooo! But if the stock goes down 4 percent, she still has to repay the loan at full dollar value, so she ends up losing 8 percent. That's not so good.

If you hold your margin position overnight or longer, you'll have to start paying interest. That will cut into your returns or increase your losses.

A trader buys $10,000 of SuperCorp with $5,000 of her own cash and a $5,000 loan
SuperCorp trades at $25/share, so the trader purchases a total of 400 shares.
The trader closes out at the end of the day, so no interest is charged.
What happens as the stock price changes?

	Ending Price	Ending Value	Loan Value	Net Equity	Trader's Rate of Return	% Change in Stock Price
Figure 14-2: Here's an example of trading stocks on margin.	$ 26.00	$ 10,400	$ 5,000	$ 5,400	8%	4%
	$ 25.50	$ 10,200	$ 5,000	$ 5,200	4%	2%
	$ 25.00	$ 10,000	$ 5,000	$ 5,000	0%	0%
	$ 24.50	$ 9,800	$ 5,000	$ 4,800	-4%	-2%
	$ 24.00	$ 9,600	$ 5,000	$ 4,600	-8%	-4%

In options markets

An *option* gives you the right, but not the obligation, to buy or sell a stock or other item at a set price when the contract expires. A *call option* gives you the right to buy, so you would buy a call if you think the underlying asset is going up. A *put option* gives you the right to sell, so you would buy a put if you think the underlying asset is going down. (You can read more about options in Chapter 3, if you are so inspired.) By trading an option, you get exposure to changes in the price of the underlying security without actually buying the security itself. That's the source of the leverage in the market.

A day trader might use options to get an exposure to price changes in a stock for a lot less money than it would cost to buy the stock itself. Suppose a call option is *deeply in-the-money*. That means that its *strike price*, the price that you would be able to buy the stock at if you exercised the option, is far below the current stock price. If this happens, the obvious thing is for the option price to be set at the difference between the current stock price and the strike price, and that's more or less what happens: more in theory, less in practice. When the stock price changes, the option price changes at almost exactly the same amount. This means that you can buy the price performance of the stock at a discount, the discount being the strike price of the stock.

Figure 14-3 shows the performance-boosting leverage from this strategy. The trader buys call options with an exercise price of $10 on a stock trading at $25. The option price changes the same amount that the stock price does, but the call holder gets a greater percentage return than the stock holder.

Figure 14-3: A trader buys deep in-the-money call options on SuperCorp. The exercise price is $10, and the stock is trading at $25.
What happens to the option value when the stock price changes?

Stock Price	Initial Option Price	Exercise (Strike) Price	New Option Price	Stock Price Change	Option Price Change
$ 26.00	$ 15.00	$ 10.00	$ 16.00	4%	7%
$ 25.50	$ 15.00	$ 10.00	$ 15.50	2%	3%
$ 25.00	$ 15.00	$ 10.00	$ 15.00	0%	0%
$ 24.50	$ 15.00	$ 10.00	$ 14.50	-2%	-3%
$ 24.00	$ 15.00	$ 10.00	$ 14.00	-4%	-7%

There are many other options strategies that day traders can use, but a discussion of them goes beyond the scope of this book. The Appendix has some resources to help you in your research.

In futures trading

A *futures* contract gives you the obligation to buy or sell an underlying financial or agricultural commodity, assuming you still hold the contract at the expiration date. That underlying product ranges from the value of treasury bonds to barrels of oil and heads of cattle, and you're only putting money down now when you purchase the contract. You don't have to come up with the full amount until the contract comes due — and almost all options and futures traders close out their trades long before the contract expiration date. Futures are discussed in Chapter 3, but here I talk about how leverage works in the futures market.

Although most options and futures contracts settle with cash long before the due date, contract holders have the right to hold them until the due date and, in the case of options on common stock and agricultural derivatives, demand physical delivery. It's rare, but the commodity exchanges have systems in place for determining the transport, specifications, and delivery of grain, cattle, or ethanol. One advantage of day trading is that you close out the same day, without ever even thinking about the fine print of physical delivery.

Because *derivatives* have built-in leverage that allows a trader to have big market exposure for relatively few dollars up front, they've become popular with day traders. Figure 14-4 shows how it works. Here, a trader is buying the Chicago Mercantile Exchange's E-Mini S&P 500 futures contract, which gives traders exposure to the performance of the Standard and Poor's 500 Index, a standard measure of the stock performance of a diversified list of 500 large American companies. The futures contract trades at 50 times the value of the index, rounded to the nearest $0.25. The minimum margin that a trader must put down on the contract is $3,500. Each $0.25 change in the index leads to a $12.50 ($0.25 × 50) change in the value of the contract, and that $12.50 is added to or subtracted from the $3,500 margin.

Figure 14-4:
Margin and the derivatives trade with built-in leverage.

A day trader buys a Chicago Mercantile Exchange E-Mini S&P 500 futures contract.
The contract price is $50 x the index level. To buy it, the trader must post margin of $3,500

Initial Index Value	Ending Index Value	Multiplier	Initial Contract Value	Contract Value	Value Change in Dollars	Value Change in Percent	Initial Margin	Ending Margin	Percent Change in Margin
1,457.50	1,458.50	$ 50.00	$ 72,875.00	$ 72,925.00	$ 50.00	0.07%	$ 3,500.00	$ 3,550.00	1.43%
1,457.50	1,458.00	$ 50.00	$ 72,875.00	$ 72,900.00	$ 25.00	0.03%	$ 3,500.00	$ 3,525.00	0.71%
1,457.50	1,457.50	$ 50.00	$ 72,875.00	$ 72,875.00	$ -	0.00%	$ 3,500.00	$ 3,500.00	0.00%
1,457.50	1,457.00	$ 50.00	$ 72,875.00	$ 72,850.00	$ (25.00)	-0.03%	$ 3,500.00	$ 3,475.00	-0.71%
1,457.50	1,456.50	$ 50.00	$ 72,875.00	$ 72,825.00	$ (50.00)	-0.07%	$ 3,500.00	$ 3,450.00	-1.43%

Some exchanges use the term *margin*, and others prefer to use *performance bond*. Either way, it's the same thing: money you put in up front to ensure that you can meet the contract terms when it comes due. If you hold the contract overnight, your account is adjusted up or down to reflect the day's profits. If it gets too low, you're asked to add more money.

In foreign exchange

The *foreign exchange*, or *forex*, market is driven by leverage. Exchange rates tend to move slowly, by as little as a tenth or even a hundredth of a penny a day. And the markets are so huge that it's easier to hedge risk. You might have trouble borrowing shares of stock to short them, but you should have no trouble ever borrowing yen. In order to get a big return, forex traders almost always borrow huge amounts of money.

In the stock market, day traders can borrow up to three times the amount of cash and securities held in their accounts (although not all firms will let you borrow the statutory maximum), and that amount is set by outside regulatory organizations. In the forex market, there is no regulation on lending, and some forex firms will allow traders to borrow as much as 400 times the amount in their accounts.

Forex firms allow such huge borrowing because they can hedge their risks, so that if you lose money, they make money. If you sell dollars to buy euros, the firm can easily go in and sell euros to buy dollars. That makes its position net neutral. If the euro goes down relative to the dollar, you've lost money, but the firm can offset its risk because its counter-trade went up.

The reason that a forex firm wants to hedge its risks against its day trading customers is that most day traders lose money. The firms know that if they bet against the aggregate trades held by their customers, they'll probably come out ahead. Don't trade in forex or any other market until you've worked out a strategy and practiced it, so that you can avoid becoming a statistic. Chapter 11 has information on testing and evaluating trading strategies.

Figure 14-5 shows how leverage in foreign exchange makes good returns possible. Here, the trader starts with a $1,000 account and borrows the maximum amount the forex firms allow, $400 for each dollar in the account. All $401,000 are put to work buying euros. Note that the euro value stays constant, but the dollar value of those euros changes by hundredths of a penny. Thanks to leverage, the return is 11 percent — not bad for a day's trading! Of course, you could lose 11 percent, which wouldn't be so good.

Figure 14-5:
Trading
foreign
exchange
on margin.

A trader has a $1,000 forex account. He borrows 400 times that amount - $400,000 - to buy euros

Initial Dollar/Euro Rate	Ending Dollar/Euro Rate	Initial Account Value	Amount Purchased ($)	Amount Purchased (€)	Ending Value (€)	Ending Value ($)	Loan Value	Ending Account Value	Trader's Rate of Return	% Change in Exchange Rate
0.7477	0.7475	$ 1,000	$ 401,000	€ 299,828	€ 299,828	$ 401,107	$ 400,000	$ 1,107	11%	-0.03%
0.7477	0.7476	$ 1,000	$ 401,000	€ 299,828	€ 299,828	$ 401,054	$ 400,000	$ 1,054	5%	-0.01%
0.7477	0.7477	$ 1,000	$ 401,000	€ 299,828	€ 299,828	$ 401,000	$ 400,000	$ 1,000	0%	0.00%
0.7477	0.7478	$ 1,000	$ 401,000	€ 299,828	€ 299,828	$ 400,946	$ 400,000	$ 946	-5%	0.01%
0.7477	0.7479	$ 1,000	$ 401,000	€ 299,828	€ 299,828	$ 400,893	$ 400,000	$ 893	-11%	0.03%

An exchange rate is just the price of money. If the dollar/euro rate is .7477, that means that $1.00 will buy 0.7477.

Borrowing in Your Trading Business

Leverage is only part of the borrowing involved in your day trading business. Like any business owner, sometimes you need more cash than your business generates. Other times, you see expansion opportunities that require more money than you have on hand. In this section, I discuss why and how day traders can borrow money over and above leveraged trading.

Margin loans for cash flow

If day trading is your job, then you face a constant pressure: How do you cover the costs of living while keeping enough money in the market to trade? One way to do this is to have another source of income — from savings, a spouse, or a job that doesn't overlap with market hours. Other day traders take money out of their trading account.

If the market hasn't been cooperative, then there might not be enough to take out of the account while still having enough capital to trade. One option is to arrange a margin loan through a brokerage firm. The firm will let you take out a loan against the securities that you hold. You can spend the money any way you like, but you will be charged interest — and you will have to repay it. Still, it's a good option to have, because day trade earnings tend to be erratic.

Borrowing for trading capital

Some day traders use a double layer of leverage: They borrow the money to set up their trading accounts and then they borrow money for their trading strategies. If the market cooperates, this can be a great way to make money, but if not, you could end up owing a lot of people money that you don't have.

If you want to take the risk, though, you have a few resources to turn to other than your relatives: You can borrow against your house, use your credit cards, or find a trading firm that will give you some money to work with.

Borrowing against your house

Yes, you can use a mortgage or a home equity line of credit to get the money for your day trading activities. In general, this carries low interest rates because your house is your collateral. In most cases, though, the interest will not be tax deductible (ask your accountant, but generally, you can only deduct interest used to purchase or improve your house). Still, it can be a relatively low-cost way to pull value stored in your house for use in trading. The risk? If you can't pay back the loan, you can lose your residence. Just don't borrow against your car, too, as you'll need a place to live when the bank evicts you.

Putting it on the card

The business world is filled with people who started businesses using credit cards. And you can do that. If you have even halfway decent credit, credit card companies are happy to lend you all the money you want.

Naturally, they charge you a mighty high rate of interest, one that even the sharpest traders will have trouble covering from their returns. If the only way you can raise the capital for day trading is through your credit card, consider waiting a few years and saving your money before taking the plunge. Because day trading income can be erratic, you may end up using your credit cards to cover your living expenses some months. You may want to save your credit for that rather than dedicate it directly for your day trading.

Risk capital from an arcade

In Chapters 6 and 7, I discuss *trading arcades*, office spaces where traders can rent space. These are usually located in major cities near established stock, bond, options, and futures exchanges. Some trading arcades offer more than just desk space. Some have training programs, whereas others give promising traders some capital to trade in exchange for a cut of the profits. This may be an option for you to consider if you are new to day trading and want to put more money to work than you currently have available.

Assessing Risks and Returns from Short Selling and Leverage

Leverage introduces risk to your day trading, and that can give you greatly increased returns. Most day traders use leverage, at least part of the time, in order to make their trading activities pay off in cold, hard cash. The challenge is to use leverage responsibly. Chapter 9 goes into money management in great detail, but here I cover the two issues most related to leverage: losing your money, and losing your nerve. Understanding those risks can help you determine how much leverage you should take, and how often you can take it.

Losing your money

Losing money is obvious. Leverage magnifies your returns, but it also magnifies your risks. Any borrowings have to be repaid regardless. If you buy or sell a futures or options contract, you are legally obligated to perform, even if you have lost money. That can be really hard. Day trading is risky in large part because of the amount of leverage used. If you don't feel comfortable with that, you may want to use little or no leverage, especially when you are new to day trading or when you are starting to work a new trading strategy.

Losing your nerve

The basic risk and return of your underlying strategy isn't affected by leverage. If you expect that your system will work about 60 percent of the time, then that should hold no matter how much money is at stake or where that money came from. However, it's likely that it does make a difference to you on some subconscious level if you have borrowed the money.

Trading is very much a game of nerves. If you hesitate to make a trade, cut a loss, or otherwise follow your strategy, you're going to run into trouble. (Chapter 8 discusses the mental aspects of day trading.)

Let's say you are trading futures and decide to accept three downticks before selling, and that you will look for five upticks before selling. This means you are willing to accept some loss, cut it if it gets out of hand, and then be disciplined about taking gains when you get them. This strategy keeps a lid on your losses while forcing some discipline on your gains.

Now, suppose you are dealing with lots and lots of leverage. Suddenly, those downticks become too real to you — it's money you don't have. Next thing you know, you only accept two downticks before closing out. But this keeps you from getting winners. Then you decide to ride with your winners, and suddenly you aren't taking profits fast enough, and your positions move against you. Your fear of loss is making you sloppy. That's why many traders find it better to borrow less money and stick to their system, rather than borrow the maximum allowed and let that knowledge cloud their judgment.

Lenders can lose their nerve, too. Your brokerage firm might close your account because of losses, even though waiting just a little longer might turn a losing position into a profit. (See the earlier sidebar "The dangers of risk: Long-Term Capital Management.") That fund was shut by lenders worried about not being repaid. There's some evidence that if the fund had been allowed to borrow more money, it would have turned a big profit in 1998.

Chapter 15

The World of Arbitrage

Day traders work fast, looking to make lots of little profits during a single day. *Arbitrage* is a trading strategy that looks to make profits from small discrepancies in securities prices. The word *arbitrage* itself comes from the French word for judgment; a person who does arbitrage is an *arbitrageur,* or *arb* for short. The idea is that the arbitrageur arbitrates among the prices in the market to reach one final level.

In theory, arbitrage is riskless. It's illogical for the same asset to trade at different prices, so eventually the two prices must converge. The person who buys at the lower price and sells at the higher one will make money with no risk. The challenge is that everyone is looking for these easy profits, so there may not be many of them out there. Good arbitrageurs have a paradoxical mix of patience, to wait for the right opportunity, and impatience, to place the trade the instant the opportunity appears. If you have the fortitude to watch the market, or if you are willing to have software do it for you (see information on research services in Chapter 7), you'll probably find enough good arbitrage opportunities to keep you busy.

True arbitrage involves buying and selling the same security, and many day traders use arbitrage as their primary investment strategy. They may use high levels of *leverage* (borrowing — see Chapter 14) to boost returns. Other traders follow trading strategies involving similar, but not identical, securities. These fall under the category of *risk arbitrage*. In this chapter, I cover the terms and strategies used by day traders who engage in arbitrage. I discuss the basics of arbitrage and how it can be put to good use by a patient trader. I outline the tools you can use to profit from price differences among similar securities. Finally, I list the many types of arbitrage you might want to include in your arsenal of trading strategies.

Obeying the Law of One Price

The key to success in any investment is buying low and selling high. But what's low? And what's high? Who knows?

In the financial markets, the general assumption is that, at least in the short run, the market price is the right price. Only investors, those patient, long-suffering accounting nerds willing to hold investments for years, will see deviations between the market price and the true worth of an investment. For everyone else, especially day traders, what you see is what you get.

Under *the law of one price*, the same asset has the same value everywhere. If markets allow for easy trading — and the financial markets certainly do — then any price discrepancies will be short-lived because traders will immediately step in to buy at the low price and sell at the high price.

Punishing violators of the law

But what happens if what you see in New York is not what you see in London? What happens if you notice that futures prices are not tracking movements in the underlying asset? How about if you see that the stock of every company in an industry has reacted to a news event except one?

Well, then, you have an opportunity to make money, but you'd better act fast — other people will probably see it, too. What you do is simple: You sell as much of the high-priced asset in the high-priced market as you can, borrowing shares if you need to, and then you immediately turn around and buy the low-priced asset in the low-priced market.

Think of the markets as a scale, and you, the arbitrageur, must bring fairness to them. When the markets are out of balance, you take from the high-priced market (the heavier side of the scale) and return it to the low-priced market (the lighter side) until both even out at a price in between.

If you start with a high price of $8 and a low price of $6, and then buy at $6 and sell at $8, your maximum profit is $2 — with no risk. Until the point where the two assets balance at $7, you can make a profit on the difference between them.

Of course, most price differences are on the order of pennies, not dollars, but if you can find enough of these little pricing errors and trade them in size, you can make good money.

Understanding arbitrage and market efficiency

The law of one price holds as long as markets are efficient. Market efficiency is a controversial topic in finance. In academic theory, markets are perfectly efficient, and arbitrage simply isn't possible. That makes a lot of sense if you are testing different assumptions about how the markets would work in a perfect world. A long-term investor would say that markets are inefficient in the short run but perfectly efficient in the long run, so they believe that if they do their research now, the rest of the world will eventually come around, allowing them to make good money.

Traders are in between. The market price and volume are pretty much all the information they have to go on. It may be irrational, but that doesn't matter today. The only thing a trader wants to know is if there is an opportunity to make money given what's going on right now.

In the academic world, market efficiency comes in three flavors, with no form allowing for arbitrage:

- ✔ **Strong form:** Everything, even inside information known only to company executives, is reflected in the security's price.

- ✔ **Semi-strong form:** Prices include all public information, so it may be possible to profit from insider trading.

- ✔ **Weak-form:** Prices reflect all historical information, so research that uncovers new trends may be beneficial.

Those efficient-market true believers are convinced that arbitrage is imaginary because someone would've noticed a price difference between markets already and immediately acted to close it off. But who are those mysterious someones? They are day traders! Even the most devout efficient markets adherent would, if pressed, admit that day traders perform a valuable service in the name of market efficiency.

Those with a less-rigid view of market activity admit that arbitrage opportunities exist, but that they are few and far between. A trader who expects to make money from arbitrage had better pay close attention to the markets to act quickly when a moment happens. And, I'd say this is the case for most arbitrage strategies open to day traders.

Finally, those who don't believe in market efficiency believe that market prices are usually out of sync with asset values. They do research in hopes of learning things that other people don't know. This mindset favors investors more than traders, because it can take time for these price discrepancies to work themselves out.

Because arbitrage requires traders to work fast, it tends to work best for those traders who are willing and able to automate their trading. If you are comfortable with programming and relying on software to do your work, arbitrage might be a great strategy for you.

Scalping for Profits

The law of one price is all well and good, but prices change constantly during the day. They go up a little bit, they go down a little bit, they move every time an order is placed. There's a way that traders can profit from those movements. It's not exactly arbitrage, it's *scalping*. Especially active in commodities markets, scalpers look to take advantage of changes in a security's *bid-ask spread*. That's the difference between the price that a broker will buy a security for from those who want to sell it (the *bid*) and the price that the broker will charge those who want to buy it (the *ask* — also called the *offer* in some markets).

In normal trading, the bid-ask spread tends to be more or less steady over time because the usual flow of supply and demand stays in balance. After all, under market efficiency, everyone has the same information, so their trading is consistent and allows the broker-dealers to generate a steady profit.

Sometimes, however, the spread is a little wider or narrower than normal, not because of a change in the information in the market, but because of short-term imbalances in supply and demand.

A basic scalping strategy looks like this:

- ✔ If the spread between the bid and the ask is wider than usual, then the ask is higher and the bid is lower than it should be. That's because slightly more people want to buy than sell, so the brokers charge the buyers higher prices. The scalper uses this as a sign to sell.

- ✔ If the spread between the bid and the ask is narrower than usual, then the ask is lower and the bid is higher than it would normally be. That happens if there are slightly more sellers than buyers, and the broker wants to find buyers to pick up the slack. The scalper would be in there buying — and hoping that the selling pressure is short lived.

The scalper has to work quickly to make many small trades. He might buy at $20.25, sell at $20.50, and buy again at $20.30. He has to have a low *trade cost structure* in place (discussed later in this chapter) or else he'll pay out all his profits and more to the broker. He also has to be sure that the price changes aren't driven by real information, because that will make market prices too volatile to make scalping profitable. Scalping is "picking up nickels in front of a steamroller," some traders say, because of the risk of focusing on small price changes when bigger changes are underway.

Many day traders rely heavily on scalping, especially on slow market days. Because each trade carries a transaction cost (discussed later in this chapter), it can contribute to more costs than profits. Done right, though, it's a nice way to make some steady profits.

Scalping, as defined here, is perfectly legal. However, the word is also used to describe some illegal activities, such as promoting a security in public and then selling it in private. If a big-name trader goes on his cable television show and talks about how great a stock is so that the price goes up and then sells it the next day when everyone else is buying, he has committed the crime of scalping.

Those Pesky Transaction Costs

Pure arbitrage works best in a world where trading is free. In reality, it costs good money to trade. Sometimes you might notice a price discrepancy that seems to last forever. You can't work it because the profit wouldn't cover your costs. And you know what? That may be true for everyone else out there.

In the real world, trading costs money. Consider all the costs of getting started: buying equipment, paying for Internet access, learning how to trade. Then there are the costs of doing business that vary with each transaction: commissions, fees, interest, the bid-ask spread, and taxes. You don't make a profit on a trade unless it covers those costs.

Even if you work with a broker that charges little or no commission, and even if your broker charges no interest on day trading margin (loans against your securities account), you can bet that your broker is making money off you. That broker's profit is showing up in the spread and the speed of execution, so there is a still a cost to arbitrage that must be covered, even on a seemingly free account. Trust me, brokerage firms are in business to make money, whether or not their customers do.

Add up those trading costs, and you can find yourself in a frustrating situation: You can see the opportunity right there staring you in the face, but you can't take it. It either sits there, taunting you, or gets picked off by a trader who has lower costs than you do.

On the other hand, if you know what your costs are, you can avoid unprofitable opportunities. Don't consider your fixed costs, like your office and your equipment. Those expenses don't change with any given trade. (Yes, you have to cover them in the long run to stay in business, but you can ignore them in the short run.) Instead, figure out how much money you give to your broker on any given trade, on an order, per share, or per contract basis. Write that number down on a sticky note, and put it on your monitor so that you remember what you have to clear before you risk a trade. Just don't get so fixated on covering your costs that you avoid exiting trades at the right time.

Risk Arbitrage and Its Tools

In its purest form, arbitrage is riskless because the purchase of an asset in one market and the sale of the asset in another happen simultaneously — you just let those profits flow right into your account. It is possible to do this, but not often. No day trader who pursues only riskless arbitrage stays in business long.

Return is a function of risk. The more risk you take, the greater the return you expect to make.

Because there are so few opportunities for true arbitrage, most day traders looking at arbitrage strategies actually practice *risk arbitrage*. Like true arbitrage, risk arbitrage attempts to generate profits from price discrepancies; but like the name says, risk arbitrage involves taking some risk. Yes, you buy one security and sell another in risk arbitrage, but it's not always the same security and not always at the same time. For example, a day trader might buy the stock of an acquisition target and sell the stock of an acquirer in the hopes of making a profit as the deal nears the closing date.

Risk arbitrage usually involves strategies that unfold over time — possibly hours, but usually days or weeks. Pursuing these strategies puts you into the world of swing trading (described in Chapter 2), which carries a little more risk than day trading.

In risk arbitrage, a trader is buying and selling similar securities. Much of the risk draws from the fact that the securities are not identical, so the law of one price isn't absolute. Nevertheless, it forms the guiding principle, which is this: If you have two different ways to buy the same thing, then the prices of each purchase should be proportional. If they are not, then there's an opportunity to make money. And what day trader doesn't want to make money?

Arbitrageurs use a mix of different assets and techniques to create these different ways of buying the same thing. This section described some of their favorites.

Derivatives

Derivatives are options, futures, and related financial contracts that draw or derive their value from the value of something else, such as the price of a stock index or the current cost of corn. They offer a lower-cost, lower-obligation method of getting exposure to certain price changes. In the case of agricultural and energy commodities, derivatives are the only practical way for a day trader to own them. Because they are so closely tied to the value of the underlying security, derivatives form a useful "almost, but not quite" asset for traders looking for arbitrage situations. A trader may see a price discrepancy between the derivative and the underlying asset, thus noticing a profitable trading opportunity.

Using a derivative in tandem with its underlying security, traders can construct a range of risk arbitrage trades (and you can read more about them later in this section). For example, a trader looking to set up arbitrage on a merger could trade options on the stocks of the buying and selling companies rather than trading the stocks themselves. The more arbitrage opportunities there are, the greater the likelihood of making a low-risk profit.

Levering with leverage

Chapter 14 covers leverage in detail, but I'm bringing it up again here. It's the process of borrowing money to trade in order to increase potential returns. The more money the trader borrows, the greater the return on capital that she can earn. Leverage is commonly used by day traders, because most trades with a one-day time horizon carry low returns unless they are magnified through borrowing.

That magic of magnification becomes especially important in arbitrage, because the price discrepancies between securities tend to be really small. The primary way to get a bigger return is to borrow money to do it.

However, leverage has a downside: Along with improving returns, it increases risk. Because even risk arbitrage strategies tend to have low risk, this may be acceptable. Just remember that you have to repay all borrowed money, no matter what happens to prices. Chapter 14 has more information on that.

Short selling

Short selling is another topic from Chapter 14, and it creates another set of alternatives for setting up an arbitrage trade. Short selling allows a day trader to profit when a security's price goes down. Instead of buying low and then selling, high, the trader sells high first and then buys back low. The short seller goes to her broker, borrows the security that she thinks will decline in price, sells it, and then buys it back in the market later so that she has the shares to repay the loan. (It all happens electronically, no office visits required!) Assuming she's right and the price does indeed fall, she pockets the difference between the price where she sold the security and the price where she bought it back. Of course, that difference is her loss if the price goes up instead of down.

By adding short selling to the bag of tricks, an arbitrageur can find a lot more ways to profit from a price discrepancy in the market. New combinations of cheap and expensive assets — and more ways to trade them — give a day trader more opportunities to make trades during the day.

The opposite of *short* is *long*. When a trader holds a security, he's said to be long.

Synthetic securities

Feeling creative? Well, then, consider creating *synthetic securities* when looking for arbitrage opportunities. A synthetic security is a combination of assets that have the same profit-and loss-profile as another asset or group of assets. For example, a stock is a combination of a *put option,* which has value if the stock goes down in price, and a *call option,* which has value if the stock goes up in price. By thinking up ways to mimic the behavior of an asset through a synthetic security, a day trader can find more ways for an asset to be cheaper in one market than in another, leading to more potential arbitrage opportunities.

A typical arbitrage transaction involving a synthetic security involves shorting the real security and then buying a package of derivatives that match its risk and return.

Many of the risk arbitrage techniques covered later in this chapter involve the creation of synthetic securities.

Complex arbitrage trading strategies require more testing and simulation trading (covered in Chapter 11) and may possibly involve losses while you fine-tune your methods. Be sure you feel comfortable with your trading method before you commit big time and big dollars to it.

An Array of Arbitrages

The tools of arbitrage — derivatives, leverage, short selling, synthetic securities — can be used in all sorts of ways to generate potentially profitable trades, and that's what this section of the chapter covers. Most day traders who decide to do arbitrage will pick a few strategies to follow. After all, it's hard enough to spot these opportunities; the trader who tries to do too much is the trader who will soon be looking for a new job. Armed with the information here, you can decide whether there's an arbitrage strategy that matches your approach to the market so that you can make it your own.

The varieties of arbitrage transactions are listed here in alphabetical order. It's not exhaustive; there are plenty of other ways to exploit price differences in the market, but some involve more time than a day trader is willing to commit. I've put them in alphabetical order. Some are more complex than others, some generate more opportunities than others, and some work best if you are willing to swing trade (hold for a few days) rather than day trade (close out all positions at the end of the day).

Many arbitrage strategies work best in combination with other strategies, such as news-driven trading (discussed in Chapter 13). For example, it might take a news announcement to cause people to pay attention to a company's stock so that there's enough trading activity that day to close a price gap. If you know about the pricing problem ahead of time, you can swoop in and make the arbitrage that day.

There are certainly other types of arbitrage out there. Wherever people pay close attention to the markets and price changes, they find small price differences to turn into large, low-risk profits. If you think you've found an arbitrage strategy not listed here, by all means, go and test it and see if it will work for you.

Capital structure arbitrage

Companies issue securities in order to finance their business, and investment bankers are in the business of helping them do just that. Some companies are nice and simple. Microsoft, for example, uses only stock for financing and has only one class of stock. Others are far more complicated, using mixtures of different classes of stock and different issues of debt to finance the growth. General Electric, for example, has one class of common stock and seven different debt securities for its parent company and its finance subsidiary. Think that's a lot? General Motors has ten different securities.

The way that a company is financed is its *capital structure*, and capital structure arbitrage looks for inappropriate price differences among all the different classes of stock and debt outstanding. Although all securities tied to the same business should trade in a similar fashion, they don't always, and that creates opportunities.

Say, for example, that SuperTech Company has two classes of stock, one on its core business and one that tracks the performance of its nanotechnology subsidiary. (A *tracking stock* is a corporate finance gimmick that goes in and out of style; it's stock on a subsidiary that is controlled by the parent company.) The parent company still has exposure to the nanotechnology subsidiary, but that is not reflected in its stock price. One day, the nanotechnology subsidiary announces great earnings, and the stock goes way up, but SuperTech stock doesn't move even though it benefits. The capital structure arbitrageur immediately shorts the nanotech subsidiary tracking stock and buys the parent company stock (matching the size of the long and short positions so that they move up and down in tandem), waiting for people to realize that the discrepancy is there.

Convertible arbitrage

As part of designing their capital structure, some companies issue *convertible bonds* (sometimes called a *convertible debenture*) or *convertible preferred stock.* These securities are a cross between stocks and bonds. Like an ordinary bond, convertibles pay regular income to those who hold them (interest for convertible bonds and dividends for convertible preferred stock), but they also act a little like stock because the holders have the right to exchange the convertible security for ordinary common stock.

Here's an example: a $1,000 convertible bond pays 7.5 percent interest and is convertible into 25 shares of stock. If the stock is less than $40 per share, the convertible holder will prefer to cash the interest or dividend checks. If the company's stock trades above $40, the convertible holder would make more money giving up the income in order to get the stock cheap. Because of the benefit of conversion, the interest rate on a convertible security is usually below that on a regular corporate bond.

Because a convertible security carries a built-in option to buy the underlying stock, it generally trades in line with the stock. If the convertible's price gets too high or too low, then an arbitrage opportunity presents itself.

Consider this case: A day trader notices that a convertible bond is selling at a lower price than it should be, given the current level of interest rates and the price of the company's common stock. So, he buys the convertibles and sells the common stock short (see Chapter 14 for more on short selling). When the stock's price moves back into line, he collects a profit from both sides of the trade.

Fixed income and interest rate arbitrage

Fixed income securities are bonds, notes, and related securities that give their owners a regular interest payment. They are popular with conservative investors, especially retirees, who want to generate a regular income from the quarterly interest payments. They are considered to be safe, predictable, long-run investments, but they can fluctuate wildly in the short term, which makes them attractive to arbitrageurs.

Interest rates are the price of money, and so they affect the value of many kinds of securities. Fixed income securities have a great deal of interest-rate exposure, because they pay out interest. Some stocks have interest-rate exposure, too. Trading in foreign exchange is an attempt to profit from the changing price of one currency relative to another, and that's usually a function of the difference in interest rates between the two countries. Derivatives have a regular expiration schedule, so they have some time value, and that's measured through interest rates.

With so many different assets affected by changes in interest rates, arbitrageurs pay attention. With *fixed-income arbitrage,* the trader breaks out the following:

- ✔ The time value of money
- ✔ The level of risk in the economy
- ✔ The likelihood of repayment
- ✔ The inflation-rate effects on different securities

If one of the numbers is out of whack, the trader constructs and executes an arbitrage trade to profit from it.

It's rarely practical for a day trader to buy bonds outright. Instead, day traders looking at fixed income arbitrage and other interest-rate sensitive strategies usually rely on interest rate futures, offered by the Chicago Board of Trade. You can read more about this in Chapter 3.

How would this work? Think of a day trader monitoring interest rates on U.S. government securities. He notices that two-year treasury notes are trading at a higher yield than expected — especially relative to five-year treasury notes. He sells futures on the two-year treasury notes and then buys futures on the five-year treasury notes. When the difference between the two rates falls back where it should be, the futures trade will turn a profit.

Index arbitrage

Market observers talk a lot about the performance of the S&P 500 Index and the Dow Jones Industrial Average. These are *market indexes*, designed to represent the activity of the market, and are widely published for market observers to follow. The performance of the index is based on the performance of a group of securities, ranging from the 3,000 largest companies in the market (the Russell 3,000) to a mere 30 large companies (the Dow Jones Industrial Average).

Sure, an arbitrageur could buy all the stocks, and there are hedge funds that do just that. But very few people can do that. Instead, they get exposure to index performance through the many different securities based on the indexes. Buy-and-hold mutual fund investors can buy funds that hold all the same stocks in the same proportion as the index. Those with shorter-term profits in mind can buy exchange-traded funds, which are baskets of stocks listed on organized exchanges (see Chapter 3), or they can trade futures and options on the indexes.

Arbitrageurs love the idea of an asset — like an index — that has lots of different securities based on its value. That creates lots of opportunities for mispricing. Unless the index, the futures, the options, and the exchange-traded funds are all in line, some canny day trader can step in and make some money.

For example, suppose the S&P 500 futures contract is looking mighty cheap relative to the price of the S&P 500 Index. A trader can short an exchange-traded fund on the index and then buy futures contracts to profit from the difference.

Garbitrage

Traders get sloppy when an exciting merger is announced. If one company in an industry gets taken over, the stock in all the companies in the industry will go up, often for no good reason. Some get so carried away that they buy the wrong stock entirely, usually because of confusion over ticker symbols. If GAP Stores, ticker symbol GPS, were to be taken over, chances are good that the stock in Great Atlantic and Pacific Tea Company — operator of the A&P grocery stores, ticker symbol GAP — would also go up. Such bad trading is known as *garbitrage*.

Merger arbitrage

Every day, companies get bought and sold, and that creates arbitrage opportunities. In fact, one of the better-known arbitrage strategies out there is *merger arbitrage*, in which traders try to profit from the change in stock prices after a merger has been announced. It starts by looking at the following details in the merger announcement:

- ✔ The name of the acquiring company
- ✔ The name of the company being taken over (and no matter what PR people say, there are no mergers of equals)
- ✔ The price of the transaction
- ✔ The currency (cash, stock, debt)
- ✔ The date the merger is expected to close

Until the date that the merger actually closes, which may be different from the date in the merger announcement, any and every one of the announced details can change. The acquiring company may learn new information about the target company and change its mind. A third company might jump in and make an offer for more money. The shareholders may agree to support the deal only if they get cash instead of stock. All that drama creates opportunity, both for traders looking for one-day opportunities and for those willing to hold a position until the merger closing date.

Here's an example. Let's say that Major Bancorp offers to buy Downtown Bank for $50 per share in cash. Major Bancorp's shares will probably fall in price, because its shareholders will be concerned that the merger will be a lot of trouble. Downtown Bank's shares will go up in price, but not all the way to $50, because its shareholders know that there is some risk that the deal won't go through. An arbitrageur would short Major Bancorp and buy Downtown Bank to profit from the concerns. If Overseas Banque decides to step in, then it might be a profitable idea to buy Major Bancorp and short Overseas Banque. (If another bidder steps in and places a higher offer for Downtown Bank, then the whole arbitrage unravels — hence, the risk.)

Option arbitrage

Options form the basis of many arbitrage strategies, especially for those day traders who work the stock market. They are discussed on Chapter 3, but here's a little refresher. First, many different types of options are available, even on the same security. The two main categories are *puts*, which bet on the underlying security price falling, and *calls*, which bet on the underlying security price rising. Puts and calls on the same security come in many different strike prices, depending on where you want to bet the price goes. Some options, known as *American options*, can be cashed in at any time between the date of issue and the expiration date, and you can exercise others, known as *European options*, only at the expiration date. (To complicate matters, American and European options can be issued anywhere.) With all those choices, there are bound to be a few price discrepancies for the alert arbitrageur.

Maybe a day trader notices that on a day when a company has a big announcement, the options exchanges seem to be assuming a slightly higher price for the stock than where the stock is actually trading. He decides to buy the underlying stock as well as a put; he also sells a call with the same strike price and expiration date as the put. This creates a synthetic security that has the same payoff as shorting the security, meaning that the trader has pulled off a riskless arbitrage transaction. He effectively bought the security cheap in the stock market and sold it at a higher price in the options market.

Pairs trading

Pairs trading, which involves buying a cheap stock and shorting an expensive stock in the same industry group, is popular with many people who day trade stocks. (It's also the core of traditional hedge-fund investing, although there are very few hedge funds that rely on it nowadays.)

A pairs trader watches an industry group and looks for situations where one company seems to be doing especially well or one is doing especially poorly. That would most likely indicate a problem in the way people are pricing the industry, because in general, what's good for one company is good for all of them. A pairs trader would pay particular attention to news events that seem to affect all but one or two companies in the same industry. If one of them appears to be overvalued relative to the others, the pairs trader shorts the pricey stock and buys the cheapest one.

The pairs trader isn't dealing with identical assets, of course, so the simultaneous purchase and sale is a lot riskier than it would be in true arbitrage. Sometimes, there's a very good reason why one stock is more expensive and one is much cheaper than the rest of the industry. Good pairs traders are willing to do a little fundamental research (see Chapter 12) so that they can avoid being short the winner and being long the loser in an industry undergoing big changes.

For Propeller-Heads Only: Statistical Arbitrage

Do you love crunching numbers? Are you comfortable with programming? Are you an actuary looking for a career change? If the answers to these questions are yes, then *statistical arbitrage* might be right for you. It involves the use of complex mathematical models to determine where a security should be priced. It's based on the notion that securities prices move randomly along a normal curve. If all results are distributed normally, then *reversion to the mean* holds. That means that a security's price will equal the average — the mean — price in the long run. If there are huge swings up, they have to be matched by huge swings down eventually, so that the mean does not change.

Here's an example. A standard die has six sides. When you roll it, you are equally likely to get any one of those six results. The mean of the six sides is 3.5, or $(1 + 2 + 3 + 4 + 5 + 6) / 6$. If you roll the die 100 times, the average of all of those results should be close to the 3.5 mean. If your mean is actually 2.1, then chances are good that your next several rolls will have an average higher than 3.5 so that the total results will begin to close in on that 3.5 mean. If not, you haven't figured out a fabulous new secret to rolling a die; it's more likely that your die is loaded.

In statistical arbitrage, the trader works with huge databases of securities prices to determine where the average should be, especially relative to market conditions such as interest rate levels. If the current price is too high, it's time to short it; if the price is too low, it's time to buy.

Here's an example of how it works: A day trader has data showing that for the past 20 years, food-processing companies have moved in a fixed percentage relative to unemployment rates. She notices that in the past month, the relationship has diverged, with the stock prices having decreased more than expected relative to the current economy. So, she buys the stocks expecting them to go up in price under the assumption that the normal relationship holds.

You might be a great statistician, but chances are good that big hedge funds and fancy brand-name brokerage firms have hired statisticians who are even better than you. (And even then, there is no guarantee of success — hedge fund Long-Term Capital Management failed in 1998 and nearly took the world's financial markets down with it despite having two Nobel Prize winners on staff.) Just remember that statistical arbitrage brings you smack against the biggest of the Big Kahunas on Wall Street.

Chapter 16

Day Trading for Investors

*I*t takes a special person to be a day trader — one who has quick reflexes, a strong stomach, and a short-term perspective on the markets. Not everyone's meant to parcel out their workdays a minute at a time. Most people do better with a long-term perspective on their finances, looking to match their investments with their goals and thinking about their investment performance over months or years rather than right now.

But those patient long-term investors can learn a thing or two from the frenetic day trader, and that's what this chapter is all about. Many day-trading techniques can help swing traders, position traders, and investors — people who hold positions for days, months, or even decades — improve their returns and make smarter decisions when it comes time to buy or sell.

Let's face it: In theory, investors might be willing to wait forever to see great stock picks play out, but in reality, they only have so much time and money. A company's stock may be ridiculously cheap, but the stock can languish a long time before everyone else catches on and bids the price up. The investor who buys and sells well can add a few extra dollars to his investment return, and who doesn't want that?

Not all day-traders close out every night, and some long-term investors will take a day-trading flyer on a hot idea. In this chapter, I cover some trading and analysis techniques used by day traders to help longer-term investors improve their returns. Then I discuss some ways that long-term investors might want to add day trading to their list of tricks to achieve better total return.

And heck, maybe a few investors want to give day trading a try, especially for those securities that they have followed long enough to know how the market reacts to news and whether those reactions are appropriate. For a long-term investor, given the time to test strategies and set limits, day trading in known markets might result in some nice incremental short-term returns.

The Trader's Discipline

Successful day traders have an innate sense of discipline. They know when to commit more money to a trade and when to cut their losses and close up shop for the day.

Unfortunately, a lot of long-term investors can get sloppy. They have done so much research and committed so much time waiting for a position to work out that they often forget the cardinal rule of the trader: The market doesn't know that you're in it. The stock doesn't know you own it, so it's not going to reward your loyalty. Securities go up and down every day for no good reason, and sometimes you are going to make a mistake and you will have to cut your losses. There's no shame in that, as long as you learn from it.

Now, how can you get that discipline? Start by developing an investment and trading plan, covered in Chapter 2. Although investing is probably not your primary occupation, you do want to have in writing what your objectives are and how you plan to meet them given other constraints: time, tax considerations, and risk tolerance. Then carefully evaluate your performance (covered in Chapter 11) and keep a trade diary so that you know what you are trading and why. Are there ways to improve? Are you making mistakes that could be avoided?

Traders have to go through these exercises in order to survive. Investors often skip these steps, but they shouldn't.

A quick way for an investor to improve her trading discipline is to set up a sell rule, a rule that tells her when to cut her losses and move on. For example, if a stock is down 20 percent from where it was purchased or where it traded at the beginning of the year, it might be time to sell, regardless of what you hope it will do.

Applying Momentum

Momentum investors look for securities that are going up in price, especially if accompanied by acceleration in underlying growth. In a sense, they are looking for the same thing day traders are — a security that is going to move big — but they have the expectation of making money over a longer period of time. The thought is that if a security is starting to go up in price, it will keep going up unless something dramatic happens to change it. In the meantime, there is plenty of money to be made.

The knock on momentum investing is that instead of buying low and selling high, the goal is to buy high and sell even higher.

Like most investors, a momentum investor starts with careful fundamental analysis (described in Chapter 12), analyzing a security to determine what will make it go up. Then the momentum investor looks for certain technical and market indicators, similar to those described in Chapters 12 and 13 and used by day traders. In addition, some momentum investors rely on chart services, especially the Value Line and William O'Neil charts, to help them identify securities that are likely to have momentum.

Earnings momentum

Earnings momentum is the province of the investor, not the trader. The investor is looking at the earnings that a company reports every quarter to see if they are going up at a faster rate, say from a steady rate of 10 percent a year to 12, 13, or more. This often happens because of a new technology or product that turns a decent company into a hot property in the stock and options markets. If the earning growth rate is accelerating, then the underlying price should go up at an accelerating rate, too.

Day traders don't look for earnings momentum, but they do look for price momentum. The two are usually related.

Price momentum

When a security goes up in price, especially at a fast clip with strong demand underneath it, it is said to have *price momentum*. Most day traders are looking for price momentum in order to make a swift profit. Many long-term investors should look for momentum in order to avoid being stuck with a position for months before it starts to move.

It pays to be patient, but it pays even better if your money is working for you while you wait.

Many momentum traders don't care why something is going up in price; they only know that it is going up and that they can profit if they're there for even part of the ride. Some of the different indicators that they look at are the following:

- ✔ **Relative strength:** There are different ways to calculate this, discussed in Chapter 12, but the basic idea is that if the security is going up faster than the market as a whole, it is showing momentum and might be a buy.

- ✔ **Moving average convergence/divergence (MacD):** This indicator looks at how the average price of the security is changing over time. Is it staying relatively level, meaning that the price is moving slowly back and forth, or is the indicator gradually going up, meaning that the price is gradually going up, too? If you plot the moving average against the actual price levels, a wide gap means that the security is moving up or down faster than the average, and if it's moving up, you'd probably want to buy it. (Otherwise, consider shorting the security, and you can learn about that in Chapter 14.)

- ✔ **Stochastics index:** This is the difference between the high and the low price for a security over a given time period. Some analysts look at days, some at weeks. The idea is that if the difference is getting bigger, that may be because the security is moving up or down in price at a faster than normal rate, creating an opportunity for a momentum buyer.

At an extreme, momentum investing leads to *bubbles*, like the infamous dot com bubble in the late 1990s. People were buying the stocks because they were going up, not because they necessarily thought that the businesses were worth much. It was fun while it lasted, but a lot of people lost a lot of money when reality set in during March and April of 2000.

For investors only: momentum research systems

Many day traders rely on different research systems to help them identify buy and sell opportunities in the course of a trading day. These systems usually don't work for an investor, simply because investors are less concerned about short-term movements. They wouldn't see the value in systems that scan the market and identify short-term price discrepancies, for example.

However, many investors use their own research services to help identify good buy and sell opportunities. Two of the more popular ones are Value Line and the William O'Neil charts.

Value Line

www.valueline.com

Value Line is one of the oldest investment research services. The company's analysts combine price and trading volume information on stocks with financial data. The numbers are crunched through a proprietary model to generate two rankings: a stock's timeliness and its safety. The higher the stock is on the timeliness ranking, the better it is to buy or hold it now. Historically, Value Line's most timely stocks have outperformed the Dow Jones Industrial Average and the S&P 500, so people are willing to pay for access to the company's data. In addition, many libraries subscribe to Value Line's print service or online database, so you may be able to get access that way. (Hey, one of the advantages of being an investor is that you have the time to go to the library to look something up, a marvel to a day trader who's afraid to go and get a cup of coffee.)

William O'Neil

www.williamoneil.com

William O'Neil started a company to distribute his technical analysis system on stocks and the stock market, started a newspaper called *Investor's Business Daily*, and wrote a book called *How to Make Money in Stocks* (see the Appendix for more information about it). The company's data services are available only to large institutional investors, such as mutual fund and insurance companies, but between the book and the newspaper, individual investors can learn a lot about identifying momentum in order to pick good times to buy or sell a stock.

Many traders — in all securities, not just stocks — find *Investor's Business Daily* to be at least as useful as *The Wall Street Journal*, because it looks at the markets from a short-term trading perspective more than from a long-term, business management angle.

The company's ranking system is based on what it calls CAN SLIM, which is a mnemonic for a list of criteria that a good stock should meet. Note that it combines both fundamental and technical indicators:

- ✓ **Current quarterly earnings** should be up 25 percent from a year ago.

- ✓ **Annual earnings** should be up 25 percent from a year ago.

- ✓ **New products or services** should be driving earnings growth, not acquisitions or changes in accounting.

- ✓ **Supply and demand,** meaning that the number of shares being purchased each day, is going up.

✔ **Leading company in leading industry** is the stock in the best position to do well.

✔ **Institutional sponsorship** means that the stock is becoming more popular with mutual funds, pension funds, and other large shareowners.

✔ **Market indexes,** such as the Dow, the NASDAQ, and the S&P 500, should all be up.

Of course, there aren't too many stocks out there that meet all the CAN SLIM criteria, but the indicators can give an investor a way of thinking about better times to buy (when more criteria are met) or sell (when fewer are being met).

The most serious momentum investors tend to be swing traders, who hold positions for a few weeks or months. Longer-term investors often rely on some momentum signals, though, to help them identify when it's a good time to buy a stock that has been languishing.

Breaking News and Breaking Markets

One reason that the markets are so volatile is that they are responding to news events. Prices reflect information. That's why prices change when any little bit of information comes into the market — even if it is just that someone wants to buy and someone wants to sell right now. The problem is that sometimes the market participants don't react in proportion to the news they receive. Good traders have an almost innate ability to discern news that creates a buy from news that creates a sell. (You can learn more about that in Chapter 13.) Sometimes traders want to go with the market and sometimes they want to go against it.

When it's your investment idea that's been affected by a news announcement, you need to consider how your position — and you — will react. After all, no matter how long your time horizon and how careful your research, things happen to companies: CEOs have heart attacks, major products are found to be defective, financial statements turn out to be fraudulent. How are you going to respond?

The first point is that you have to respond. The market doesn't know your position, and the market doesn't care. (Have I mentioned that already?) You need to assess the situation and decide what to do. Given the information, is it time to buy, sell, or stay put? It's often okay to hold your long-term position in the face of long-term news, but that should be an active decision, not a fallback. The trick is to be objective, and that's not easy when real dollars are at stake.

Successful day traders are able to keep their emotions under control and keep the market separate from the rest of their lives. Good investors should be able to do the same. Chapter 8 has some ideas that might help.

When evaluating news, day traders look at how the news is different from expectations. Investors can also consider how the news is different relative to the known facts about the company to date.

For example, let's suppose that The Timely Timer Company is expected to report earnings of $0.10 per share. Instead, the news hits the tape saying that earnings will be only $0.05 because of accounting charges. The trader might see that the earnings are below expectations news and sell all his shares to minimize his losses for the day, moving on to another position. The investor might know that the accounting charges were expected and go in and buy more shares while the price is depressed.

The fact that there is a way for a buyer and a seller to match their differing needs is the whole reason that the financial markets exist!

To a day trader, perception is reality. To a keen-eyed investor, the difference between perception and reality might be an opportunity to make money.

Day traders have to think about the psychology of the market, because everything moves so quickly. Investors sometimes forget about psychology because they can wait for logic to prevail. When it comes time to place a buy or sell order, however, understanding the psychological climate that day can give the investor a price advantage, and every bit of profit improvement goes straight to the bottom line.

Day traders keep their sanity by closing out positions at the end of the day, so that they get on with their lives until the next market open. Investors, on the other hand, might want to know what's happening to their positions at other times. Many brokerage firms offer mobile phone alert services, which I think are a terrible idea for a day trader but might not be a bad idea for an investor.

Setting Targets and Limits

Good day traders set limits. They often place stop and limit orders to automatically close out their positions when they reach a certain price level. They have profit targets in mind and know how much they are willing to risk in the pursuit of those gains.

Good investors should set similar limits. It can be harder for them, because they have often done so much research that they feel almost clairvoyant. Why worry about the downside when the research shows that the stock has to go up?

Well, the research might overlook certain realities. And even if the analysis was thorough, things change. That's why even the most ardent fundamentalist needs to have a downside risk limit. In most cases, stop and limit orders are bad ideas for a long-term investor because they'll force the sale of a security during a short-term market fluctuation and they'll force the sale when it's really a good time to buy more. Investors have a different risk profile than day traders, so they need to manage risk differently. They still need to manage risk, though.

With a *stop* order, the broker buys or sells the security as soon as a predetermined price is met, even if the price quickly moves back to where it was before the order took effect. A *limit* order is only executed if the security hits the predetermined level, and it stays in effect only if the price is at that level or lower (for a buy limit order) or at that level or higher (for a sell limit order).

Martha Stewart's defense in her insider trading case was that she sold her ImClone stock because she had a pre-arranged sell order in place with her broker, but it was not actually a stop order. The phone call with possible inside information had nothing to do with it, she said, and in fact, the prosecutors could not disprove her. She was found guilty of obstruction of justice, not insider trading.

Day traders close out their positions at the end of each day, so they rarely review their limits. A swing trader or an investor, holding for a longer period of time, needs to review those limits frequently. How much should a position move each month, quarter, or year before it's time to cover losses or cash out with a profit? How has the security changed over time, and do the limits need to change with it?

When the position is working out, an investor will think of letting it ride forever. But, alas, few investments work that long into the future, so the investor also needs to think in term of relative performance. Is it time to sell and put the money into something else with greater potential?

When managing money, day traders usually think about maximizing return while minimizing the risk of ruin. For an investor, the goal is maximizing return relative to a list of long-term objectives, including a target for risk. But because long-term objectives change, the portfolio will have to as well. That means that a position that has been working out fine might have to be changed in order to meet the new portfolio goals. The discussion is starting to get beyond the scope of this book, but the point remains: Like successful day traders, successful investors have a plan for how they will allocate their money among different investments, and they adjust it as necessary.

Although investing is a long-term proposition and lacks the frenzy of trading, it is still an active endeavor. Instead of putting energy into buying and selling, the investor puts it into monitoring.

When an Investor Should Go Short Term

Many day traders are also long-term investors. Sure, they trade for the short term, but they regularly take some of their profits and put them toward investments that have a longer time frame. It's smart risk management for a business that has a high wash-out rate. After all, even a short-term trader has long-term goals.

But does it ever make sense for a long-term investor to take up short-term trading? It might. There are three reasons: the idea proves itself to be short-term, the research shows short-term trading patterns that might be profitable, and fundamental analysis supports short selling.

Don't try riskier trading strategies unless your portfolio can handle the risk. As with full-time day trading, part-time and occasional trading strategies should only be done with risk capital, which is money that the trader can afford to lose. Money needed to pay the mortgage this month or pay for retirement in 30 years is not risk capital.

The idea proves to have a short shelf life

It happens to every long-term investor once or twice: He buys a security intending to hold it forever, and within a few days or weeks, some really bad news comes out. Or he buys only to see two days later that the company is being sold. That great long-term buy-and-hold idea no long fits the original parameters, so it's time to sell. Despite the goal of holding forever, it's time to get out and move on, even if it's only a day later.

Your research shows you some trading opportunities

Good investors monitor their holdings, and some become intimate with the nuances of a security's short-term price movements even though the objective is to hold the position for the long term. An investor who gets a feel for the trading patterns of a specific holding might want to turn that into swing trading and day trading opportunities. Yes, it adds risk to the portfolio (and the risks of day trading are covered extensively throughout this book), but it can also increase return.

For example, suppose that an investor who is fascinated with technology stocks notices that the stocks always rise in price right before big industry conferences and then fall when the conference is over. She might not want to change any of her portfolio holdings based on this, but she might also want a way to profit. So, she buys call options on big technology companies before the conference and then sells them on the meeting's first day. That short-term trade allows her to capture benefits of the price run-up without affecting her portfolio position.

You see some great short opportunities

Short selling allows a trader to profit from a decline in the price of a security. The trader borrows a security from the broker, sells it in the market, and then waits in hopes that the price goes down. When it does, the trader buys the security back at the lower price and repays the loan, keeping the difference between the purchase price and the sale price.

Because the broker charges interest on the loaned securities, short selling can get expensive. Traders who sell short are usually looking for a relatively short-term profit, not necessarily over a single day, but over months rather than years.

In addition to the interest, short selling faces another risk, which is that the security can go up in price while the trader is waiting for it to go down. In order to reduce that risk, most short sellers do careful research to make sure that they're right about the security being all wrong. And who else does careful research? Many long-term investors.

For the investor who loves to do research and who has some appetite for risk, short selling is a way to make money from those securities that would make terrible long-term holdings because it seems obvious that they aren't going to do well. When these investors come across securities that are headed for trouble, they can short them in the hope of making a nice short-term profit.

Judging Execution Quality

Day traders rely on outstanding trade execution from their brokers. They need to keep costs as low as possible in order to clear a profit from their trading, especially because their profits are relatively small.

Investors may have a greater likelihood of making a profit, given that they are waiting for a position to work out rather than closing it out every night. Even then, better execution will lead to better profits. The magnitude of the few extra cents might be smaller relative to the entire profit, but it still counts.

Your broker makes money three ways. The first is on the commission charged to make the trade. The second is on the *bid-ask spread* (also called the *bid-offer*), which is the difference between the price that the broker buys the security from customers and the price that the broker sells it to customers. The third is any price appreciation on the security between when the broker acquired it and when the firm sold it to the customer. Because three sources of profit are available, some brokers don't even charge commission. But note that the broker can still make money — lots of money — even without a commission.

When choosing a broker, consider *total execution costs*, not just commission. Some brokers offering deep commission discounts make money from high levels of trading volume, but others make their money from execution.

The broker has a few tricks for improving execution. The first trick is to invest heavily in information systems that can route and match orders, as even one second can make a difference if the markets are moving. The second is to have a large enough customer base to be able to match customer orders quickly. Finally, and most importantly, the firm has to decide that execution is a strategic advantage it can use to keep customers happy. Many brokerage firms would rather concentrate on research, financial planning, customer service, or other offerings to keep customers happy instead of offering excellent execution.

In general, a firm that offers low commissions and emphasizes its services to active traders will have better execution than a firm that emphasizes its full-service research and advisory expertise. But there are exceptions, and in some cases, the exceptions vary with account size.

Brokerage firms use several numbers to evaluate their execution, including the following:

- ✔ **Average execution speed:** This is the amount of time it takes the firm to fill the first share of an order. Firms also track — and sometimes disclose — how long it takes to fill an entire order, on average.

- ✔ **Price relative to National Best Bid or Offer:** At any time, there is a list of bid and ask prices in the market, and your broker might not have the best spread. The National Best Bid or Offer is the best price in the market. You might not be able to get this price for all sorts of reasons, usually because of the number of shares you want to buy or sell. For example, if the best bid is for 100 shares, and you want to sell 500, you won't be able to get it. Brokerage firms track and report how close the price you received was to the best bid or offer at the time.

> ✔ **Price improvement:** Most brokerage firms buy and sell securities for their own account. In fact, working as a trader at a brokerage firm might be a great alternative to day trading (you can read about this and other alternatives in Chapter 20). Because the firm might own the security or want it for its own account, it might give you a slightly better price than what is in the market.
>
> ✔ **Average Effective Spread:** This measures how much the spread between the bid and the offer differed from the National Best Bid or Offer, on average. The lower the Average Effective Spread, the better.

Certainly, your results will vary based on what types of securities you are trading, what market conditions are like when you are trading, and how big of an account you have with the firm. But investigating the averages for a brokerage firm can help long-term investors decide whether it makes sense to change firms in order to improve profits.

So what can you do to improve your execution? Here are three suggestions:

> ✔ Ask the brokerage firm for its policies. The firm should be willing to provide this, as well as to give you some of its recent data, so that you can decide whether the total value of the firm's services matches the total cost.
>
> ✔ Check the weekly "Electronic Trader" column in *Barron's* as well as the magazine's annual review of online brokerage firms. Execution cost is a key component of *Barron's* evaluation.
>
> ✔ Update your own hardware and Internet connection so that it's as fast as possible. If you are a day trader, it's imperative to have good data (see Chapter 6 for more information). If you are not a day trader but actively manage your investment account, you might want to consider an upgrade as well. A few seconds can make a difference.

Part IV
The Part of Tens

The 5th Wave   By Rich Tennant

"Oh Martin, you scared me half to death! Next time let me know when you're picking a new stock."

In this part . . .

In this *For Dummies*-only part, you get to enjoy some top-ten lists. I present ten reasons to day trade, ten reasons to not, ten common mistakes that day traders make, and ten alternative careers for people who love the excitement of trading but who don't want to work for themselves as day traders. I also include an appendix full of references so that you can get more information to help you build your trading business.

Chapter 17

Ten Good Reasons to Day Trade

*D*ay trading is a great career option for the right person in the right circumstances. It requires a strong, decisive personality who wants to be running the show every step of the way, from backing up the PCs to collecting all the profits. And good day traders have some financial cushion and good personal support systems to get them through the tough times.

In this chapter, I list ten really good reasons to take up day trading. (For balance, I cover ten bad reasons in Chapter 18.) Think you have what it takes? Are you ready to go into business for yourself as a day trader? See how many of these characteristics fit your life right now.

You Love Being Independent

Day trading is like owning any small business. You're the boss and you call the shots. Each day's successes — and failures — are due to you and you alone. Most likely, you're working by yourself all day, so you're responsible for everything from the temperature in the office, to the functioning of the computers, to the accounting for trades.

Good day traders are independent. They don't want someone to tell them what to do; they want to figure it out for themselves. They love that challenge, whether it's finding a good bargain on office supplies or developing a profitable way to arbitrage currency prices.

If you would like to work for yourself and control your own destiny, keep reading. Day trading might be for you. And if not, go to Chapter 20 to see some alternative careers that involve the markets but do not put all of the onus on you for success.

You Want to Work Anywhere You Like

All you need to day trade is a computer, an account with an online brokerage firm, and high-speed Internet access. Nowadays you can find these tools almost anywhere: at home, at the library, in a bar; in a big city, in a small town, in the mountains, or in another country. Day trading offers a lot of geographic flexibility, which few other businesses do. You can trade while traveling as easily as you would trade at home. You have the luxury of setting up shop wherever you please, and if you decide to move, you can pack up your laptop and move your trading activities to your new destination.

You Are Comfortable with Technology

NASDAQ is the precursor to the Internet. Long before everyone and her grandmother were online, securities traders were using complex electronic communications networks to buy and sell securities. The financial services industry was one of the first to embrace computer technology in a big way in the 1960s, and it is still a technology-intensive industry. For all the images of people in colored cotton jackets running around the exchange floor, waving their hands and yelling at each other, most trading takes place over computer networks via machines.

Day traders use software to develop and refine their trading strategies. They trade online, using software to monitor and automate their trades. They track their trades in spreadsheets and other software. They spend their days in front of a screen, communicating online with other traders all over the world. They don't interact much with human beings during the trading day. It's all about the hardware boxes and the software interface between the trader and the market data.

Day traders are also self-employed, and many work from home. That means that if their software crashes, they have to fix it. They have to handle the upgrades, install the firewalls, back up the data. Sure, it may be possible to pay someone to do it, but that cost is probably prohibitive — and the tech consultant probably won't be able to drop everything to get you up and trading again immediately.

If you spill Diet Coke on your keyboard, don't even bother trying to fix it. It's ruined. Get in the car and go to the office supply store and get a new one. Better yet, keep a spare keyboard on hand. Don't ask me how I know this. Just trust me.

Good day traders are comfortable with technology. If you like to mess around with programs, don't mind maintaining your computer, and understand how to set up your hardware for maximum efficiency, you're in good shape for day trading. (Chapter 6 has some more on this, too.)

Day trading is like any other entrepreneurial business. You, the entrepreneur, are responsible for everything! Some days, it's wonderful, but some days, it's a real drag.

You Want to Eat What You Kill

You don't have to be a self-employed day trader to trade securities. Brokerage firms, hedge funds, and exchange traders employ people to trade for them, and in fact most securities trading takes place through such larger organizations. But maybe you don't want to share your profits with someone else. Maybe you don't want someone dictating your strategy, placing limits on your trades, or determining your bonus based as much on factors such as teamwork and firm profitability as on what you brought in. You want to eat what you kill, as they say, and day trading is one way you can do that.

When you day trade, you're responsible for your profits and your losses. That means that you reap the rewards and you don't have to share them with anyone else. That's a powerful incentive for independent people.

You Love the Markets

Good day traders have always been fascinated with the markets and how they move. If you watch CNBC for fun and have been following the securities business for years, no matter what your day jobs have been, then you might be a good candidate for day trading. Of course, I hope you've picked up more than "some people make a lot of money doing this!" A lengthy immersion in the cycles and systems that drive securities prices will give you a good foundation for developing your own trading strategies and knowing what you are up against.

And the markets are amazing, aren't they? All these buyers and sellers, with all their different needs, come together and find the price that gets the deal done. The prices assimilate all kinds of information about the state of the world, the desires of the people trading, and the future expectations for the economy. It's capitalism in its purest form, and it's almost magical to watch how it works. If you love how the markets work and want to learn first-hand what they tell you about making money, then by all means keep reading.

The market isn't your opponent, because the market doesn't know that you are out there. The market is simply a playing field for your trading strategies and execution style.

You Have Investing Experience

If you have never opened an account with a brokerage firm, purchased a stock, or invested in a mutual fund, you might not be suited for day trading. It's not that those activities are adequate preparation for day trading — they aren't — but they can help you understand what all can happen that can cause you to make or lose money. If you've made some trades in the past, you know some of the language and some of the limitations of the markets. And that will give you a base to work from.

If you have not made any trades before, don't quit your day job to day trade. Instead, flip back to Chapter 16 for some ideas on how you can use short-term trading in an investment portfolio. That way, you can learn more and build up your savings before taking the plunge.

You Have Studied Trading Systems and Know What Works for You

Much of the work of day trading takes place long before entering the buy or sell order. You have to define your trading system, see how it would have worked in the past, and tested it to see how it works now. It's not as exciting as actually doing the day trading, because you won't be making real money — but you won't be losing money, either.

Short-term trading has a huge potential for loss, and many traders are chasing the exact same ideas. The more you know about how your strategy works in different market conditions, the better prepared you will be to act appropriately and profitably.

Backtesting a strategy, which means checking it against historic securities prices to see what would have happened if you had used the strategy in the past, can give you a sense of how realistic and effective your strategy is. Maybe you find that it's profitable, but the conditions to make it work don't happen enough for you to make good money. Maybe you find that it's too complex to remember. Maybe you find that it worked when most of the security's trading took place in open-outcry pits on the exchange floor, but now that more of the trading is electronic, it no longer works well. Such information is power, because it can help you be a better trader.

It can take a long time to find a strategy that works enough of the time to make it worth your while. Many day traders spend months developing, testing, and refining their day trading strategy. You can read more about the process of strategy testing in Chapter 11.

If you've taken the time to create and test a good strategy, then you're ready to go.

Because backtesting uses historic prices, you can do much of the work on the side, at night and on weekends, before you start day trading full time. It's a good way to get prepared for your trading business while you save your money and make other preparations for your new day trading venture.

You Are Decisive and Persistent

Can you make a decision and act on it? Can you assimilate information quickly into a good strategy? If you screw up, do you figure out what you did wrong so that it doesn't happen again and then move on? If so, you have the basic personality of a good day trader. Traders see a lot of information come at them quickly, and they have to be able to discern what the market is saying so that they can find their entry points and then exit at a good time.

Short-term traders don't have the luxury of thinking too much about what they are doing. Trading has to become intuitive. They have to be able to act on what they see when they see it. There's no room for second guessing, for hesitation, for choking or panic attacks.

Good day traders are also persistent. Once they find a strategy that they trust, they stick with it no matter how things are going. That's how they're able to buy low and sell high.

Even great traders go through bad periods, but if they trust their system and continue to stick with it, they usually pull out of it, often with money ahead. If you've been able to stick things out other times in your life when things went wrong, you know what to expect when day trading.

You Can Afford to Lose Money

Obviously, you want to be a day trader to make money. That's the whole idea. But day trading is difficult. Most traders quit in the first year. Some can't take the stress, some lose all their money, and some simply don't make enough money to make it worth their time.

Like any small business, you're taking a risk when you set up shop as a day trader. That risk is easier if you can afford to lose money. I'm not saying you need to have so much money that you won't miss it when it's gone, but you shouldn't be day trading with money you need to live on, any more than you would open a store or start a law practice with money you need to buy groceries and pay the mortgage.

If your household does not have a second source of income, be sure to set aside enough money to cover your living expenses while you get started. And you should keep a second pot of money, your *walk-away* fund (see Chapter 8), so that you are free to quit day trading and move on to your next adventure if you decide it's not for you.

It's especially important to have a financial cushion when you are day trading so that you can ride your winners, stay in the market when things get bad, and better handle the stress.

You can afford to commit to your trading

Having your living expenses covered, at least at first, isn't just about dealing with losses. It's also about being able to stick with your trading. If you have a constant need for cash to pay your bills, you may be tempted to take money out of the market whenever you are doing well. This may keep you from re-investing your profits. You won't be sticking to your strategy, and your trading capital will not grow as fast. Think of this as building a long-term asset, not as generating a steady stream of current income.

You can stay in the market through the rough times

You know the old saw that the best way to make money is to buy low and sell high, right? Well, this means that the best time to buy is usually when securities prices have been beaten up and you've lost a lot of money. If you can afford to lose some money, it will be easier for you to stay in the game and stick to your strategy so that you can profit big when the market finally turns.

You can better handle the stress of losses

Not all your trades are going to work out. You are going to lose money. That's a given. If you have enough money that you do not fear loss, you'll be able to make better decisions. You're less likely to panic if you know that you'll still be able to eat, that your lights are still going to turn on when you flip the switch, and that you'll have a roof to sleep under at night. You'll be better able to view the markets clearly and follow a winning strategy. Trading is very much a game of psychology. Give yourself an edge by waiting until you can afford to do it.

You Have a Support System

Trading is stressful. The markets gyrate with news events that no one can foresee. Things just happen, and no one else who's trading that day cares how these events affect you. It's enough to make you crazy some days — and unfortunately, some traders do get crazy. Alcoholism, depression, divorce, and suicide seem to be occupational hazards, often because day traders have trouble separating what's happening to them in the market with who they are as people.

The securities markets are wonderful mechanisms for bringing together diverse buyers and sellers. They are not wonderful for propping up your ego, helping you through a rough time in your life, or slipping you a little extra money when you most need it. The markets are not human. They are ruthless machines designed to generate the best price for the aggregate of the buyers and sellers participating that day, and some days, you're going to suffer.

Good day traders are psychologically strong. They understand how their weaknesses come out when they are stressed. They have people and activities in their lives who help give their brains a break from trading, ranging from regular exercise routines to good friends to hobbies.

If you are going to be a day trader, you need to have some support in your life for when things go wrong. Because some days, they will go wrong, and real money will be lost, and it will feel terrible.

Chapter 8 talks about managing the stress of day trading, and in many ways, I think it's the most important chapter in this book.

Chapter 18

Ten Good Reasons to Avoid Day Trading

Day trading isn't right for everyone. In fact, it's a bad idea for most people. It requires a strong personality, someone who can face the gyrations of the markets day in and day out. And it also requires someone with enough attention to detail to run a business. It's a great career option for the right person in the right circumstances. But for people who have trouble keeping cool, who don't have the patience to learn how to trade, and for anyone who has a gambling problem, day trading can be a quick road to ruin.

In this chapter, I list ten signs that maybe day trading isn't right for you right now. Take them seriously. Most day traders lose money, in part because a lot of people who aren't cut out for day trading try it anyway. Don't fret if it turns out that you aren't day trader material. Most people aren't. That's why Chapter 16 and Chapter 20 offer alternatives that might be better for your money and your career.

You Want to Learn Investing by Day Trading

Many people want to manage their own investments, and it's certainly possible. It requires taking the time to learn about the basics of finance, such as the relationship between risk and return, proper diversification, and figuring out your time horizon. In fact, there's a great book called *Investing For Dummies*, 4th Edition, by Eric Tyson (Wiley) that can help.

Some people confuse investing with day trading, though, and they are not the same. I list tons of information on the differences in Chapter 4, but here's the condensed version: Day trading involves rapid buying and selling of securities to take advantage of small movements in prices. This can be a successful strategy for part of your investment account, but it is not a good idea to day trade with all your money.

It is entirely possible to buy and sell securities on your own without being a day trader. And if you don't know another good term for "self-employed person managing her own money," just tell people you run your own hedge fund. You'll get better tables at restaurants that way.

In modern usage, a *hedge fund* is a private investment partnership that does not have to register with the Securities and Exchange Commission. You wouldn't be stretching the truth much to say that you're running a hedge fund!

You Love Fundamental Research

Fundamental research, discussed in Chapter 12, is the process of analyzing a company to see how good its business is and what the company's securities are worth. Fundamental analysts crunch numbers, build forecasts, check out products, and look for stocks that are going to do well over the long term. They dream of uncovering the next Microsoft or the next Wal-Mart and holding the stock all the way up.

Fundamental research is antithetical to day trading. Day traders look for profit opportunities in short-term price movements. They often do not know what industry a company is in, nor do they care. If you love the fundamentals, you're probably too analytical to be a good day trader.

You're Short on Time and Capital

Getting started in day trading is a lot like buying a small business. It takes commitment of both time and of money. If you don't have enough time, it is difficult to learn technical patterns. If you don't have the money, you won't be able to work through rough cycles.

And there will be rough cycles. That's day trading's only sure thing.

Some day traders are able to trade part time. If you are disciplined, you can be successful at it. The key is to close out your positions at the end of your designated trading period as though the market day were ending. If your plan is to trade for two hours a day, then trade for two hours a day and no more. Use an alarm clock as your personal trading bell.

You Like Working as Part of a Group

A decade ago, most large cities had day trading offices, called *trading arcades*, where traders could go each day to buy and sell securities. The big advantage these firms offered was high-speed Internet access. Now almost everyone can get high-speed Internet access at home, so there's little need for day traders to go elsewhere, and most of these offices are closed.

Working at home is great for some people. If you prefer camaraderie during the day, like the support of a team, and want friendly faces around you, you're likely to be miserable day trading. It's just you and the market, and the market doesn't have a great sense of humor.

You Can't Be Bothered with the Details of Running a Business

Day traders are small-businesspeople, and their entrepreneurial flair goes beyond making their own buy and sell decisions. They also buy equipment, shop for supplies, and maintain careful income tax records. To some, this is exhilarating: no more mean office manager who decides how many and what kind of pens must be used. No more going through hoops and bringing in letters from a doctor to get a fancy ergonomic chair. You're the boss, and if you want it, you can have it.

But to others, all this responsibility is overwhelming. Picking out pens? Creating backup procedures? Worrying about accounting software? It's too much. If the mere thought of standing at the office supply store gives you the heebie-jeebies, you might want to consider trading as an employee rather than trading for your own account.

You Crave Excitement

Trading *seems* so exciting. You've seen the stereotypical picture of the people on the floor at the Chicago Board of Trade, wearing bright-colored jackets and loud ties, screaming and waving their arms. It gets my blood running to just think about it. Of course, they may be shouting out coffee orders and waving their arms in a debate over the Cubs versus the Sox. With so many people together, they can make their own excitement on days when the market isn't doing anything interesting.

For that matter, the number of people trading on exchange floors is small and getting smaller. The Chicago Board of Trade is merging with the Chicago Mercantile Exchange, partly because of changes in how people trade. Nowadays, most traders sit in offices in front of computer screens. They have to stay focused on the little blips in front of them, and it can be deathly dull. Some days few, if any, opportunities come up to trade using your system.

If you crave excitement and have trouble staying focused, you might find that day trading is too boring for you. It can involve intense stress with few opportunities to work it off during the day.

You're Impulsive

With the frenzy of trades and the rapid-fire decisions involved, day trading might seem like a perfect career for an impulsive person. It's all about instinct, about acting on your hunches, about pulling the trigger and seeing what happens. Right? Uh, no. To be a good day trader, you have to trust your trading system more than your hunches. Sometimes you'll make trades when it doesn't seem right and you'll sit out periods even though you are itching to get in. Good day traders are quick thinkers, but they do think. If you like to act now and deal with the consequences later, day trading isn't a good idea for you.

You Love Going to the Casino

Do get a big rush out of gambling? Do you love trying to beat the odds? Does day trading seem like it would like a visit to Vegas without the airfare? Then you know what? You shouldn't be day trading. Unlike at a casino, no one is even going to give you free drinks in exchange for your massive losses.

A lot of traders like to gamble. Every trader has some crazy story about playing Liar's Poker, played with the serial numbers on dollar bills instead of with cards, or about a friend of a friend who bet on whether the person walking in front of him would turn right or left. And that's fine if they keep their gambling in perspective and bet no more than they can afford to lose.

Trading isn't necessarily gambling, but it can be, especially if you get carried away with the market and don't stick to your trading and money management systems. But remember this: in gambling, the odds always favor the house. When you cross the line, you hand your profit potential over to someone else.

The line between day trading and gambling is thin. Check the questions at www.gamblersanonymous.org/20questions.html to see whether you might have a gambling problem. Substitute *day trading* for *gambling* and see what you come up with. And by all means, get help if you have a problem. Don't take up day trading.

You Have Trouble Setting Boundaries

Successful day traders are disciplined. They have set trading hours, which they stick to, and set systems for planning trades and managing their money. They took the time to carefully test their trading strategy (see Chapter 11 for more on how you can do that). They understand that if they don't have a system and manage their risk, they are more likely to become one of those numerous day traders who lose everything early on.

The whole idea behind day trading is that you limit risk by closing out your positions at the end of the day. The financial markets are global, though, so in theory, the trading day never ends. If you have a hard time turning off the lights at the end of the day, you might not be the best day trader. If you resent rules, you might rebel against the rules that you've set for yourself.

Good day traders know that they are cut out for day trading before they even begin. They've taken the time to assess how their personality and psychological makeup mix with the demands of the job. And one key trait is discipline.

You Want to Get Rich Quick

Day traders look for short-term profit opportunities, so it follows that day trading leads to big, fast profits, right? Wrong. Day traders make money by collecting a large number of small profits. Those who make money usually do it through patience and persistence. Yeah, there may be one or two out there who managed to make a killing in a week, but they are the exception.

Research shows that 80 percent of day traders lose their capital and are gone from the business within one year. Instead of getting rich, you are more likely to go broke quick from day trading. If you don't like those odds, try something else with your money.

The Guy on the Infomercial Said It Would Work

A lot of money can be made in day trading, but sometimes it seems like more money is made selling day trading training systems. Some of these are heavily marketed, even through television infomercials. The sales pitch makes day trading seem like an easy, safe, fun way to make money using your own smarts. It leaves out pesky details about researching and testing systems, high levels of risk, and the pressure trading can place on a person. And the wash-sale rule is never mentioned.

Day trading is great for some people. But like anything, if it sounds too good to be true, it probably is. Don't let a strong-arm sales pitch cost you your hard-earned money.

Chapter 19

Ten Common Day Trading Mistakes

Day trading is tough. Many popular markets are *zero-sum games*, meaning that for every winner, there's a loser. Other markets, such as the stock market, have a *positive bias*, meaning they have a tendency to increase in value over time, but you may rarely see big moves in any one day. And the whole point of day trading is to close your positions each night. Most day traders lose money, in part because they make obvious, avoidable mistakes.

This list of ten mistakes will help you avoid the most serious ones so that you can be more successful from the get-go. Following them is no guarantee that you will make money trading, but it will certainly reduce your risk and improve your odds. And that's half the battle.

Starting with Unrealistic Expectations

Most day traders lose money. Some research shows that 80 percent of day traders wash out in the first year. Brokerage firms that deal with day traders are constantly figuring out ways to attract new customers, because it is so hard to retain the ones they have for the long term.

Yes, some traders make money. A few make a lot of money. But they are the exception. It is tough to make money day trading, and even tougher to make enough money to cover the value of your time. If you go into trading knowing that it's hard, that you should only risk money that you can afford to lose, and that you need to think about it as a business, you'll have a leg up on those who think that they've found an easy way to make millions from the comfort of their own home — and who are then stunned to discover they are broke.

Starting Without a Business Plan

Trading is a business. When you decide to day trade, you are committing capital to an entrepreneurial business with a high risk of failure. You are no different from your brother-in-law, who decides to open a sandwich shop franchise; your neighbor, who joined a startup company for little salary and lots of equity; or your college buddy, who has been trying to make a go of it as a full-commission life insurance salesman. You are all out on your own, risking your capital in the hope of great success but knowing that many others doing the same thing fail.

Successful businesses have business plans, and your trading business is no different. You need to specify what you are going to trade, and when, and how, and with how much money, before you get started. You need to determine what equipment you need, what services and training you want, and how you will measure your success. Chapter 2 can help you with a business plan, and the rest of the book can help you fill in the appropriate sections of it. Having the plan will keep your expectations in line and create a professional starting point for your new trading venture.

Failing to plan is planning to fail, as the cliché goes. You are risking too much of your hard-earned money to skip careful upfront planning. Take responsibility for your trading.

Starting Without a Trading Plan

A business plan sets the framework for your trading business, but you need to fill in the details. How are you going to trade? What signals will you watch for? Why will you enter a position, and why will you close it? That's your trading plan. Good traders have trading plans, so that they know exactly what they will do as they see opportunities in the market. This reduces the fear and doubt that can unsettle most traders and it heads off the panic that destroys more than a few. Read Part III for ideas on how to trade.

Good trading plans have to be tested and evaluated. Chapter 11 has good information on testing and evaluation so that you have enough confidence in your system to follow it, even when the market gets squirrelly on you.

Failing to Manage Risk

Day trading is risky business, and most day traders quit because of losses. (Have I told you that already?) Even traders who stick with it have many losing trades. That's why they have risk management systems in place. Their trading plans include *stops*, which automatically execute buy or sell orders when securities reach predetermined levels. (Stops are discussed in Chapter 2.) They also have a money management system (discussed in Chapter 9) so that they risk their capital appropriately.

The day trader looking for trouble places orders without thinking about how much of a security to buy or sell at any one time, and she thinks that she'll just know when to sell. And then she second-guesses herself and finds herself with bigger losses than she intended.

If you're going to day trade, be safe. You know what the risks are (that's why you picked up this book), so use the protection offered by stops and sound money management.

Most day traders lose money. Don't risk money you can't afford to lose, and plan for the risks that you take.

Not Committing the Time and Money to Do It Right

Day trading is a job. It's a small business endeavor that requires research and training well in advance of the first trade. It's not something you can squeeze into an hour a day as a hobby. To do well, you need to set regular hours and have enough money to generate reasonable returns without unreasonable risks.

Many people think day trading is something that's easy to enter, and that they can generate profits while their kids are napping. That's a mistake. If you can't dedicate the time to studying the markets and understanding how you react to them, you will have trouble staying in the trading business.

Successful traders start out with enough money to last through periods of drawdown and are still able to generate meaningful dollar returns. Day trading is a business of frequent trades with small percentage gains and a high potential for loss. If you have days of losses, a small account will quickly end up with too little money to meet minimum order sizes. On the upside, a 1 percent return on $1,000 is equal to $10, and a 1 percent return on $100,000 is $1,000. If you have more money to begin with, the dollars you make from day trading will seem more real to you. The U.S. Securities and Exchange Commission and the National Association of Securities Dealers define day traders in part as customers with $25,000 in their accounts. If you have $25,000 you can afford to lose, you are more likely to be a successful day trader than if you have only $2,500.

You are going to lose money. All day traders have bad days, and they are more likely to lose money early in their trading career before they get a feel for the markets and their own reactions to it. If you have enough money when you begin, you can consider these losses to be part of your apprenticeship.

Chasing the Herd

Everyone in the market is looking at the same data and the same technical indicators (like those discussed in Chapter 12). Good day traders follow market trends, but with the goal of being early or on time. Those who get in late get crushed — they buy too high, they sell too low. It's an easy temptation, because it's so hard to watch the market moving away from you.

Day trading requires quick reactions. It's video games and psychology, some people joke, because the trader who can figure out what others in the market are doing and then click on the mouse button fastest has a huge advantage. The trader who hesitates or goes along for the ride is likely to be ruined.

There's no easy solution for this. It helps if you know that you are psychologically cut out for day trading (covered in Chapter 8) and have confidence in the long-term performance of your trading system (covered in Chapter 11). But to a big extent, you just have to have some experience in the markets to know how your trading system matches what's in your head.

Switching Between Research Systems

Day traders lose money, at least part of the time. That can cause a day trader to lose trust in his trading system. And many day traders do what seems logical, which is move to a trading system that seems to be working. The problem is that no system works all the time — if one did, everyone would use it.

And sometimes things look worst before they turn. By switching systems whenever things look bad, the trader never learns the nuances of how a given system works for him. And he's likely to get stuck on another down trend, picking up the new system right when the old one starts to work again.

Markets go in cycles. No system will work for you all the time, but if you panic and start trying new things without doing a lot of upfront work, you're likely to make things worse. Chapter 11 covers performance evaluation and system testing in great detail. The more you understand your system and how it works, the less likely you are to be brought down by floundering around for new systems all the time.

Anyone who has a magic trading system that works in all markets is retired and living on a beach in Maui. Everyone else has to live through a few rough stretches.

Overtrading

Because day traders don't hold positions for long periods of time, they rarely enjoy big and profitable price moves. Instead, they make money from lots of transactions with small profits. They are crazy people, moving in and out for short periods. But believe it or not, the day trader who trades too much will lose out. She won't be in the market for large intra-day moves, and she'll get killed on commissions and other transactions costs.

As paradoxical as it seems, many day traders do better by making fewer trades each day. That way, commissions and fees take a smaller bite of the profit. One way to profit from fewer trades is with better money management, discussed in Chapter 9. A trader who puts money to work appropriately can often make more money than one who trades frenetically.

Sticking Too Long with Losing Trades

This a corollary to the overtrading mistake. Day traders are often overcome with fear, doubt, greed, and hope. They are afraid to recognize a loss. They wonder if they are good traders. They don't want to pay the commission to get out of the loser. And if the security was a good buy at the higher price, it's surely a better buy now that it's gone down in price. These traders think that if they just keep a positive mental attitude, everything will work out all right in the end.

Good traders have systems in place to limit their losses. They use stop orders (Chapter 2) to force themselves out of bad trades. They would rather put the money to work on a good trade than stick out a bad one.

The market doesn't know your position. Therefore, no amount of wishing and hoping will cause it to reward you for your patience. If a trade isn't working, get out. Tomorrow is another day.

Getting Too Emotionally Involved

Trading is a stressful business. You're up against an impersonal market that moves seemingly at random (and many academics would say that it moves truly at random.) It involves money, which to some people is a way to keep score in life and to others is their primary source of security. Losing trades mean a loss of status and a loss of safety. It's easy to think that the entire market is conspiring against you — you specifically — and it's no wonder so many traders are head cases.

The best traders are almost Zen-like in their lack of attachment to the market. They are able to remove themselves from the frenzy of the trading day so that they are not susceptible to fear, doubt, greed, and hope. Chapter 8 has some advice that can help you approach the trading day in a calmer manner. Only you know whether you are capable of that.

Chapter 20

Ten Alternatives to Day Trading

In This Chapter

▶ Considering careers options for traders

▶ Finding other ways to manage your money

▶ Getting the excitement without the risk of ruin

Maybe you like the idea of trading, but after reading this book, you've decided that working for yourself making large numbers of short-term trades isn't exactly what you want to do. But then what options are there? In this chapter, I put forward several ideas for alternative activities that might better match your interests than day trading. These include other career options, different ways to invest your money, and entertainment that gives you the excitement of trading without the same amount of risk.

Proprietary Trading for an Investment Company or Hedge Fund

Day trading is a solitary pursuit, and not everyone who wants to trade also wants to run his own business and work by himself all day. Good thing many companies need people to trade for them. Investment companies, brokerage firms, and hedge funds hire traders. These people are often known as *prop traders*, short for *proprietary*, and their job is to trade money for the firm's account. These traders may have to follow a set style, or they may be free to trade as they see fit. Prop traders don't keep all their profits, but they get a small salary, benefits, and a bonus that represents a generous cut of the money they make.

Proprietary trading lets you combine the safety net and camaraderie of a job with the excitement and potential huge returns of trading. It's a good option for those who want to spend their days with other people.

Many firms have training programs that pay entry-level employees low salaries, no matter how much money they may have made at other jobs. These junior staffers often do a lot of clerical work and run errands for the senior traders. If they show an aptitude for the business, they'll be promoted quickly. The market is a meritocracy.

Trading for an Agricultural, Energy, or Commodities Company

The options and futures markets (discussed in Chapter 3) were developed to help commodity companies manage their income and expenses better. That's why the traditional products on those exchanges almost seem funny in the era of modern finance: pork bellies, soybeans, and orange juice.

But you know what? Those traditional customers for those traditional products are still active, and they need people to help them. Energy companies, growers, food processors, and metals companies need someone to trade barrels of oil, bushels of corn, live cattle, and silver futures. They are often more interested in *hedging* — using trading to reduce risk rather than increase return — than in trading to maximize return, but depending on market conditions and firm philosophies, they may be open to traders who want to take on risk.

Joining an Exchange

In the olden days, day trading was impossible because individuals could not afford to get a data feed, let alone execute orders. People who wanted to trade for themselves had to move to a city with an exchange, submit their membership application, pay their fees, and go to work on the floor.

Although floor trading is going away, the exchanges are not. They still have members — who can trade on the floor or electronically — and they have a lot of services for their members. If you really want to be close to the action, you can join. It's not cheap; for example, membership (also known as a seat) at the Chicago Board of Trade is running around $700,000 and requires background checks, financial statements, and licensing. (The membership itself has value, and people have been known to buy it as an investment.) Many exchanges will allow you to lease membership in order to have access to the floor and the electronic exchange at a lower cost, and that runs $3,000 to $4,000 a month at the Chicago Board of Trade.

Many of the exchanges are now public companies. Instead of buying a membership or a seat, those who want trading privileges buy a special class of stock that can only be sold to someone who is qualified to trade on the exchange. You can buy regular shares of the exchanges through your brokerage firm — you can even day trade those exchange shares, if you like, but owning them won't give you membership privileges.

In Chapter 3, you can find out more about the different exchanges. If you are interested in membership, go to each exchange's Web site, as the policies and prices vary greatly.

Traditional Investing for Your Own Account

I'm thinking that some people who buy this book don't really want to day trade. Instead, they want to manage their own investment accounts during the day instead of having a regular job. You can manage your money yourself without making a high volume of short-term trades, and given the huge numbers of day traders who wash out (80 percent, according to some studies), you might be better off. True, you won't have the drama of day trading, and you won't need to focus your attention for hours on end. Instead, you'll be researching stocks and mutual funds, allocating your portfolio among several different assets, and tracking your tax liabilities. If you aren't sure where to start, consider picking up a copy of *Investing For Dummies*, 4th Edition, by Eric Tyson (Wiley).

In addition, Chapter 16 has some ideas for ways that you can use day trading techniques for long-term accounts.

Joining an Investment Club

One reason why day trading is so risky is that traders are by themselves, learning as they go along. Unlike working for a company that might have paid apprentices or junior employees who get paid to stay up to speed, a day trader often pays others for training, coaching, and research (discussed in Chapter 7) that are of varying degrees of helpfulness. It can be scary, and expensive, and disheartening.

There is a good option, though. Before you take up day trading, consider forming or joining an *investment club*. These are groups of people who want to learn more about investing. They may be neighbors, members of the same church, or participants in the same community organization. Club members pool small amounts of money, such as $50 a month, meet regularly, and learn about different types of securities, methods of research, and styles of trading.

One place to get more information on how to join, start, and operate an investment club is that National Association of Investors Corporation (www.better-investing.org), a nonprofit organization dedicated to promoting investment clubs and individual investing. If you are relatively new to investing, you may want to check out an investment club before taking up day trading.

Taking a Swing at Swing Trading

Swing trading is a cross between day trading and longer-term investing. Instead of closing out their positions at the end of each day, swing traders may hold their positions for a few days or even weeks. It's a way to change the risk and return profile. Price changes can happen overnight when you are away from your computer monitors, but the luxury of time means that there are more opportunities for your position to work out.

Swing trading favors traders with a little bit of patience, who can handle the risk of holding open positions overnight, and who have some interest in industry news and fundamental information. It's discussed a little bit in Chapter 2.

Gambling for the Fun of It

Sloppy day traders are often gamblers: they aren't following a strategy; they just like the rush and the expectation of the positive return. This means that they aren't always paying attention to the market, nor are they ready to commit to the discipline of spending days in front of a screen and evenings reviewing market activities. If you are more of a gambler than a trader, why not just admit it?

Assuming that you are not a problem gambler (see www.gamblersanonymous.org/20questions.html), keep your day job, contribute to your retirement plan, and set aside a portion of your spending money to take to the casino. And don't gamble more money than you bring.

When you gamble, the odds always favor the house, so you'll probably lose money. When you day trade, the odds on each particular trade are even or slightly in your favor, at least before considering commissions, but not so much that you are guaranteed an easy return. So if it's the rush and not the return you want, admit it and book a flight to Las Vegas.

In a casino, you get some of your losses returned to you in the form of drinks, show tickets, and other comps. Of course, it's cheaper to hold on to your money and pay cash for your drinks. That's my strategy. I hate to lose, so I don't gamble in the first place.

Play Day Trading Video Games

Want the excitement of day trading without the risk of losing your money, either to the markets or to the casino owner? Think you can figure out the markets, but don't want to put real money or your job on the line to find out? Then why not play a day trading video game?

Well, okay, it's not exactly a game; it's a simulator designed to teach you to day trade. The RapidSP Day Trading Simulator, available at www.trading simulatorsoftware.com, gives you all the excitement of day trading without risk to your capital and without the sales pitch. It's a low-cost, low-risk way to enjoy the day trading experience.

A simulation doesn't involve real money. Many traders find that when their own money is on the line, they don't trade as well as when they trade for fake money or for someone else. That's part of the psychology of facing the markets, and you can get some tips for managing that in Chapter 8.

Trade in Demo Accounts

Simulators are a good way to learn day trading, but they cost money. If you're looking for a free way to try day trading in general, or if you are a day trader thinking of adding new securities to your repertoire, you can trade in demo accounts. Many brokerage firms (see Chapter 6 for a list of some that deal with day traders) allow prospective customers to start with a demonstration account, both to check out the broker's capabilities and to see if day trading is right for you. Some brokers even run contests, where prospective traders trade paper accounts (that is, not real money), and the winners receive money for a real trading account.

If you are thinking of day trading, you owe it to yourself to do some simulation to work through your trading system. And if you just like the idea of playing around with trading, paper trading in a demonstration account can help you have fun without risking your hard-earned money.

Brokerage firms offer demo accounts to entice you to buy, and you can expect that someone will call or email you to see how things went. You can cut down on clutter in your email in-box by opening a free Web mail account just for your demo trading. Google Mail (www.gmail.com), Hotmail (www.hotmail.com), and Yahoo! (www.yahoo.com) are among the companies offering free email accounts.

Sign Up for a Trading Contest

Each year, some prominent financial media companies offer trading contests. People can sign up for them, manage a paper portfolio (investing or day trading, as they please), and the participant with the greatest return wins a cash prize.

Three popular ones are

 ✔ Forbes Stock Game: www.forbesstockgame.com.

 ✔ TheStreet.com's Beat the Street Contest: www.thestreet.com.

 ✔ CNBC's Million Dollar Portfolio Challenge: www.cnbc.com.

These offer all the fun of trading with none of the risk — although cheating scandals in 2007 mean that the future of these contests is up in the air. Consider also that they offer all the fun of trading with none of the oversight of the Securities and Exchange Commission or the Commodity Futures Trading Commission.

Appendix

Resources for Day Traders

. . . .

*A*s much as I hate to admit it, *Day Trading for Dummies* doesn't tell you all you need to know to get started in day trading. This appendix lists books, Web sites, periodicals, and other resources offering trading strategies and techniques and ideas on managing risk, taxes, and stress.

Great Books for Great Trading

Have a shelf that looks a little bare? Fill it up with a few of these beauties.

Basic trading guides

The following books offer nuts-and-bolts information on day trading.

Barron's Dictionary of Finance and Investment Terms, by John Downes and Jordan Elliott Goodman (Barron's Educational Series)

This is not the same *Barron's* as the weekly newspaper, but it's about as indispensable to investors. This dictionary is a handy guide to the technical terms and jargon you'll come across when trading. It's especially good when you are almost, but not quite, sure of what a word means.

Capital Gains, Minimal Taxes, by Kaye A. Thomas (Fairmark Press)

Every profitable trade triggers a taxable event, and a trader who is not paying attention can end up giving up all her returns to the Internal Revenue Service. That's not good. When writing your business plan and developing your trading strategy, you need to consider the tax implications. This book helps.

Day Trading the Currency Market: Technical and Fundamental Strategies to Profit from Market Swings, by Kathy Lien (Wiley)

The foreign exchange (forex) market is becoming popular with day traders, but it's a little different from the stock and futures markets. It relies heavily on leverage, and market participants have more motivations than simply hedging or speculating. If you are interested in trading currencies, this book can help you get started.

The Electronic Day Trader: Successful Strategies for On-line Trading, by Marc Friedfertig and George West (McGraw-Hill)

This book is mostly about day trading in the stock market. It covers technical analysis, trading strategies, and some of the market psychology that affects buy and sell decisions.

Mastering the Trade, by John F. Carter (McGraw-Hill)

The author, an experienced trader, walks day traders and swing traders through the ins and outs of the markets, including specific advice on different trading opportunities. He includes charts and data that explain when to place a trade and when to close it out. It's practical, useful, and detailed.

The New Money Management: A Framework for Asset Allocation, by Ralph Vince (Wiley)

Money management can keep traders in the game longer while maximizing potential returns. It's a key discipline that can mean the difference between long-run success and failure. Unfortunately, many day traders completely overlook money management. (I cover this topic in Chapter 2.)

The Tax Guide for Traders, by Robert A. Green (McGraw-Hill)

This detailed book will help you plan your trading strategy with tax efficiency in mind, and it will save you time and money when working with your tax accountant. Green writes specifically for the professional trader, so he knows what tricks and traps await you when it comes to the IRS.

Trading Rules that Work: The 28 Lessons Every Trader Must Master, by Jason Jankovsky (Wiley)

If it were possible to get rich knowing a handful of specific trading indicators, every trader would retire and run huge charitable foundations. But it's not that easy. Instead, a disciplined, professional approach to the market makes a difference over the long run. This book is a useful overview of different trading rules, why they work, and how traders should apply them.

Technical analysis guides

Technical analysis is a system of looking at price and volume trends to determine supply and demand levels in the market. Supply and demand, of course, drive price changes, so it's pretty darn useful. Here are a few books that cover technical analysis in depth.

Candlestick Charting Explained, by Gregory Morris (McGraw-Hill)

Candlestick charts were developed in Japan and are the basis of a system of technical analysis that's popular with short-term traders, including day traders. This book explains how to identify and use candlestick patterns.

Mind Over Markets: Power Trading with Market Generated Information, by James Dalton, Eric Jones, and Robert Bevan Dalton (Traders Press)

Don't let the title fool you. This book is not about trading psychology. Instead, it covers a price charting and technical analysis system in great depth, especially the relationships between price changes and volume changes. The system, called *market profile*, is especially useful for day traders working in futures markets.

Tape Reading and Market Tactics, by B. Neill Humphrey (Marketplace Books)

In the early part of the 20th century, traders looked at price and volume information that came across ticker tapes. Traders still rely on an analysis of price and volume information, just with different tools. This book was originally written in 1931, but many day traders find Humphrey's advice on what to look for and what to avoid when looking at price data still holds true.

Technical Analysis for Dummies, by Barbara Rockefeller (Wiley)

Day traders use technical analysis to help gauge market activity, and this book is a detailed guide on reading charts and applying the information to trading in an intelligent way. What else would a *For Dummies* book offer?

Schools of price theory

Most day traders take an eclectic approach to the markets. They find a few indicators that help them and apply them to the situation in the market. Over time, they refine their system, but some traders rely on specific theories for how prices should move. Here are some basic texts on them.

Dow Theory Today, by Richard Russell (Fraser Publishing)

The Dow Theory, developed by Charles Dow, publisher of *The Wall Street Journal*, predicts overall market performance based on the performance of different industry sectors. These essays from the 1950s and 1960s explain the theory and how market analysts can use it to figure out where prices are going.

Elliott Wave Principle: Key to Market Behavior, by A.J. Frost and Robert R. Prechter, Jr. (Wiley)

The Elliott Wave theory is a strange animal. It looks for really long-term patterns in the markets — over decades and even centuries — based on the *Fibonacci series*, a number series found in nature. It's not widely used, but some traders swear by it.

How to Make Profits in Commodities, by W.D. Gann (Lambert Gann)

It's not exactly an easy read, but many analysts believe that Gann's system can help them figure out how prices change over time. Reissued in 1976, the text dates from the 1940s. Some find it dated, others think it's timeless.

How to Make Money in Stocks: A Winning System in Good Times or Bad, by William J. O'Neill (McGraw-Hill)

William O'Neill's system will be of most interest to people who are swing trading or investing in common stock, but it might help day traders understand what other participants in the market are looking at when they place orders. The book explains *momentum* investing, which looks for stocks of companies with improving business trends and performance.

Trading psychology

Good traders are mentally tough. They need the confidence to face the market, the decisiveness to place orders, and the fortitude to take losses — and do it against a faceless mix of everyone else trading that day. Several books address trading psychology specifically; others on mental strength are also popular with traders because their lessons can be applied to the markets.

The Art of War, by Sun Tzu

It seems like every trader I've ever met has a copy of *The Art of War*. It's a Chinese text describing military strategy, including the importance of mental toughness and strict discipline. First translated into a European language in 1782, several different versions and translations are in print.

Awaken the Giant Within, by Anthony Robbins (Pocket Books)

This is a basic self-help book that's popular with all sorts of folks. Many traders find that Robbins' methods give them confidence and help them control their minds when they are trading.

The Crowd: A Study of the Popular Mind, by Gustave LeBon (Dover Books)

In the 19th century, Gustave LeBon wrote this treatise on crowd psychology. He didn't think much of his fellow human being, but many traders have found that his insights explain some short-term irrational behavior in the markets. Understanding why traders make mistakes can help you make profits.

The Disciplined Trader: Developing Winning Attitudes, by Mark Douglas (Prentice Hall)

Mark Douglas is a trader who lost a lot of money and tried to figure out why. As he did that, he developed a great deal of insight into the psychological aspects of trading. Namely, the market doesn't care about who is trading in it, so every trader is responsible for his or her own results. Many experienced day traders swear by the information in this book.

The Inner Game of Trading, by Robert Koppel (McGraw-Hill)

Day trading requires a lot of mental discipline. A trader has a short time to make a profit, and some panic at the idea. Others succumb to doubt, fear, greed, and hope, using emotion to avoid making good trading decisions. This is a classic guide to managing the emotional aspects of trading. The author has written other books on different aspects of trading psychology as well.

History and memoir

I'm not willing to accept the Elliott Wave and say that all market movements are part of overarching trends, but market history — like all history — tends to repeat. Why? Because people are people, and no matter how commerce and the economy changes, people do the same things over and over again.

Double Down: Reflections on Gambling and Loss, by Frederick and Stephen Barthelme (Harvest Books)

Want to see what a gambling addiction looks like? The Barthelme brothers are writers and English professors who inherited $250,000 from their father's estate and then lost it all playing casino blackjack. It's a story of how complicated relationships with money cause people to make bad decisions. For a day trader, this book tells what happens when people cannot place limits for emotional reasons, a route to ruin in the casino or during the trading day.

Fortune's Formula: The Untold Story of the Scientific Betting System that Beat the Casinos and Wall Street, by William Poundstone (Hill and Wang)

Claude Shannon and John Kelly were Bell Labs scientists working on queuing theories for long-distance calls when they stumbled on what is known as the Kelly Criterion: the ideal proportion of money to bet can be found by the ratio of your edge in the market divided by the odds of winning. The "edge/odds" formula can be used by day traders to figure out how much money to allocate to a trade. This book explains how the system works, though it never quite proves that it works when applied to legitimate casinos or to trading.

Reminiscences of a Stock Operator, by Edwin LeFevre (Wiley)

This classic, written before the 1929 market crash, tells of the adventures of Jesse Livermore, one of the most successful traders of his time. It's a disguised memoir of speculation, with a character named Larry Livingston standing in for Livermore. Some traders like it for the lessons they can learn from Livermore, others are just amused by how unchanged the art of day trading is despite dramatic changes in technology.

Organizations for Day Traders

Okay, let's face it: Day traders are an independent lot, and there aren't many organizations for them, nor many trade associations or lobbying groups. Still, if you are trying to find other day traders out there, here are a few ideas.

Security Traders Association

The STA (www.securitytraders.org) represents traders at brokerage firms and investment companies. Much of its focus is regulatory, but on occasion, local chapters sponsor meetings and events that might be of interest to a day trader.

Market Technicians Association

Day traders rely on technical analysis to help them make trading decisions. If you really want to study the subject in depth, the MTA (www.mta.org) will help you. The organization is mostly aimed at people who do technical analysis for large trading firms, but anyone interested in the topic may join. Local chapters bring in successful traders to talk about their techniques.

Meetups

Meetup.com is a Web site that lets people with similar interests find each other and get together wherever they live. Many Meetup groups are designed for day traders. Go to http://daytraders.meetup.com to find day traders, and to www.meetup.com/topics/fin/inv/ to find groups that cover foreign exchange (forex), commodities, or other aspects of trading and investing.

The Trader's Internet

Day trading was made possible by the Internet. When high-speed connectivity to market data became affordable, almost anyone could trade with the same speed as folks working on the exchange floor or a brokerage trading desk. And yet, the Internet can be a terrible distraction to a day trader or to anyone else working alone. Here are some good Web sites for day traders, but you might want to limit your use of them to before and after trading hours.

Bill Cara

Bill Cara isn't a day trader, but he is a full-time investor who pays careful attention to the markets. Each day, he records his observations about what's happening on his blog, www.billcara.com. It's good reading.

IndexArb.com

Interested in trading futures on the market indexes? This site, http://indexarb.com, has useful information. It lists the premiums on different contracts, offers strategies for different market conditions, and gives you some good background information to help you make your own decisions.

MyPivots.com

This site, www.mypivots.com, runs through key price and economic data every morning, with trading calculators and a forum. It's of most interest to people working with eMini index futures.

TraderInterviews.com

Looking for something educational and inspirational for your MP3 player? TraderInterviews.com (www.traderinterviews.com) features discussions with different traders.

Trader Mike

Every day, Michael Seneadza, a day trader, updates his blog at www.tradermike.net. It includes his trading journal, thoughts on the markets, and his own advice on day trading, which he admits is not definitive. This blog is often thought-provoking.

Traders Laboratory

If you are interested in meeting other day traders online, finding Web-based seminars, reading traders' blogs, or checking out economic release calendars, then Traders Laboratory, www.traderslaboratory.com, is the site for you.

Other Mainstream Media

Even though traders are hooked to real-time market data through the Internet, they still look to some old-style sources for information.

Barron's

Barron's (www.barrons.com) is a weekly financial newspaper published by Dow Jones & Company. The primary emphasis is on long-term investing, but it carries in-depth market analysis and often interviews outstanding traders. In addition, the regular "Electronic Trader" column carries news and ratings of online brokerage firms, many of which specialize in services for day traders.

CNBC

CNBC (www.cnbc.com) is a cable channel that carries news and information about the markets. Some traders keep it running in the background while they trade. Others watch the shows before and after market hours.

Investor's Business Daily

This newspaper, www.investors.com, is published by the William O'Neill Company, which also publishes charts and technical analysis systems used by stock investors. (See Chapter 16.) Every morning, *IBD* has new trade ideas and market analysis for active traders, especially those in the stock market.

Index

• D •

• *M* •

BUSINESS, CAREERS & PERSONAL FINANCE

0-7645-9847-3

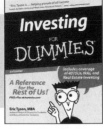

0-7645-2431-3

Also available:
- Business Plans Kit For Dummies
  0-7645-9794-9
- Economics For Dummies
  0-7645-5726-2
- Grant Writing For Dummies
  0-7645-8416-2
- Home Buying For Dummies
  0-7645-5331-3
- Managing For Dummies
  0-7645-1771-6
- Marketing For Dummies
  0-7645-5600-2

- Personal Finance For Dummies
  0-7645-2590-5*
- Resumes For Dummies
  0-7645-5471-9
- Selling For Dummies
  0-7645-5363-1
- Six Sigma For Dummies
  0-7645-6798-5
- Small Business Kit For Dummies
  0-7645-5984-2
- Starting an eBay Business For Dummies
  0-7645-6924-4
- Your Dream Career For Dummies
  0-7645-9795-7

HOME & BUSINESS COMPUTER BASICS

0-470-05432-8

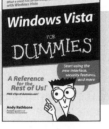

0-471-75421-8

Also available:
- Cleaning Windows Vista For Dummies
  0-471-78293-9
- Excel 2007 For Dummies
  0-470-03737-7
- Mac OS X Tiger For Dummies
  0-7645-7675-5
- MacBook For Dummies
  0-470-04859-X
- Macs For Dummies
  0-470-04849-2
- Office 2007 For Dummies
  0-470-00923-3

- Outlook 2007 For Dummies
  0-470-03830-6
- PCs For Dummies
  0-7645-8958-X
- Salesforce.com For Dummies
  0-470-04893-X
- Upgrading & Fixing Laptops For Dummies
  0-7645-8959-8
- Word 2007 For Dummies
  0-470-03658-3
- Quicken 2007 For Dummies
  0-470-04600-7

FOOD, HOME, GARDEN, HOBBIES, MUSIC & PETS

0-7645-8404-9

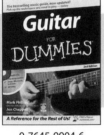

0-7645-9904-6

Also available:
- Candy Making For Dummies
  0-7645-9734-5
- Card Games For Dummies
  0-7645-9910-0
- Crocheting For Dummies
  0-7645-4151-X
- Dog Training For Dummies
  0-7645-8418-9
- Healthy Carb Cookbook For Dummies
  0-7645-8476-6
- Home Maintenance For Dummies
  0-7645-5215-5

- Horses For Dummies
  0-7645-9797-3
- Jewelry Making & Beading For Dummies
  0-7645-2571-9
- Orchids For Dummies
  0-7645-6759-4
- Puppies For Dummies
  0-7645-5255-4
- Rock Guitar For Dummies
  0-7645-5356-9
- Sewing For Dummies
  0-7645-6847-7
- Singing For Dummies
  0-7645-2475-5

INTERNET & DIGITAL MEDIA

0-470-04529-9

0-470-04894-8

Also available:
- Blogging For Dummies
  0-471-77084-1
- Digital Photography For Dummies
  0-7645-9802-3
- Digital Photography All-in-One Desk Reference For Dummies
  0-470-03743-1
- Digital SLR Cameras and Photography For Dummies
  0-7645-9803-1
- eBay Business All-in-One Desk Reference For Dummies
  0-7645-8438-3
- HDTV For Dummies
  0-470-09673-X

- Home Entertainment PCs For Dummies
  0-470-05523-5
- MySpace For Dummies
  0-470-09529-6
- Search Engine Optimization For Dummies
  0-471-97998-8
- Skype For Dummies
  0-470-04891-3
- The Internet For Dummies
  0-7645-8996-2
- Wiring Your Digital Home For Dummies
  0-471-91830-X

* Separate Canadian edition also available
† Separate U.K. edition also available

Available wherever books are sold. For more information or to order direct: U.S. customers visit www.dummies.com or call 1-877-762-2974.
U.K. customers visit www.wileyeurope.com or call 0800 243407. Canadian customers visit www.wiley.ca or call 1-800-567-4797.

SPORTS, FITNESS, PARENTING, RELIGION & SPIRITUALITY

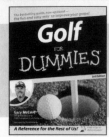

0-471-76871-5

0-7645-7841-3

Also available:
- Catholicism For Dummies
  0-7645-5391-7
- Exercise Balls For Dummies
  0-7645-5623-1
- Fitness For Dummies
  0-7645-7851-0
- Football For Dummies
  0-7645-3936-1
- Judaism For Dummies
  0-7645-5299-6
- Potty Training For Dummies
  0-7645-5417-4
- Buddhism For Dummies
  0-7645-5359-3

- Pregnancy For Dummies
  0-7645-4483-7 †
- Ten Minute Tone-Ups For Dummies
  0-7645-7207-5
- NASCAR For Dummies
  0-7645-7681-X
- Religion For Dummies
  0-7645-5264-3
- Soccer For Dummies
  0-7645-5229-5
- Women in the Bible For Dummies
  0-7645-8475-8

TRAVEL

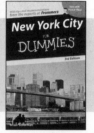

0-7645-7749-2

0-7645-6945-7

Also available:
- Alaska For Dummies
  0-7645-7746-8
- Cruise Vacations For Dummies
  0-7645-6941-4
- England For Dummies
  0-7645-4276-1
- Europe For Dummies
  0-7645-7529-5
- Germany For Dummies
  0-7645-7823-5
- Hawaii For Dummies
  0-7645-7402-7

- Italy For Dummies
  0-7645-7386-1
- Las Vegas For Dummies
  0-7645-7382-9
- London For Dummies
  0-7645-4277-X
- Paris For Dummies
  0-7645-7630-5
- RV Vacations For Dummies
  0-7645-4442-X
- Walt Disney World & Orlando
  For Dummies
  0-7645-9660-8

GRAPHICS, DESIGN & WEB DEVELOPMENT

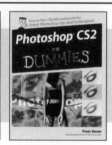

0-7645-8815-X

0-7645-9571-7

Also available:
- 3D Game Animation For Dummies
  0-7645-8789-7
- AutoCAD 2006 For Dummies
  0-7645-8925-3
- Building a Web Site For Dummies
  0-7645-7144-3
- Creating Web Pages For Dummies
  0-470-08030-2
- Creating Web Pages All-in-One Desk
  Reference For Dummies
  0-7645-4345-8
- Dreamweaver 8 For Dummies
  0-7645-9649-7

- InDesign CS2 For Dummies
  0-7645-9572-5
- Macromedia Flash 8 For Dummies
  0-7645-9691-8
- Photoshop CS2 and Digital
  Photography For Dummies
  0-7645-9580-6
- Photoshop Elements 4 For Dummies
  0-471-77483-9
- Syndicating Web Sites with RSS Feeds
  For Dummies
  0-7645-8848-6
- Yahoo! SiteBuilder For Dummies
  0-7645-9800-7

NETWORKING, SECURITY, PROGRAMMING & DATABASES

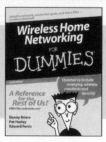

0-7645-7728-X

0-471-74940-0

Also available:
- Access 2007 For Dummies
  0-470-04612-0
- ASP.NET 2 For Dummies
  0-7645-7907-X
- C# 2005 For Dummies
  0-7645-9704-3
- Hacking For Dummies
  0-470-05235-X
- Hacking Wireless Networks
  For Dummies
  0-7645-9730-2
- Java For Dummies
  0-470-08716-1

- Microsoft SQL Server 2005 For Dummies
  0-7645-7755-7
- Networking All-in-One Desk Reference
  For Dummies
  0-7645-9939-9
- Preventing Identity Theft For Dummies
  0-7645-7336-5
- Telecom For Dummies
  0-471-77085-X
- Visual Studio 2005 All-in-One Desk
  Reference For Dummies
  0-7645-9775-2
- XML For Dummies
  0-7645-8845-1